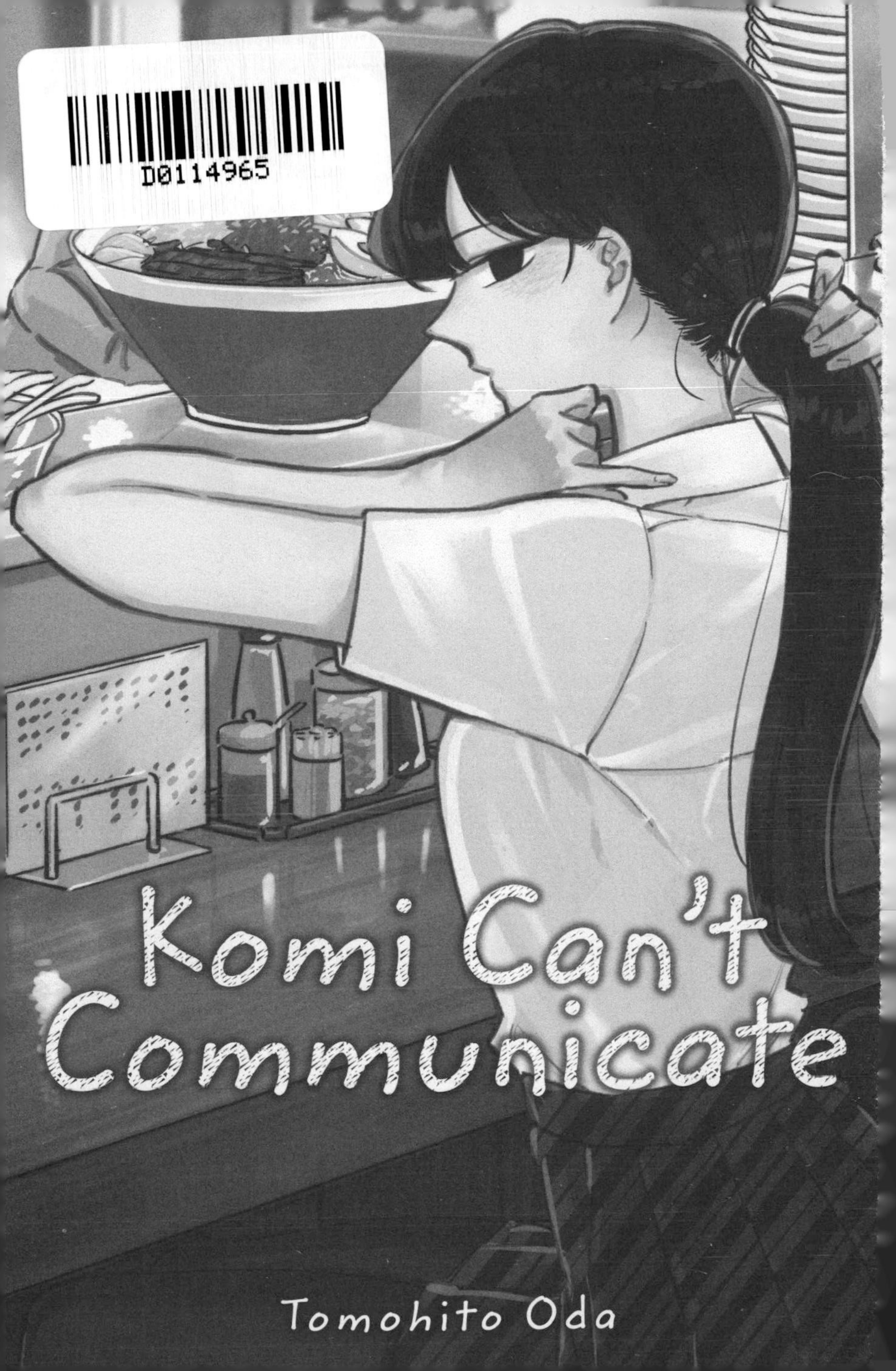
Komi Can't Communicate
Tomohito Oda

Contents 2

Komi Can't Communicate

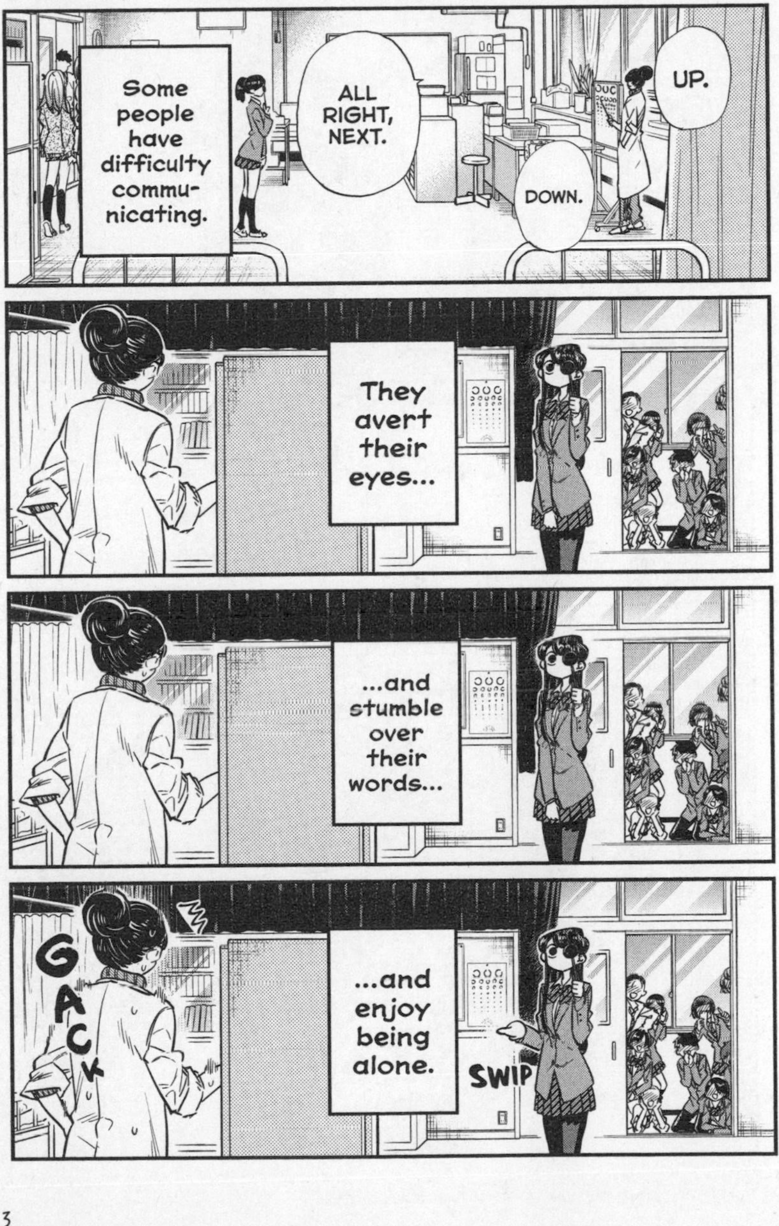
UP.
DOWN.
ALL RIGHT, NEXT.
Some people have difficulty commu-nicating.
They avert their eyes...
...and stumble over their words...
...and enjoy being alone.
SWIP
GACK

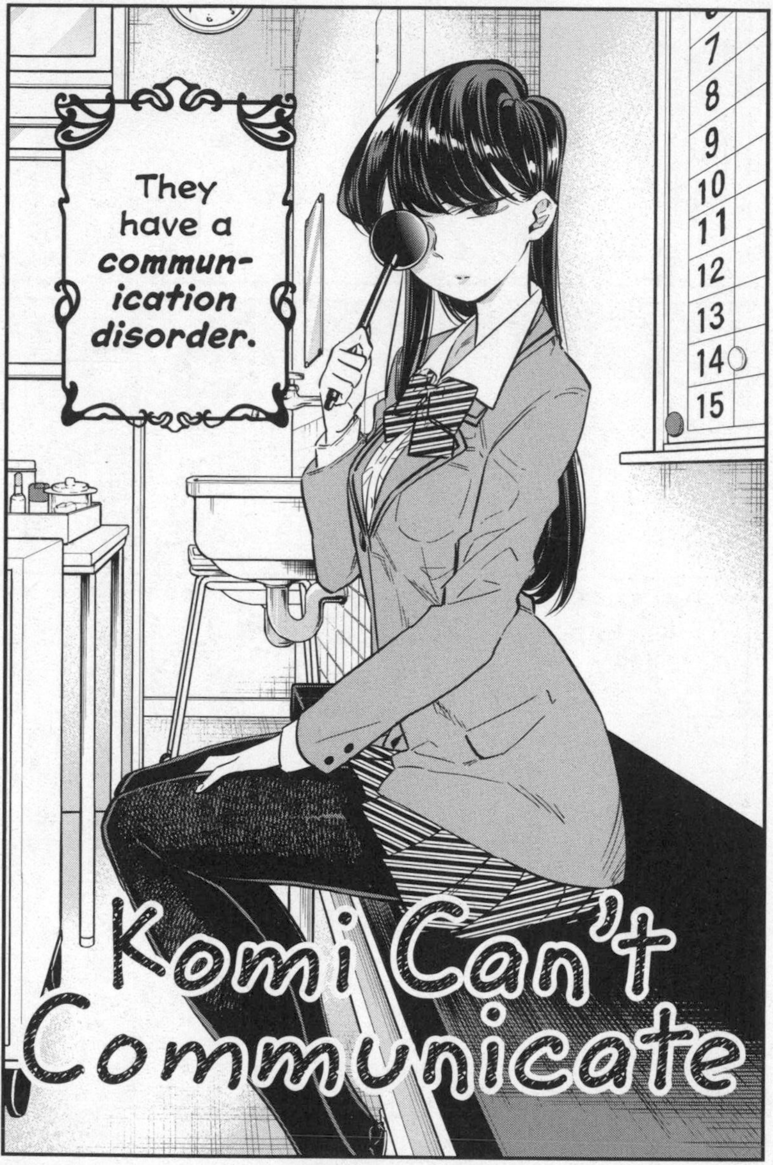
They have a communication disorder.
7
8
9
10
11
12
13
14
15
Komi Can't Communicate

Communication 20: The Physical

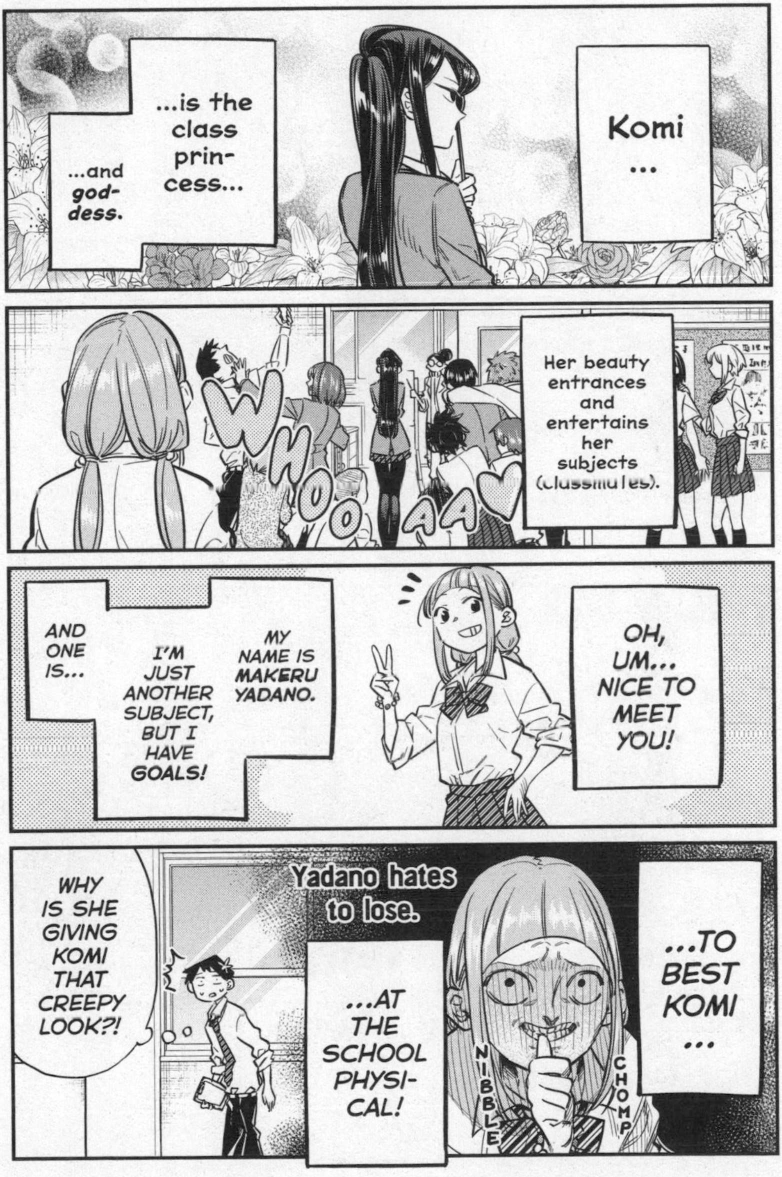
Komi ...
...is the class prin-cess...
...and god-dess.
Her beauty entrances and entertains her subjects (classmates).
WHOOAA♥
OH, UM... NICE TO MEET YOU!
MY NAME IS MAKERU YADANO.
I'M JUST ANOTHER SUBJECT, BUT I HAVE GOALS!
AND ONE IS...
...TO BEST KOMI ...
CHOMP
NIBBLE
...AT THE SCHOOL PHYSI-CAL!
Yadano hates to lose.
WHY IS SHE GIVING KOMI THAT CREEPY LOOK?!

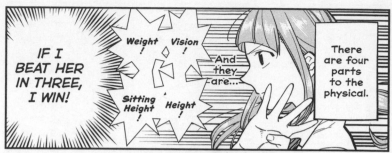

There are four parts to the physical.
And they are...
Vision!
Weight!
Height!
Sitting Height!
IF I BEAT HER IN THREE, I WIN!
KOMI IS THE MOST SPLEN-DIFEROUS BEING IN OUR CLASS ...
PWOO
CHEW CHEW
*Her imagination
...SO BEATING HER WILL MAKE ME THE COOLEST!
WHAT'S UP? WHY ISN'T KOMI ANSWER-ING?
...
MY EYESIGHT ISN'T GREAT, BUT IT LOOKS LIKE THIS'LL BE A CINCH!!
About 0.7
GOOD, KOMI! YOU'RE 1.5!
Using finger to point
HUH ?!
Can't see from back there

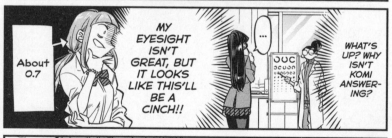

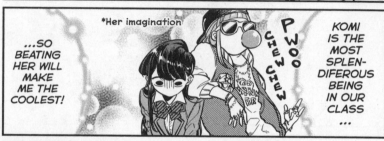

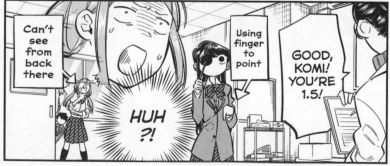

WHAT?! HOW'D THAT HAPPEN?!
Huh? Y...
Yada-no?
BUT SHE DIDN'T EVEN ANSWER!
GASP
DID SHE BRIBE THE REF (TEACHER)?!
PWOO
CHEW CHEW
W-WHAT A LOW-DOWN TRICK!!
*Her imagination
DOES SHE WANT TO BEAT ME THAT BADLY?!
Impor-tant
GRRRRR-P
Hey... That hurts...
That hurts, Yada-no!!
NO MATTER! I'LL TOTALLY THRASH YOU!!
HG
URRR
Result: 0.7

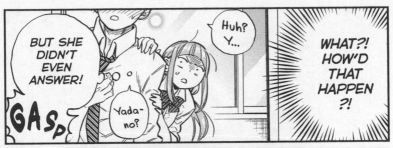

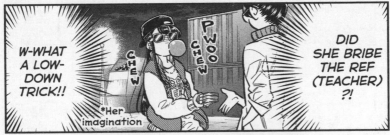

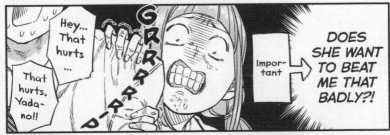

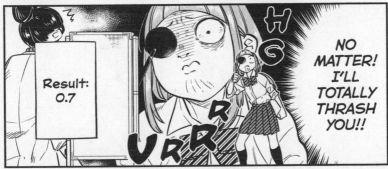

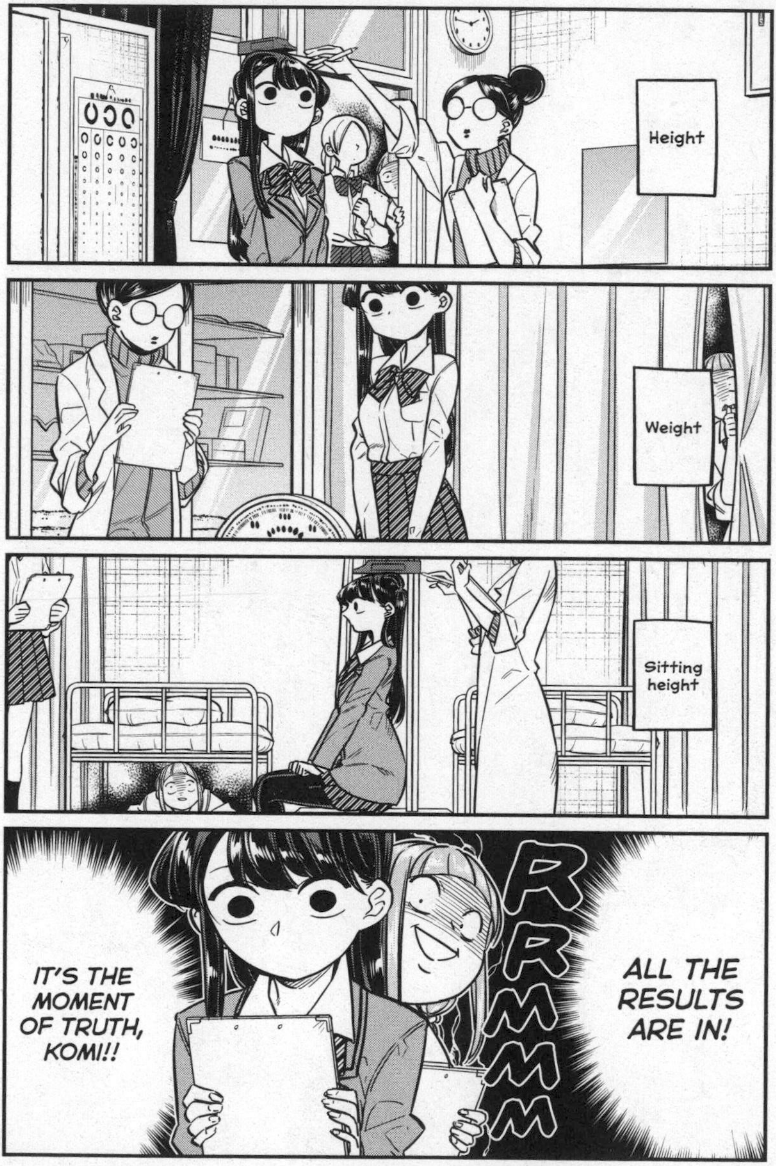
Height
Weight
Sitting height
ALL THE RESULTS ARE IN!
RRMMMM
IT'S THE MOMENT OF TRUTH, KOMI!!

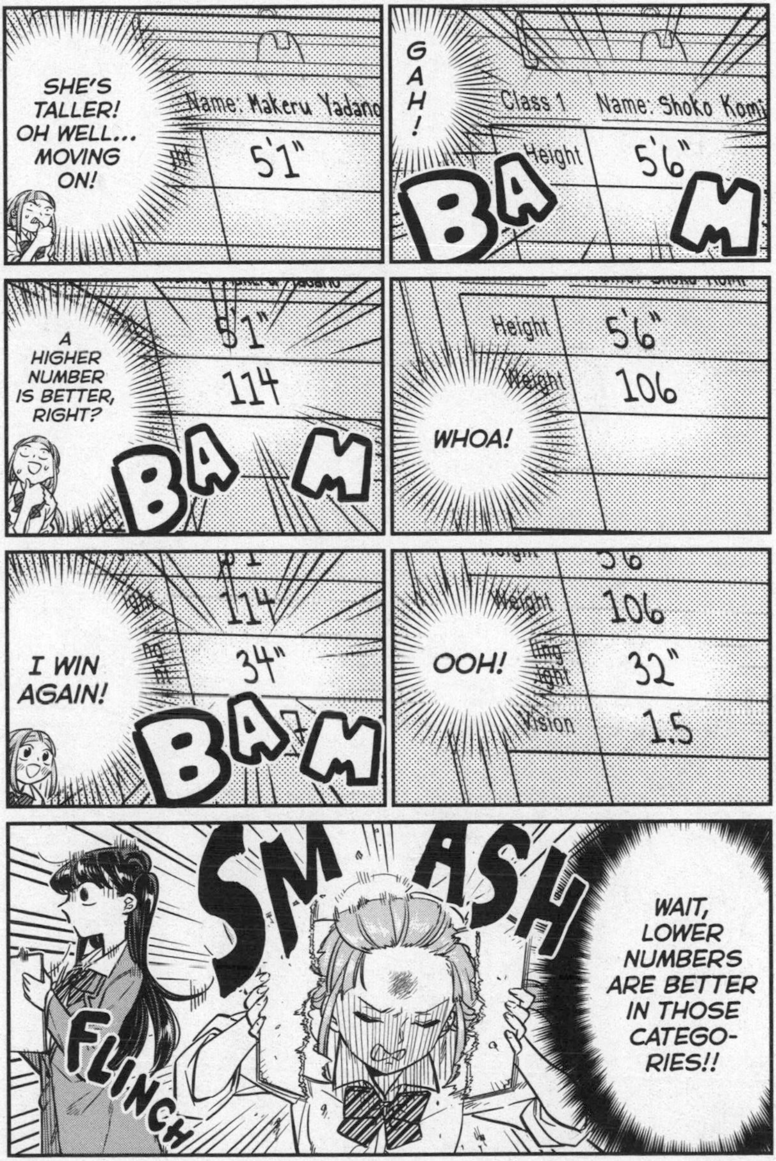
GAH!
Class 1
Name: Shoko Komi
Height
5'6"
BAM
SHE'S TALLER! OH WELL... MOVING ON!
Name: Makeru Yadano
5'1"
Height
5'6"
Weight
106
WHOA!
5'1"
114
A HIGHER NUMBER IS BETTER, RIGHT?
BAM
Weight
106
32"
Vision
1.5
OOH!
114
34"
I WIN AGAIN!
BAM
SMASH
WAIT, LOWER NUMBERS ARE BETTER IN THOSE CATEGO-RIES!!
FLINCH

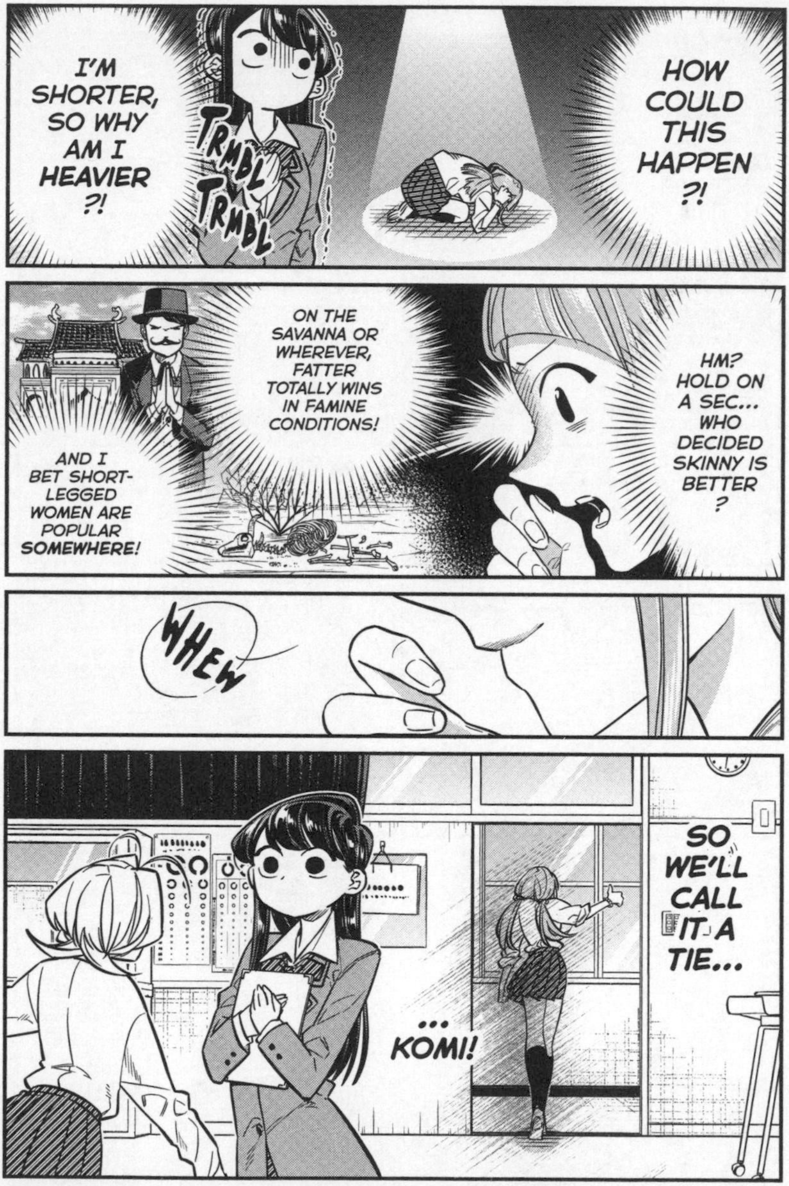
HOW COULD THIS HAPPEN ?!
I'M SHORTER, SO WHY AM I HEAVIER ?!
TRMBL TRMBL
HM? HOLD ON A SEC... WHO DECIDED SKINNY IS BETTER ?
ON THE SAVANNA OR WHEREVER, FATTER TOTALLY WINS IN FAMINE CONDITIONS!
AND I BET SHORT-LEGGED WOMEN ARE POPULAR SOMEWHERE!
WHEW
SO WE'LL CALL IT A TIE...
...KOMI!

Communication 20 — The End

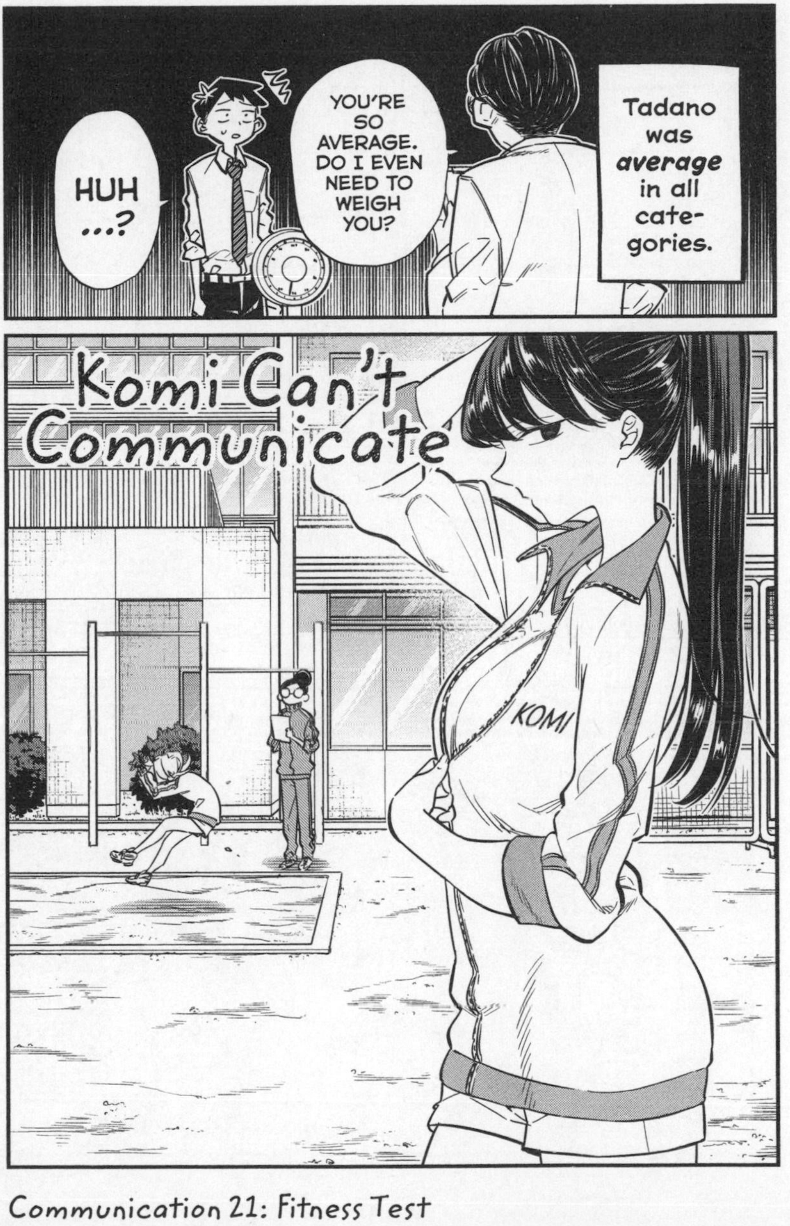
Tadano was *average* in all categories.
YOU'RE SO AVERAGE. DO I EVEN NEED TO WEIGH YOU?
HUH ...?
Komi Can't Communicate
KOMI

Communication 21: Fitness Test

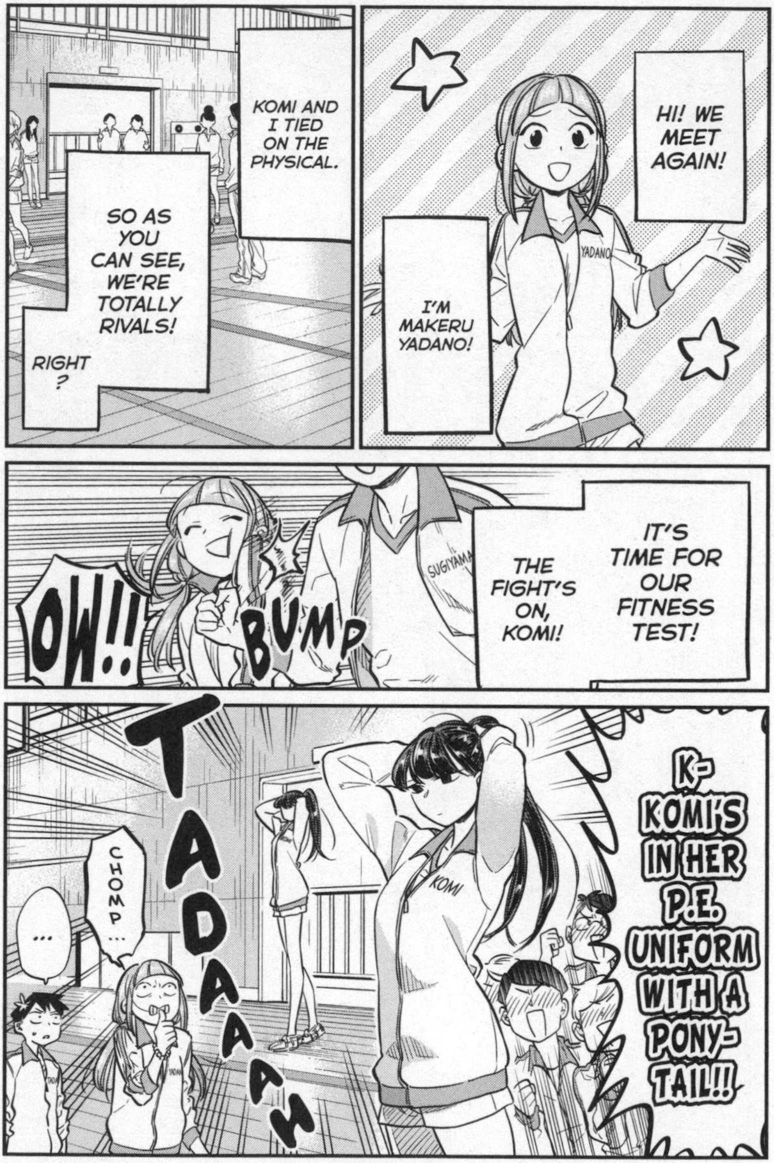
HI! WE MEET AGAIN!
I'M MAKERU YADANO!
KOMI AND I TIED ON THE PHYSICAL.
SO AS YOU CAN SEE, WE'RE TOTALLY RIVALS!
RIGHT?
IT'S TIME FOR OUR FITNESS TEST!
THE FIGHT'S ON, KOMI!
BUMP
OW!!
K-KOMI'S IN HER P.E. UNIFORM WITH A PONY-TAIL!!
TADAAAAAH
CHOMP...
...

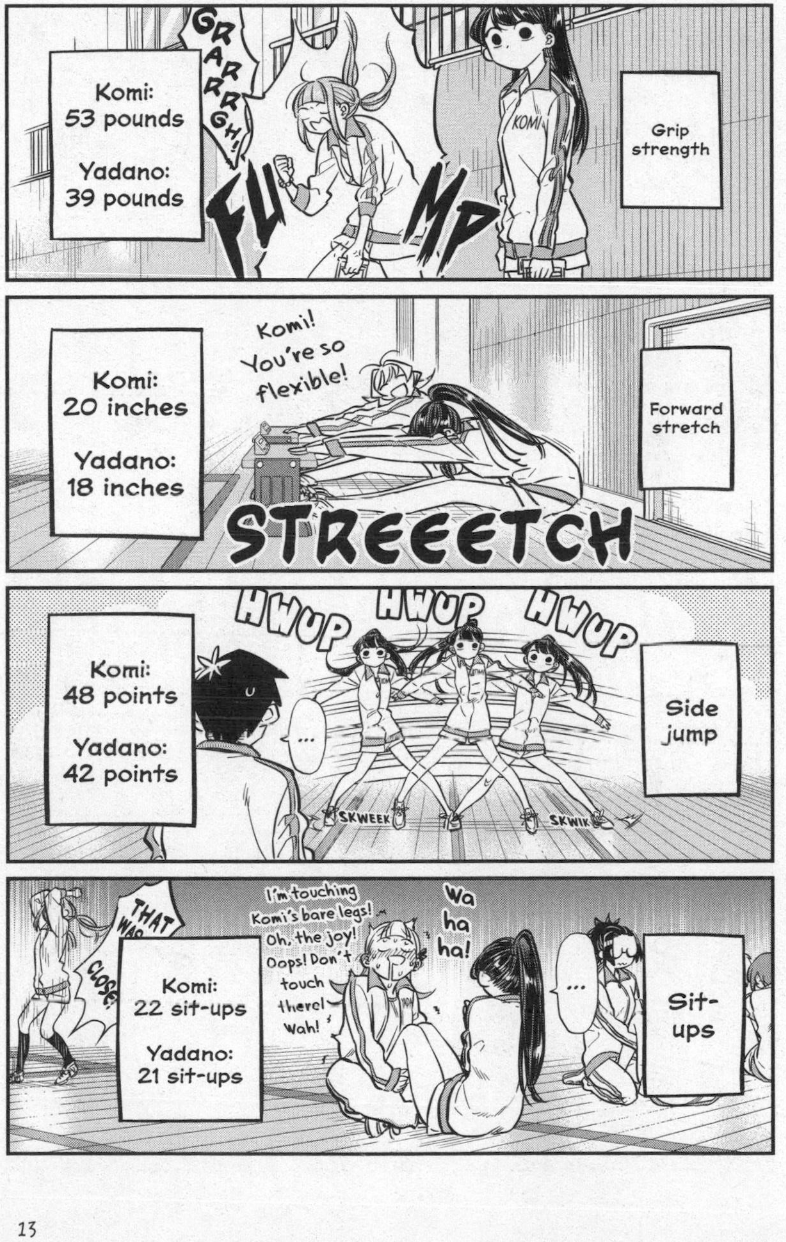

Grip strength
GRARRRGH!!
FUMP
Komi: 53 pounds
Yadano: 39 pounds
Forward stretch
Komi! You're so flexible!
STREEETCH
Komi: 20 inches
Yadano: 18 inches
Side jump
HWUP HWUP HWUP
SKWIK
SKWEEK
...
Komi: 48 points
Yadano: 42 points
Sit-ups
...
Wa ha ha!
I'm touching Komi's bare legs! Oh, the joy! Oops! Don't touch there! Wah!
THAT WAS CLOSE!
Komi: 22 sit-ups
Yadano: 21 sit-ups

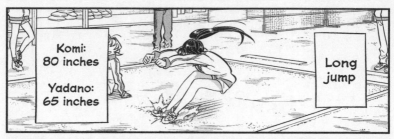

Long jump
Komi: 80 inches
Yadano: 65 inches
Hand-ball toss
I messed up!
Komi: 26 meters
Yadano: 5 meters
Lost every-thing so far
GLOOM
HM?
WHAT'S WRONG, YADANO?
ARE YOU SICK?
I'M SO FRUS-TRATED !!
SNORT
?!

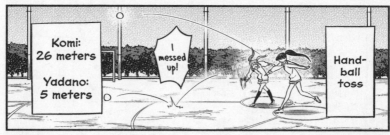

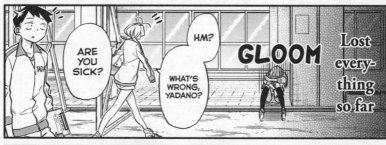

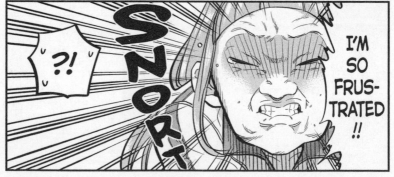

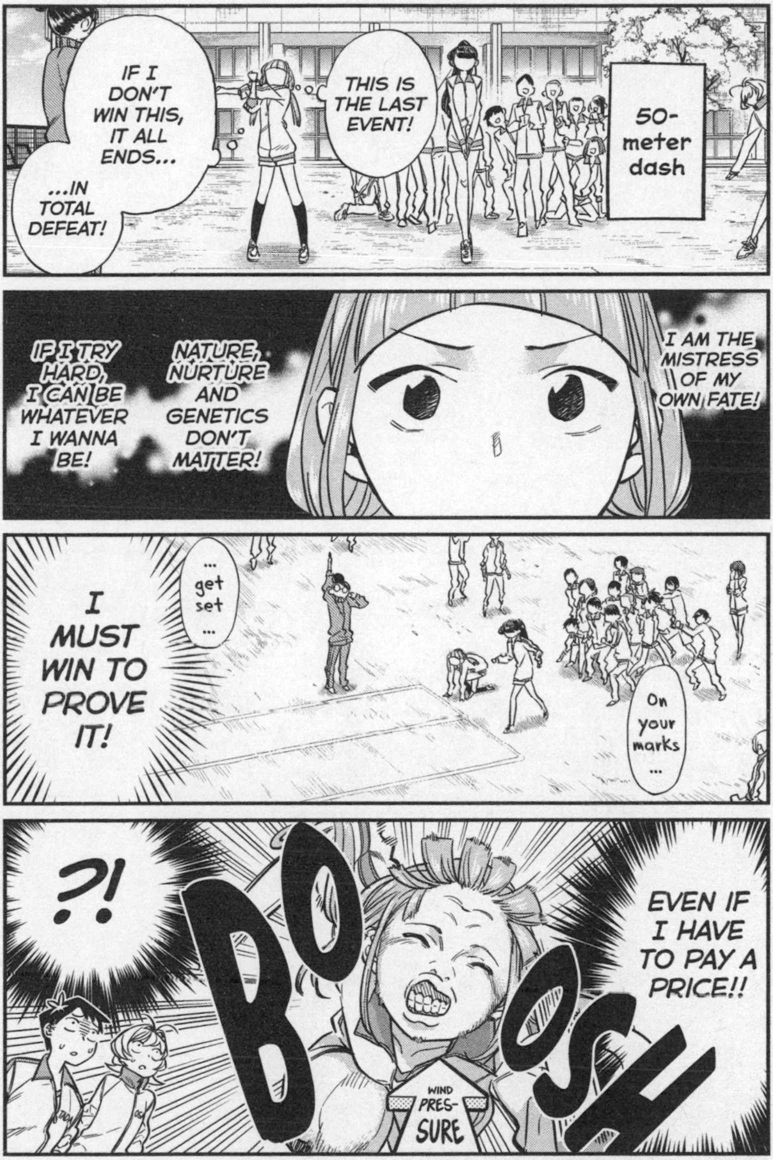
50-meter dash
THIS IS THE LAST EVENT!
IF I DON'T WIN THIS, IT ALL ENDS...
...IN TOTAL DEFEAT!
I AM THE MISTRESS OF MY OWN FATE!
NATURE, NURTURE AND GENETICS DON'T MATTER!
IF I TRY HARD, I CAN BE WHATEVER I WANNA BE!
On your marks ...
... get set ...
I MUST WIN TO PROVE IT!
EVEN IF I HAVE TO PAY A PRICE!!
BOOOSH
WIND PRES-SURE
?!

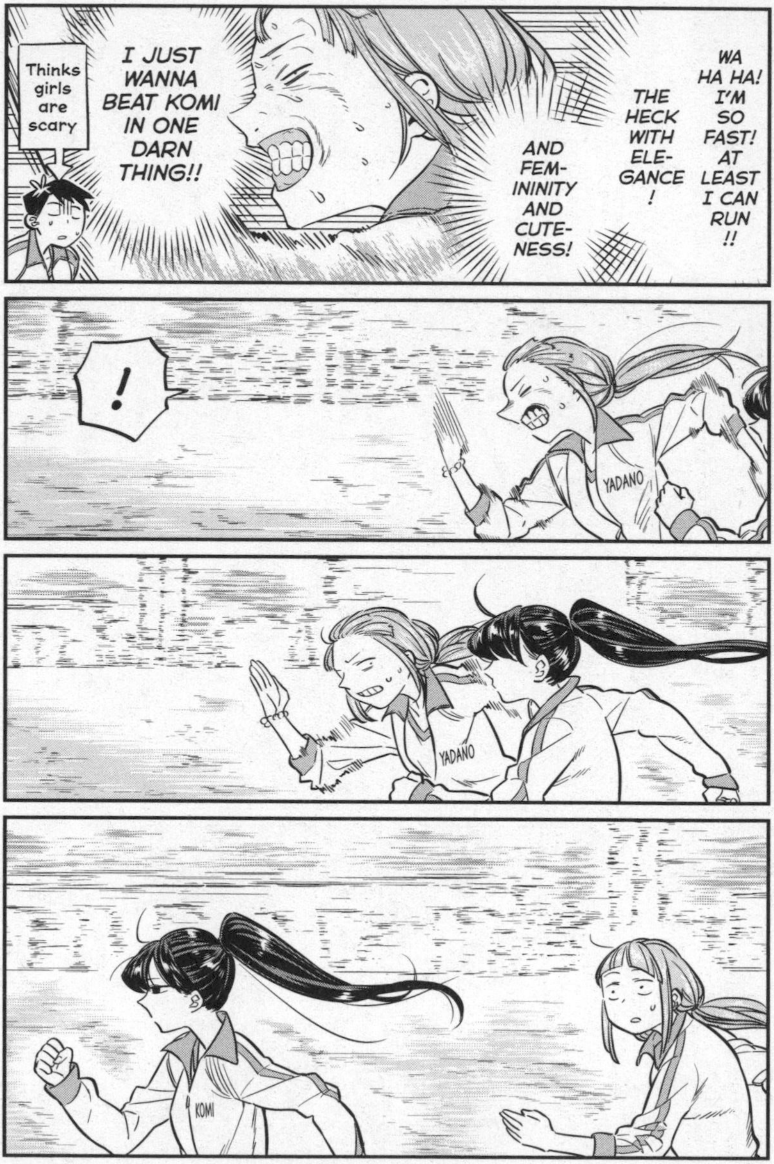
WA HA HA! I'M SO FAST! AT LEAST I CAN RUN!!
THE HECK WITH ELEGANCE!
AND FEMININITY AND CUTENESS!
I JUST WANNA BEAT KOMI IN ONE DARN THING!!
Thinks girls are scary
!
YADANO
YADANO
KOMI

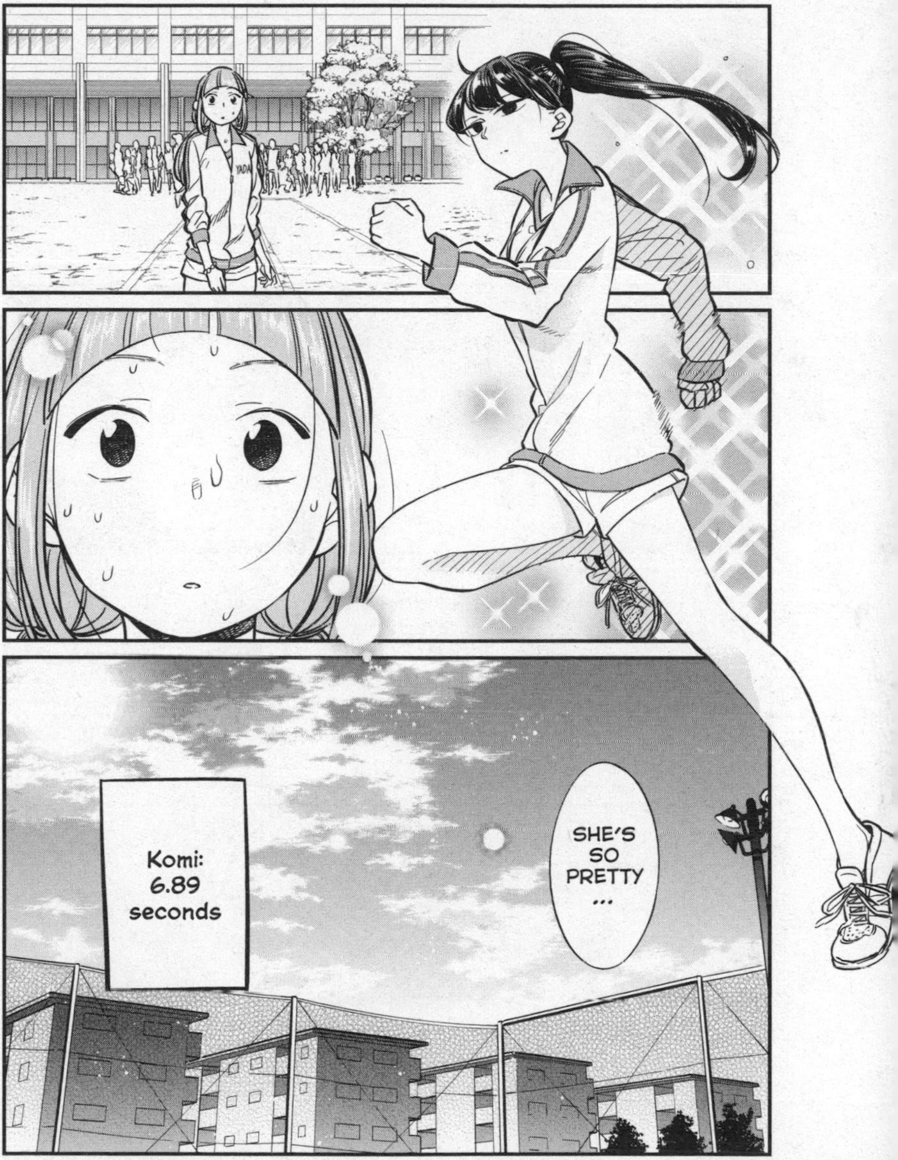
YADA
SHE'S SO PRETTY ...
Komi: 6.89 seconds

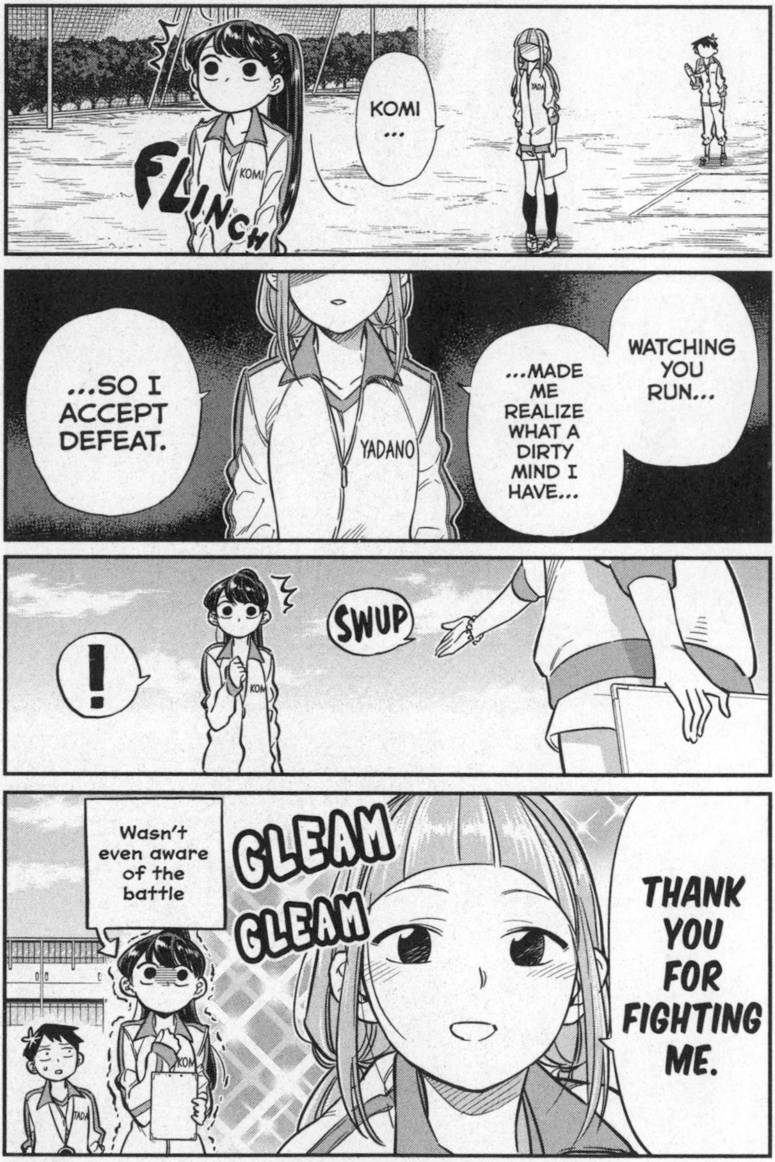
YADA
KOMI...
KOMI
FLINCH
WATCHING YOU RUN...
...MADE ME REALIZE WHAT A DIRTY MIND I HAVE...
YADANO
...SO I ACCEPT DEFEAT.
SWUP
!
THANK YOU FOR FIGHTING ME.
GLEAM
GLEAM
Wasn't even aware of the battle

YOU ...
... DON'T WANT TO SHAKE HANDS ?
...!
I SUPPOSE YOU THINK I'M GIVING UP...
YADA
...AND YOU WANT ME TO KEEP WORKING HARD.
WHICH MEANS YOU VIEW ME AS A FORMID-ABLE OPPO-NENT!!
?!
RIVALS

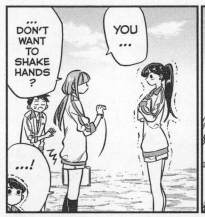

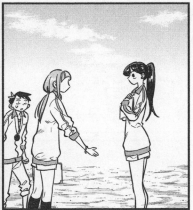

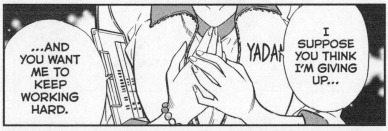

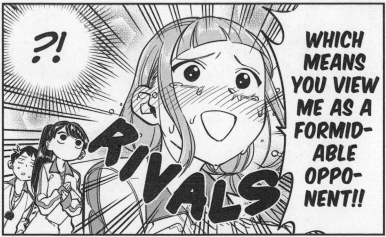

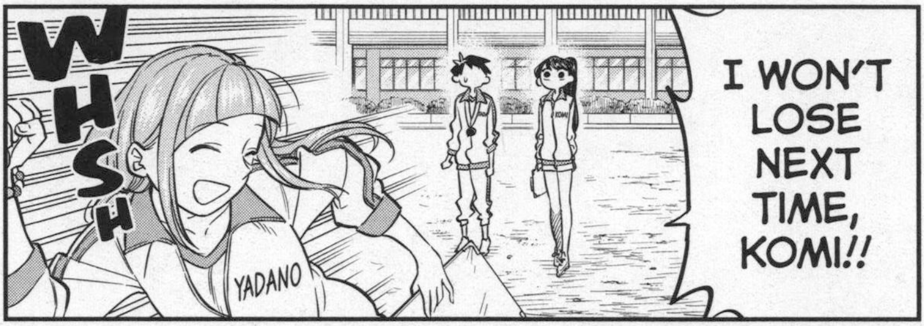
I WON'T LOSE NEXT TIME, KOMI!!
WHSH
YADANO

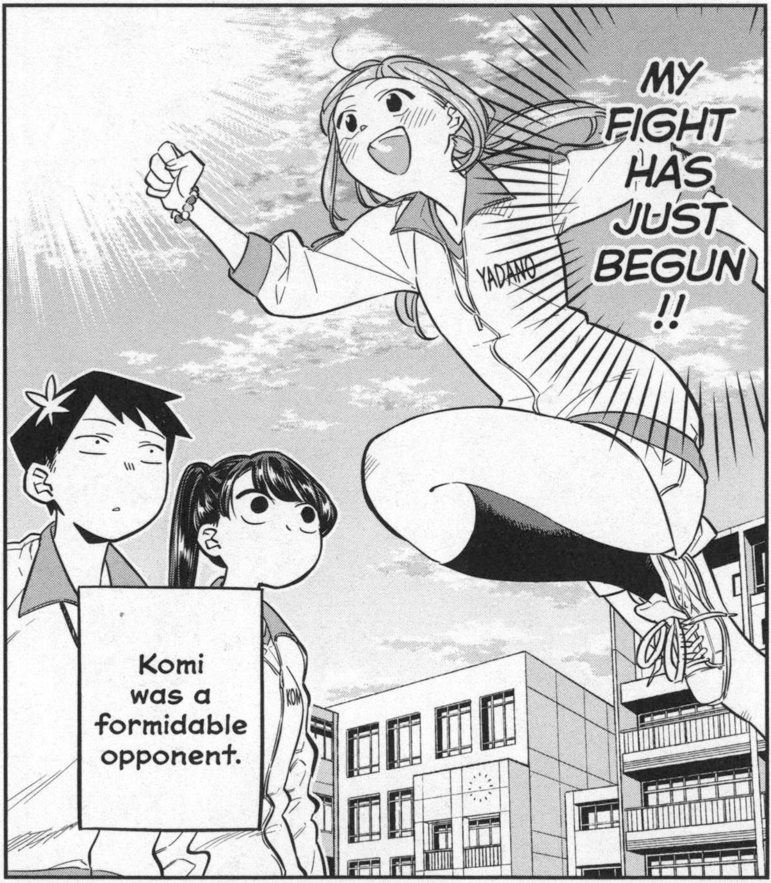
MY FIGHT HAS JUST BEGUN!!
YADANO
Komi was a formidable opponent.

Communication 21 — The End

Komi Can't Communicate

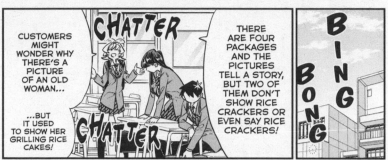

BING
BONG
THERE ARE FOUR PACKAGES AND THE PICTURES TELL A STORY, BUT TWO OF THEM DON'T SHOW RICE CRACKERS OR EVEN SAY RICE CRACKERS!
CHATTER
CUSTOMERS MIGHT WONDER WHY THERE'S A PICTURE OF AN OLD WOMAN...
...BUT IT USED TO SHOW HER GRILLING RICE CAKES!
CHATTER
APPARENTLY, THEIR BRAINS ARE COMPARABLE TO A HORNED BEETLE'S, EVEN THOUGH THEY'RE MAMMALS, SO HAMSTERS ARE SMARTER!
YADA YADA
AND A WHALE SHARK'S BRAIN IS THE SIZE OF A PEANUT, EVEN THOUGH THEY'RE SO BIG!
YADA YADA
BUT LOBSTERS DON'T LIVE VERY LONG!
YOU CAN'T PARK YOUR BIKE AT THE STATION, BUT FIVE MINUTES SHOULD BE ENOUGH TO BUY FAST FOOD, RIGHT?
BLAH
SO I THOUGHT I WAS SAFE, BUT THERE'S AN OLD MAN WHO WATCHES THE PLACE LIKE A HAWK!
AND HE SAID, "Y–"
BLAH
Hey! Can I hang at your house today, Komi?
FWIP
HUH? HOW DOES THAT STORY END?!

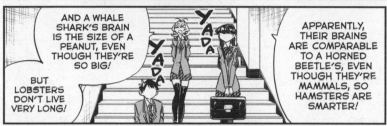

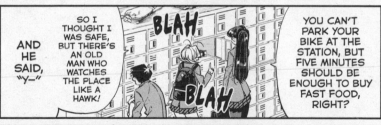

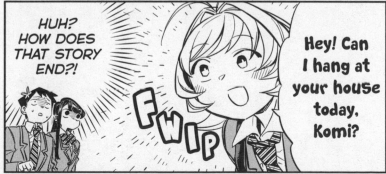

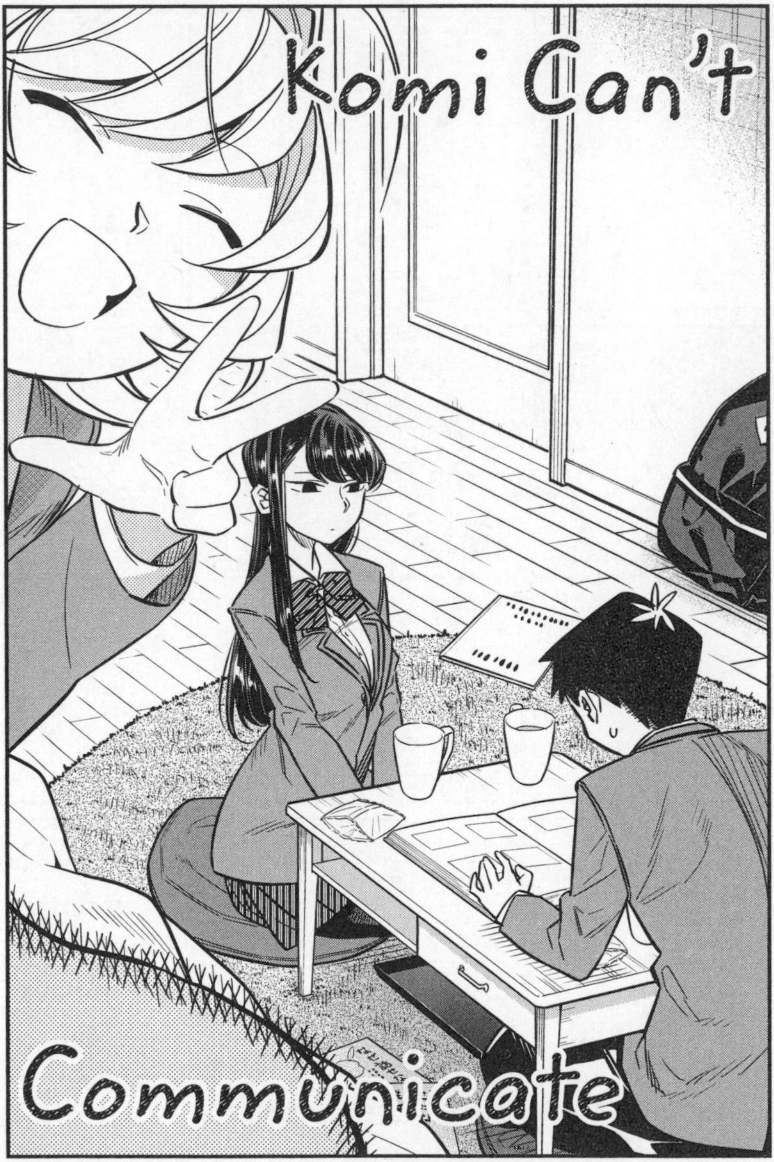
Komi Can't
Communicate

Communication 22: Home Visit

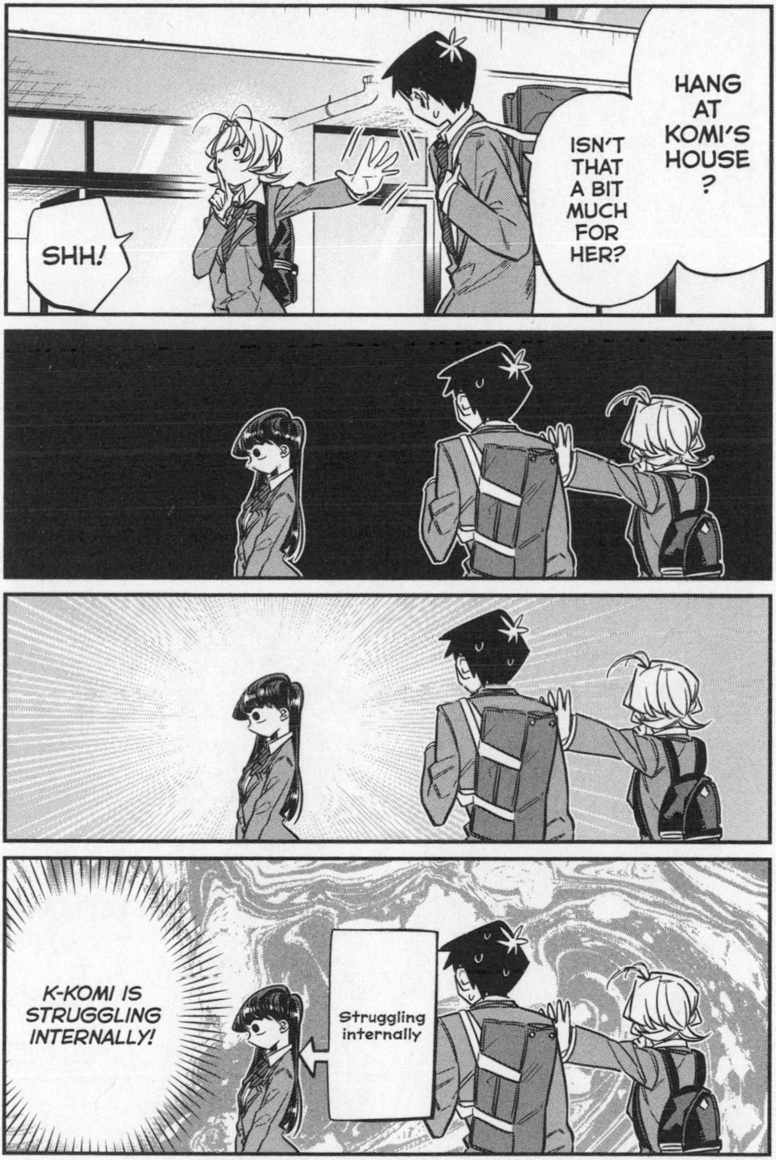
HANG AT KOMI'S HOUSE?
ISN'T THAT A BIT MUCH FOR HER?
SHH!
Struggling internally
K-KOMI IS STRUGGLING INTERNALLY!

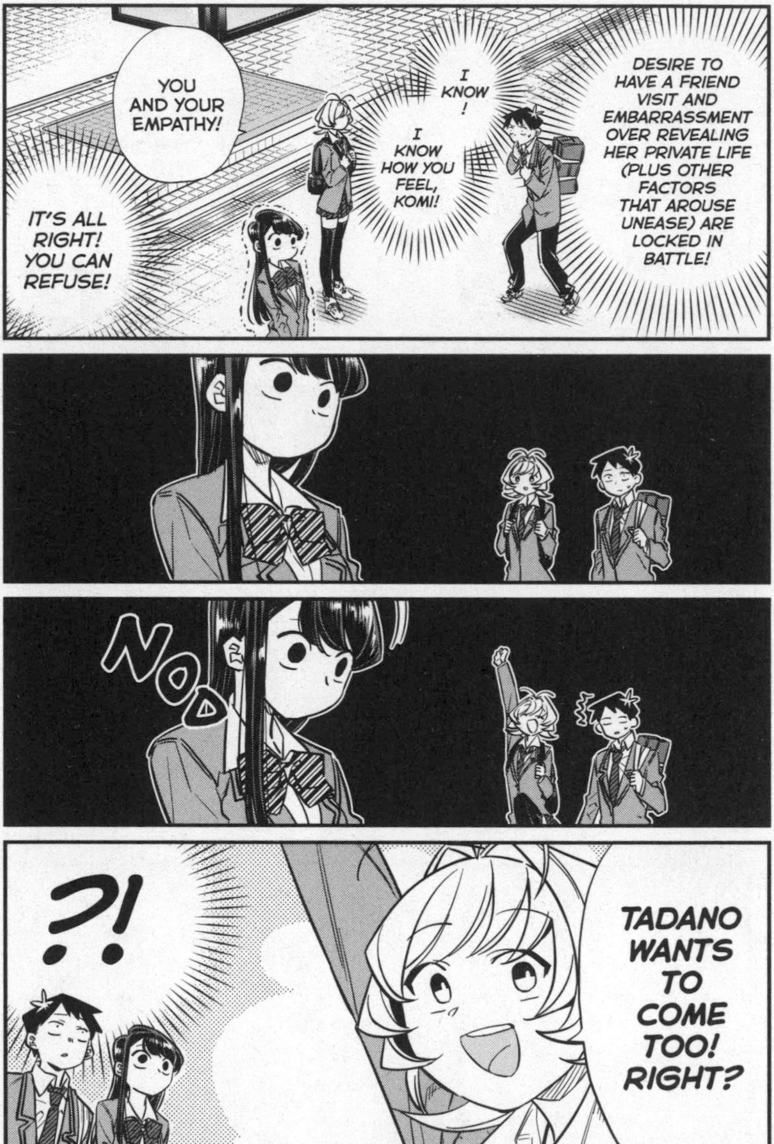
DESIRE TO HAVE A FRIEND VISIT AND EMBARRASSMENT OVER REVEALING HER PRIVATE LIFE (PLUS OTHER FACTORS THAT AROUSE UNEASE) ARE LOCKED IN BATTLE!
I KNOW!
I KNOW HOW YOU FEEL, KOMI!
YOU AND YOUR EMPATHY!
IT'S ALL RIGHT! YOU CAN REFUSE!
NOD
TADANO WANTS TO COME TOO! RIGHT?
?!

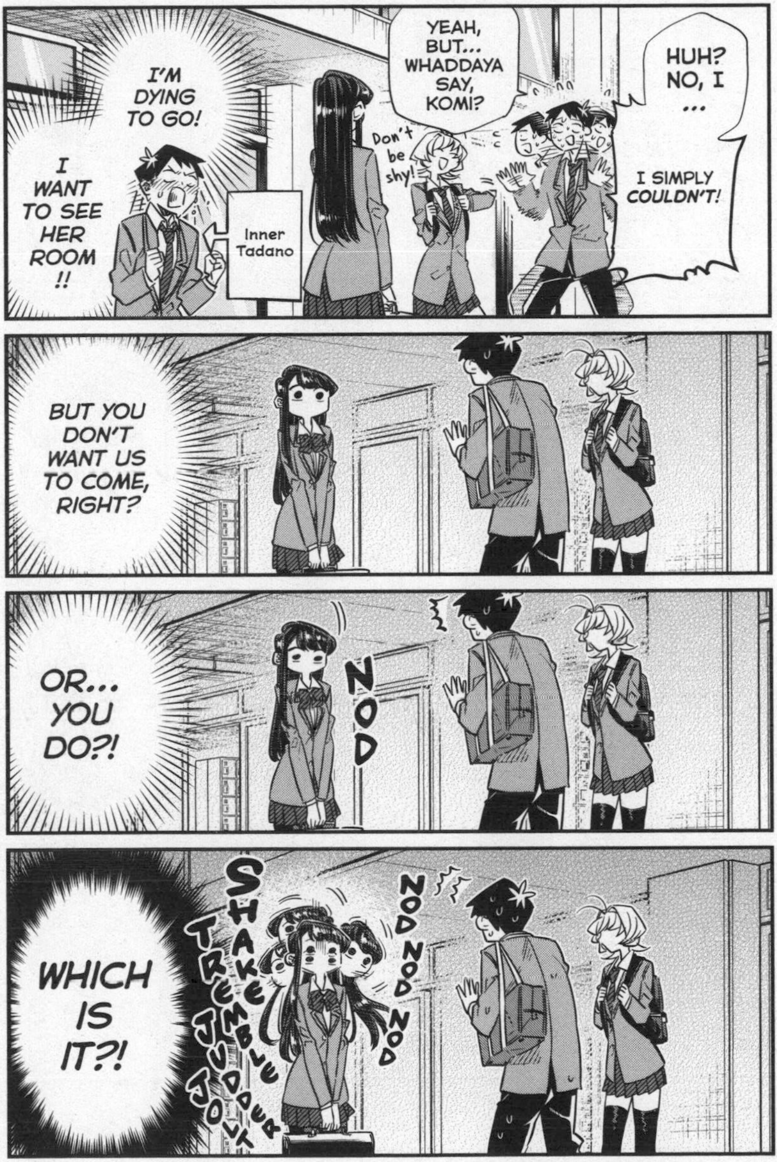
HUH? NO, I ...
I SIMPLY COULDN'T!
YEAH, BUT... WHADDAYA SAY, KOMI?
Don't be shy!
Inner Tadano
I'M DYING TO GO!
I WANT TO SEE HER ROOM !!
BUT YOU DON'T WANT US TO COME, RIGHT?
NOD
OR... YOU DO?!
NOD NOD NOD NOD
SHAKE
TREMBLE
JUDDER
JOLT
WHICH IS IT?!

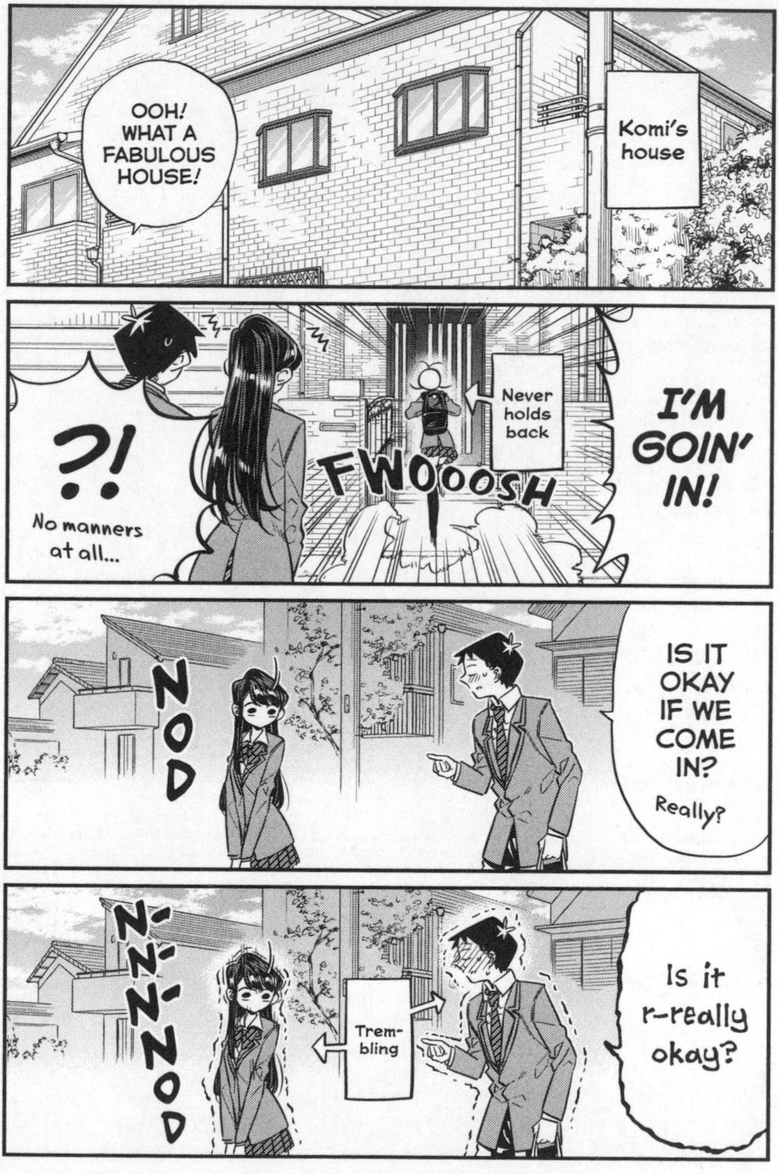

Komi's house
OOH! WHAT A FABULOUS HOUSE!
I'M GOIN' IN!
Never holds back
FWOOOSH
?!
No manners at all...
IS IT OKAY IF WE COME IN?
Really?
NOD
Is it r-really okay?
Trem-bling
N-N-N-NOD

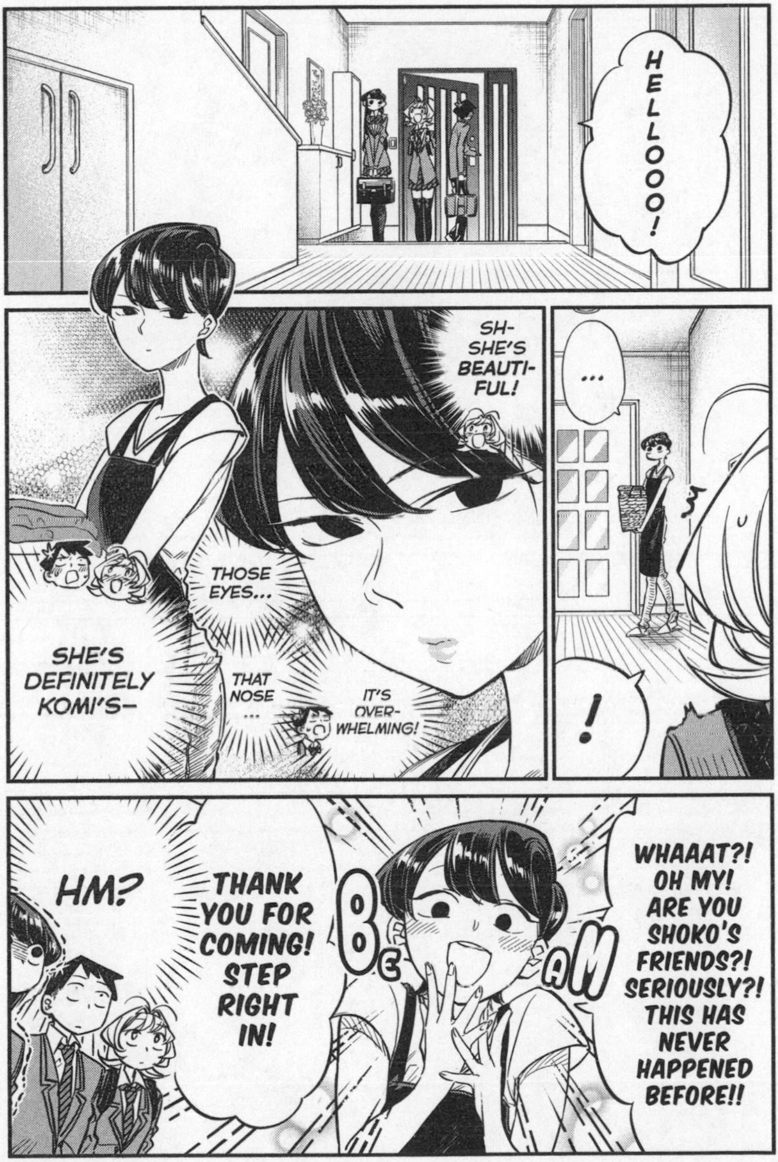

HELLOOO!
...
!
SH-SHE'S BEAUTIFUL!
THOSE EYES...
THAT NOSE...
IT'S OVERWHELMING!
SHE'S DEFINITELY KOMI'S—
WHAAAT?! OH MY! ARE YOU SHOKO'S FRIENDS?! SERIOUSLY?! THIS HAS NEVER HAPPENED BEFORE!!
BEAM
THANK YOU FOR COMING! STEP RIGHT IN!
HM?

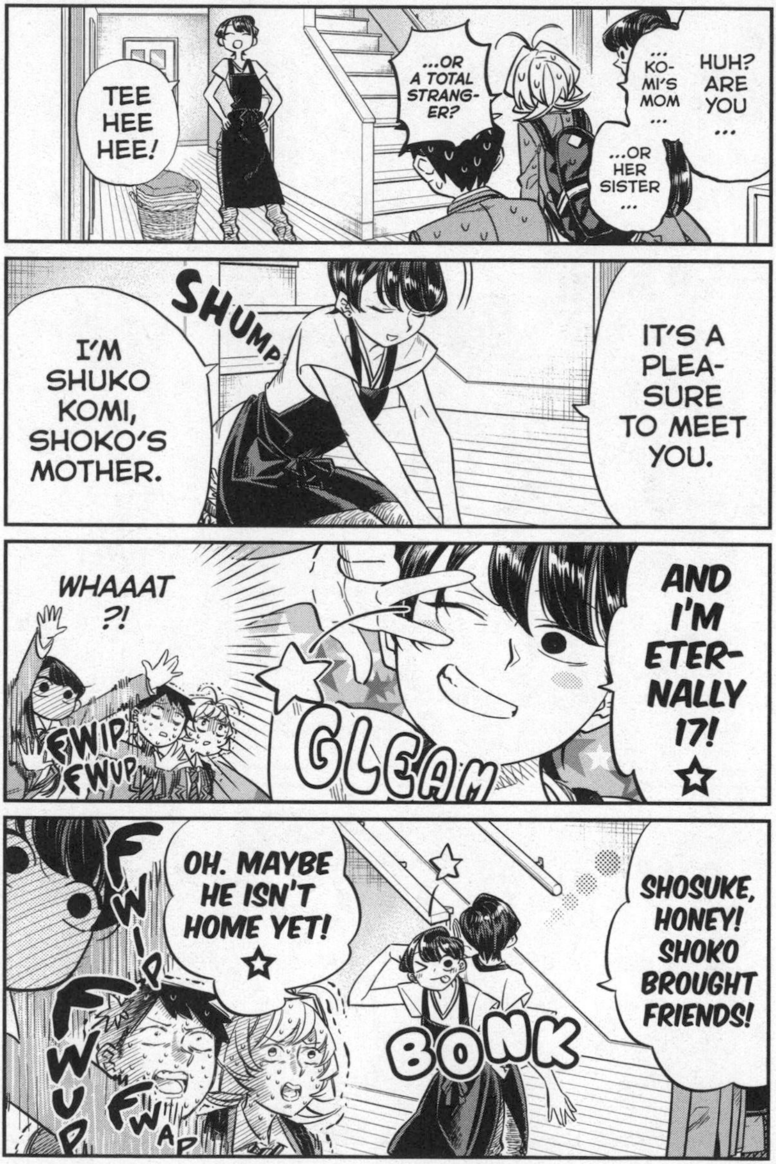
HUH? ARE YOU ...
...KO-MI'S MOM ...
...OR HER SISTER ...
...OR A TOTAL STRANGER?
TEE HEE HEE!
IT'S A PLEASURE TO MEET YOU.
SHUMP
I'M SHUKO KOMI, SHOKO'S MOTHER.
AND I'M ETERNALLY 17! ☆
GLEAM
WHAAAT?!
FWIP FWUP
SHOSUKE, HONEY! SHOKO BROUGHT FRIENDS!
BONK
OH. MAYBE HE ISN'T HOME YET! ☆
FWIP FWUP FWAP

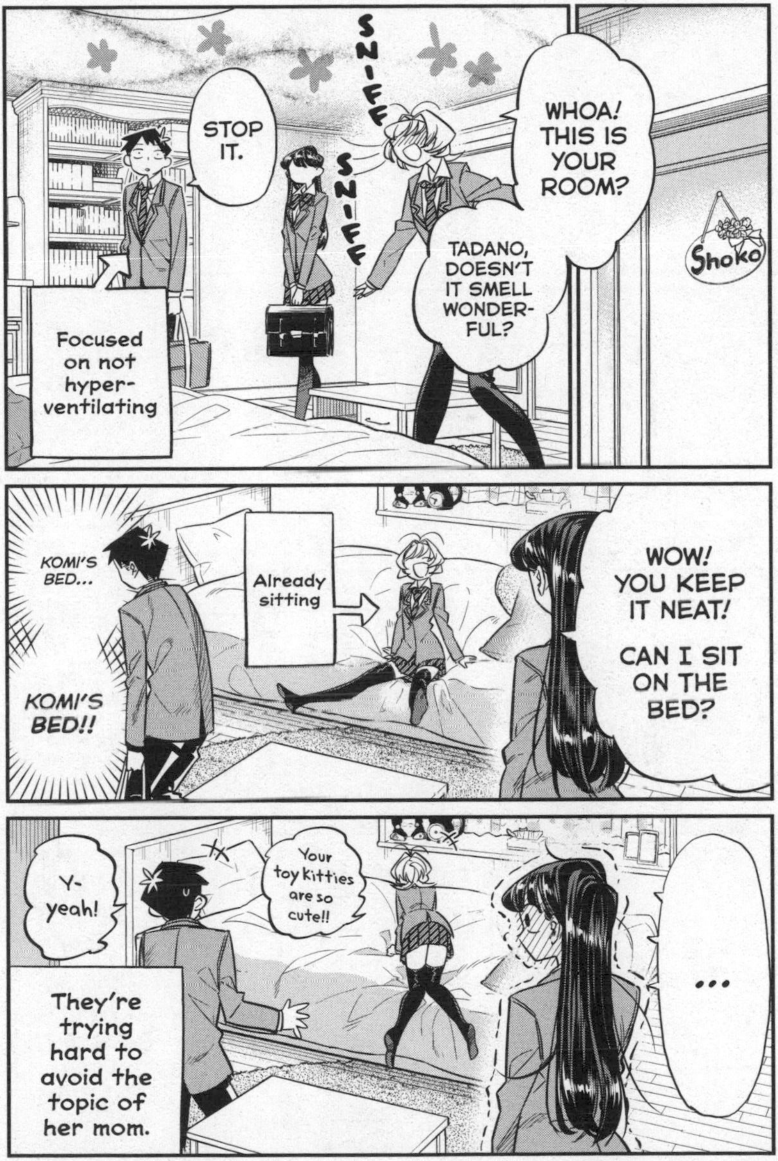
Shoko
WHOA! THIS IS YOUR ROOM?
SNIFF SNIFF
TADANO, DOESN'T IT SMELL WONDERFUL?
STOP IT.
Focused on not hyper-ventilating
WOW! YOU KEEP IT NEAT!
CAN I SIT ON THE BED?
Already sitting
KOMI'S BED...
KOMI'S BED!!
...
Your toy kitties are so cute!!
Y-yeah!
They're trying hard to avoid the topic of her mom.

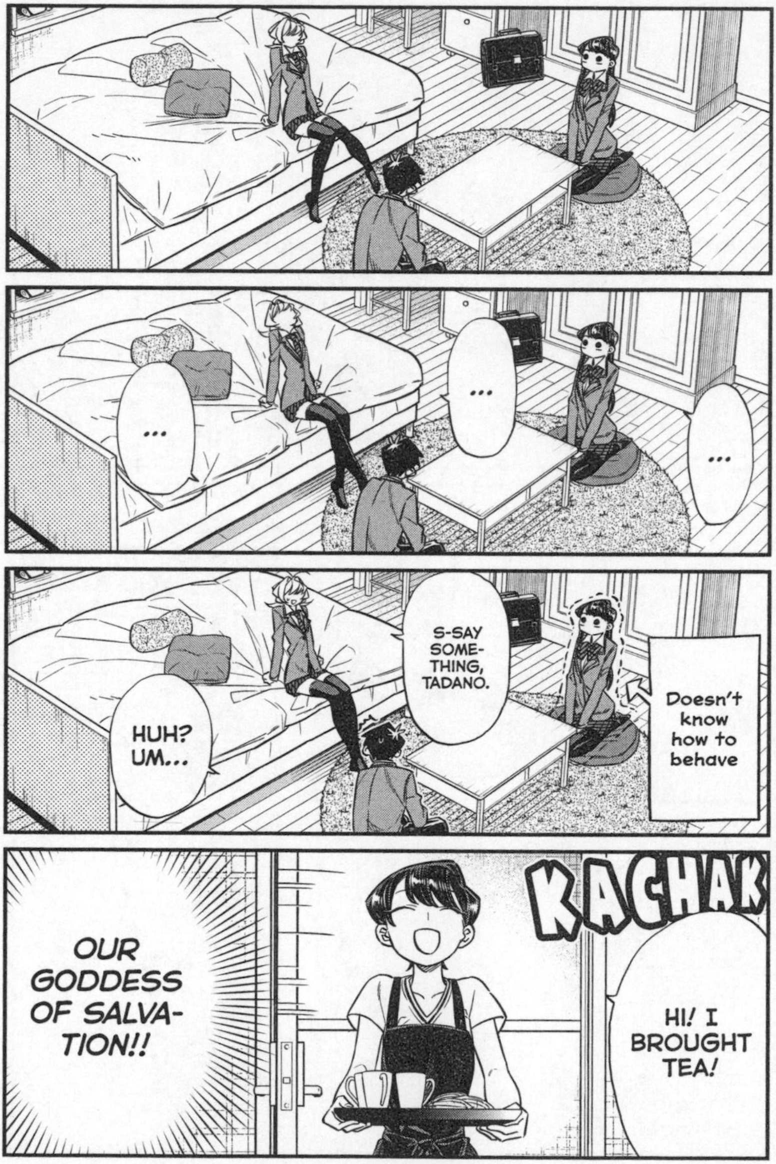
...
...
...
Doesn't know how to behave
S-SAY SOME-THING, TADANO.
HUH? UM...
KACHAK
HI! I BROUGHT TEA!
OUR GODDESS OF SALVA-TION!!

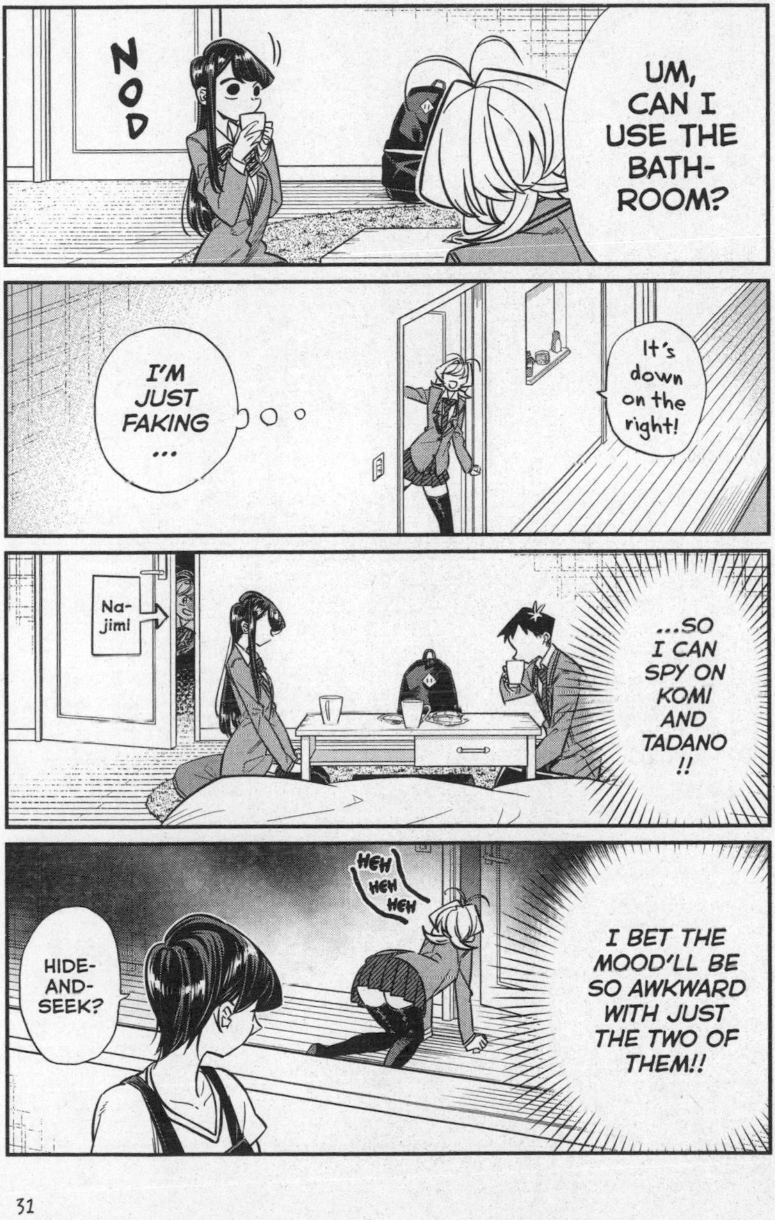
UM, CAN I USE THE BATH-ROOM?
NOD
It's down on the right!
I'M JUST FAKING ...
...SO I CAN SPY ON KOMI AND TADANO !!
Na-jimi
I BET THE MOOD'LL BE SO AWKWARD WITH JUST THE TWO OF THEM!!
HEH HEH HEH
HIDE-AND-SEEK?

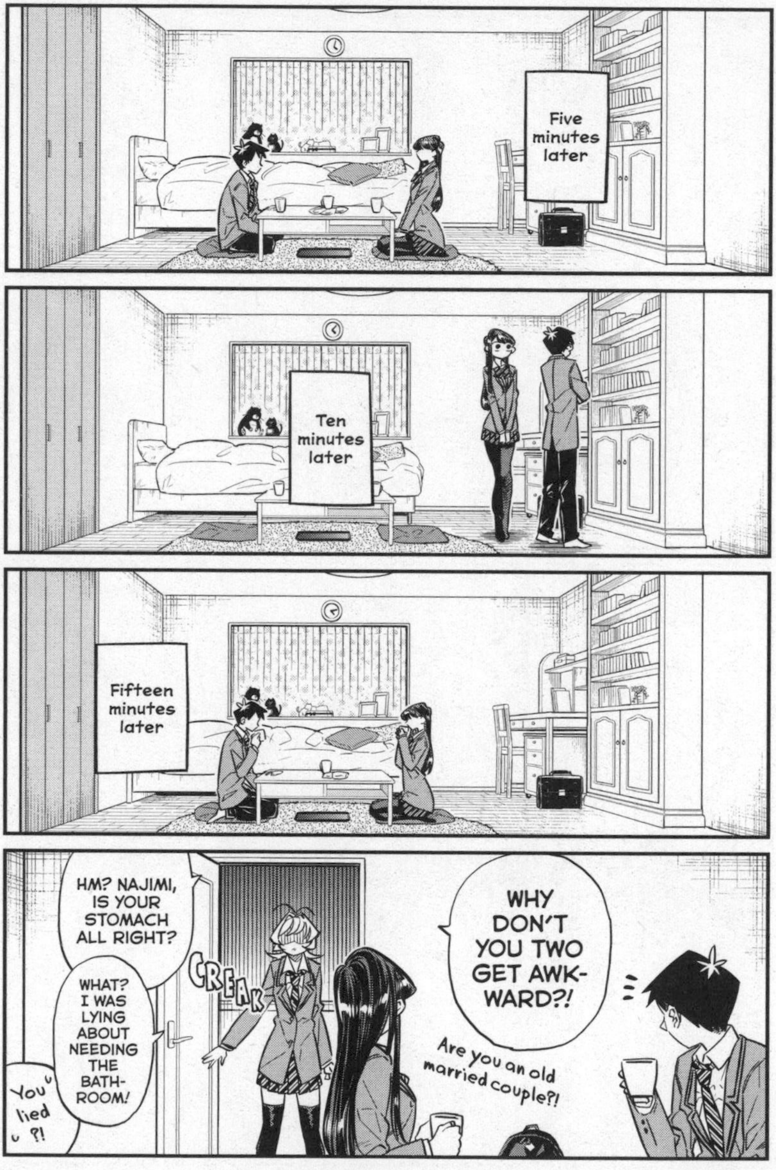
Five minutes later
Ten minutes later
Fifteen minutes later
WHY DON'T YOU TWO GET AWK-WARD?!
Are you an old married couple?!
CREAK
HM? NAJIMI, IS YOUR STOMACH ALL RIGHT?
WHAT? I WAS LYING ABOUT NEEDING THE BATH-ROOM!
You lied ?!

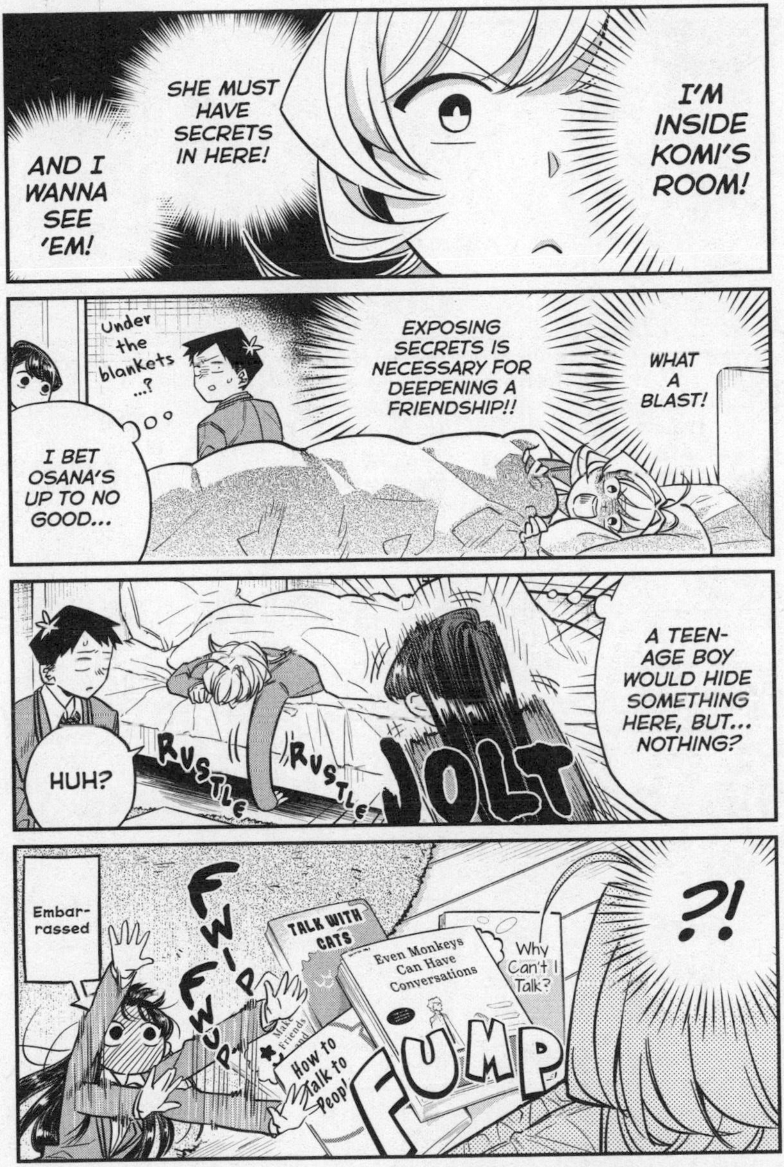
I'M INSIDE KOMI'S ROOM!
SHE MUST HAVE SECRETS IN HERE!
AND I WANNA SEE 'EM!
WHAT A BLAST!
EXPOSING SECRETS IS NECESSARY FOR DEEPENING A FRIENDSHIP!!
Under the blankets ...?
I BET OSANA'S UP TO NO GOOD...
A TEEN-AGE BOY WOULD HIDE SOMETHING HERE, BUT... NOTHING?
JOLT
RUSTLE
RUSTLE
HUH?
?!
Why Can't I Talk?
Even Monkeys Can Have Conversations
FUMP
TALK WITH CATS
FWIP
How to Talk to Peop
FWUP
Embar-rassed

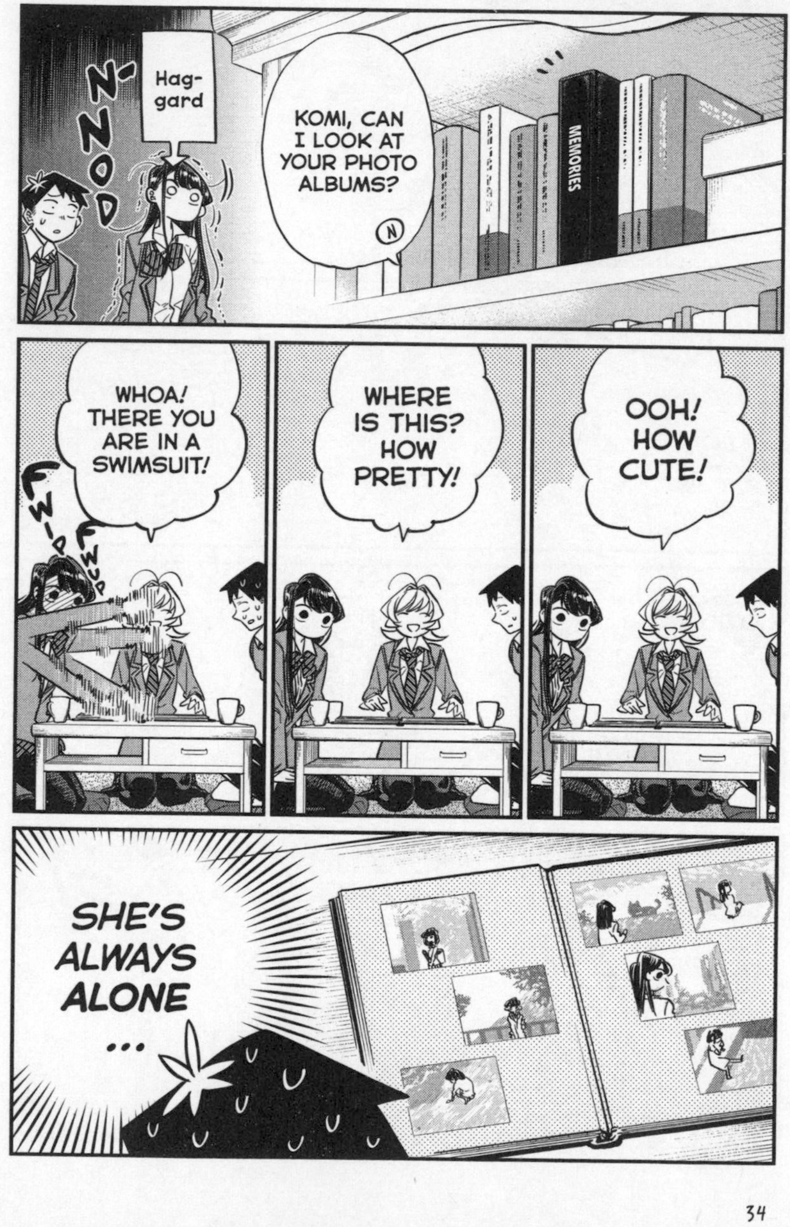
MEMORIES
KOMI, CAN I LOOK AT YOUR PHOTO ALBUMS?
N
Hag-gard
N-NOD
OOH! HOW CUTE!
WHERE IS THIS? HOW PRETTY!
WHOA! THERE YOU ARE IN A SWIMSUIT!
FWIP
FWUP
SHE'S ALWAYS ALONE ...

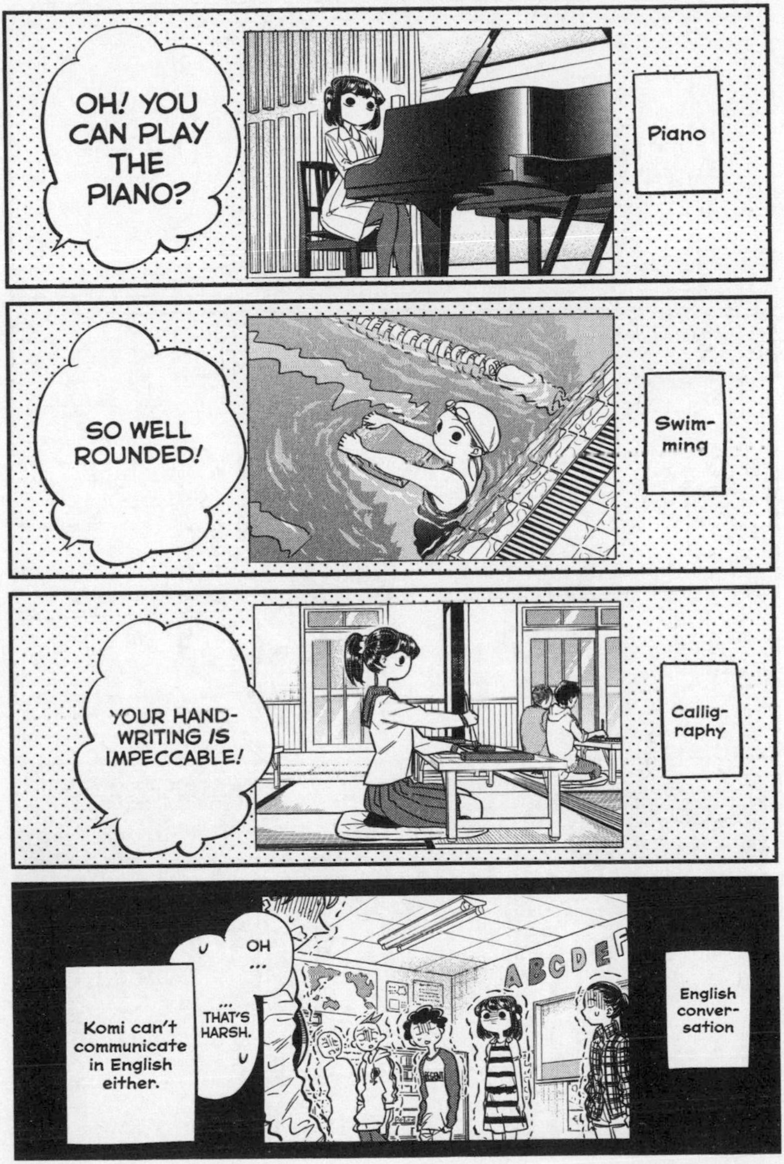
Piano
OH! YOU CAN PLAY THE PIANO?
Swim-ming
SO WELL ROUNDED!
Calligraphy
YOUR HAND-WRITING IS IMPECCABLE!
English conver-sation
OH ... ... THAT'S HARSH.
Komi can't communicate in English either.

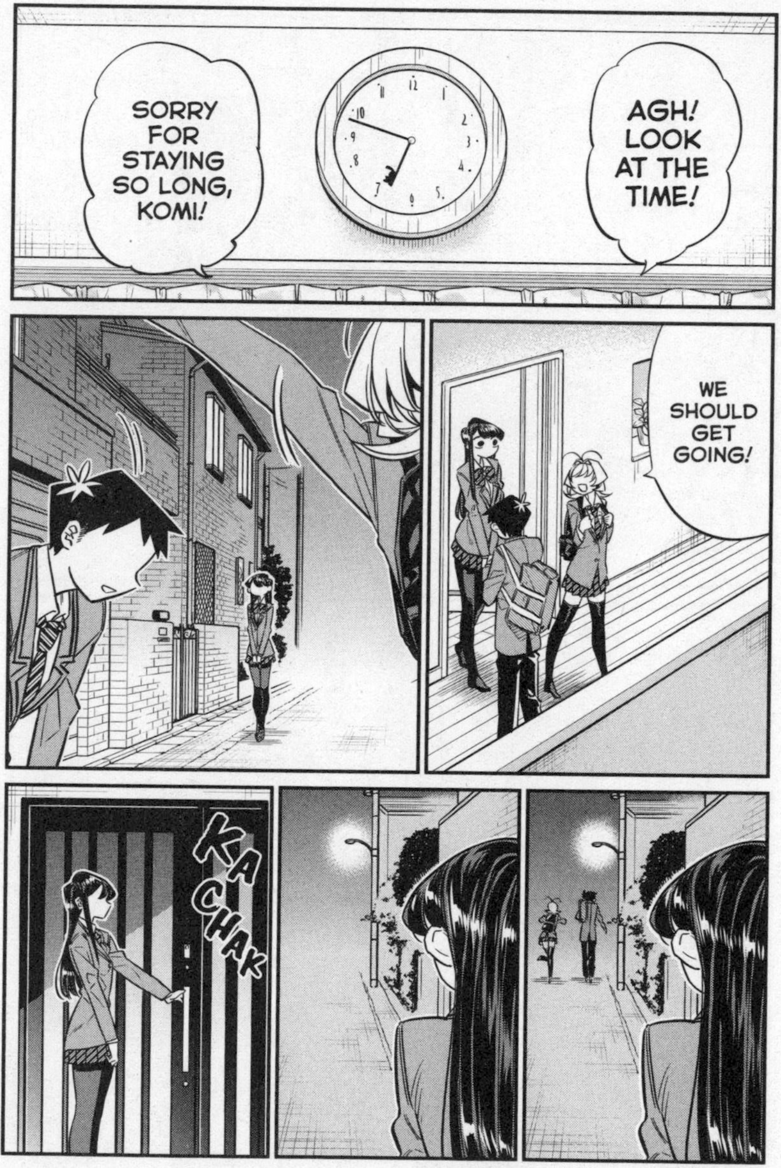
AGH! LOOK AT THE TIME!
SORRY FOR STAYING SO LONG, KOMI!
WE SHOULD GET GOING!
KA CHAK

KA CHAK

TMP TMP

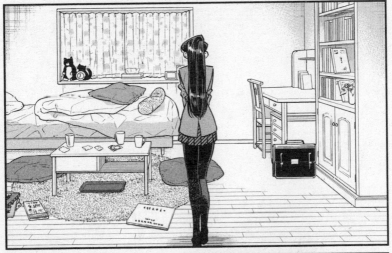

37

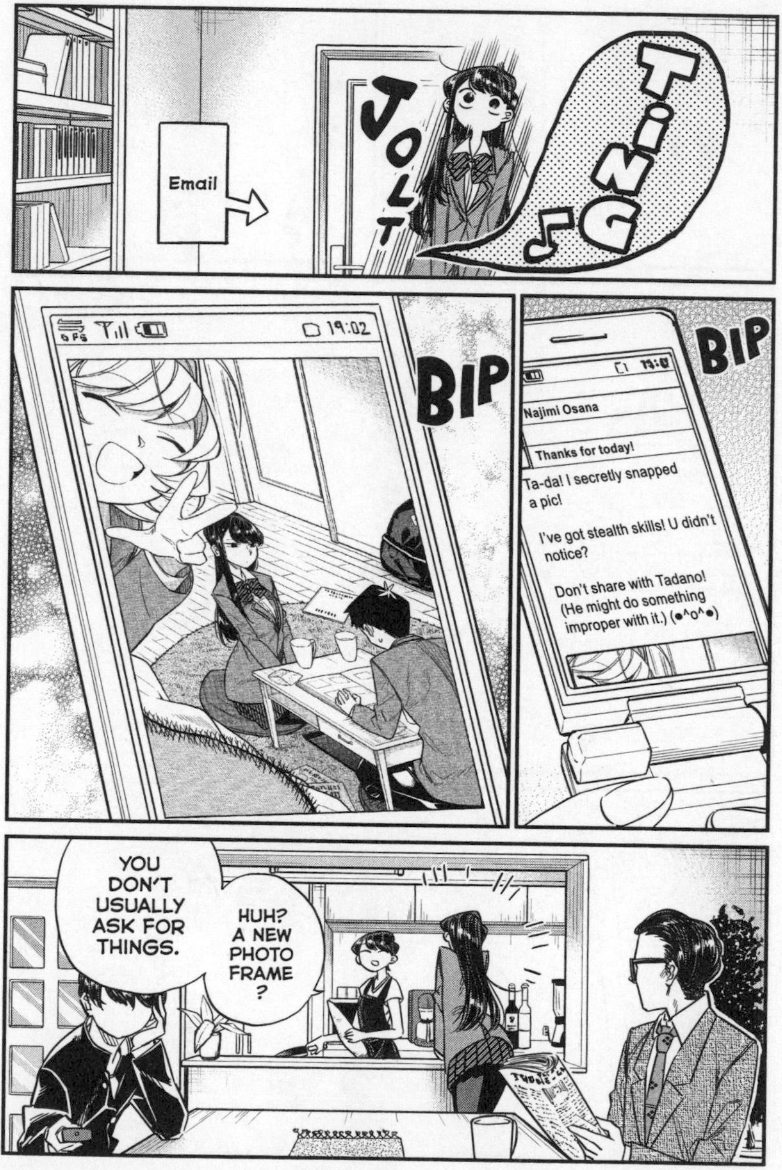
TING
JOLT
Email
BIP
Najimi Osana
Thanks for today!
Ta-da! I secretly snapped a pic!
I've got stealth skills! U didn't notice?
Don't share with Tadano! (He might do something improper with it.) (●^o^●)
19:02
BIP
HUH? A NEW PHOTO FRAME?
YOU DON'T USUALLY ASK FOR THINGS.

Communication 22 – The End

Komi Can't Communicate

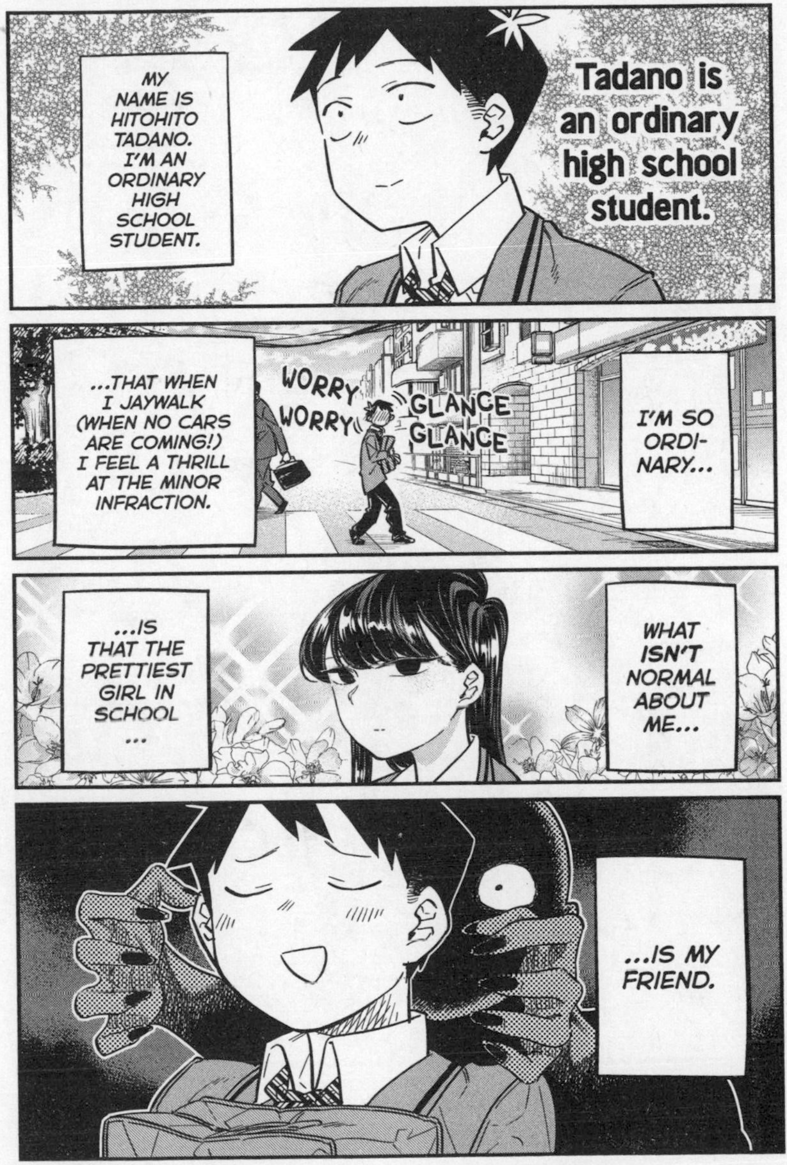
Tadano is an ordinary high school student.
MY NAME IS HITOHITO TADANO. I'M AN ORDINARY HIGH SCHOOL STUDENT.
I'M SO ORDINARY...
GLANCE GLANCE
WORRY WORRY
...THAT WHEN I JAYWALK (WHEN NO CARS ARE COMING!) I FEEL A THRILL AT THE MINOR INFRACTION.
WHAT ISN'T NORMAL ABOUT ME...
...IS THAT THE PRETTIEST GIRL IN SCHOOL...
...IS MY FRIEND.

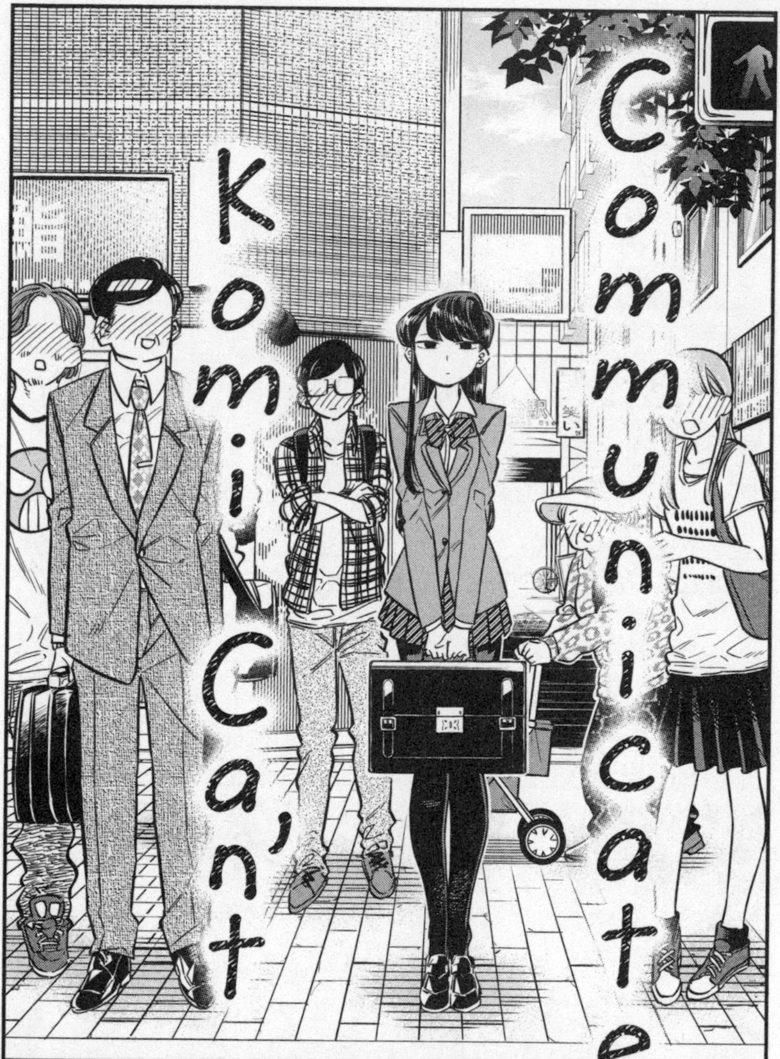
Komi Can't
Communicate

Communication 23: Ren

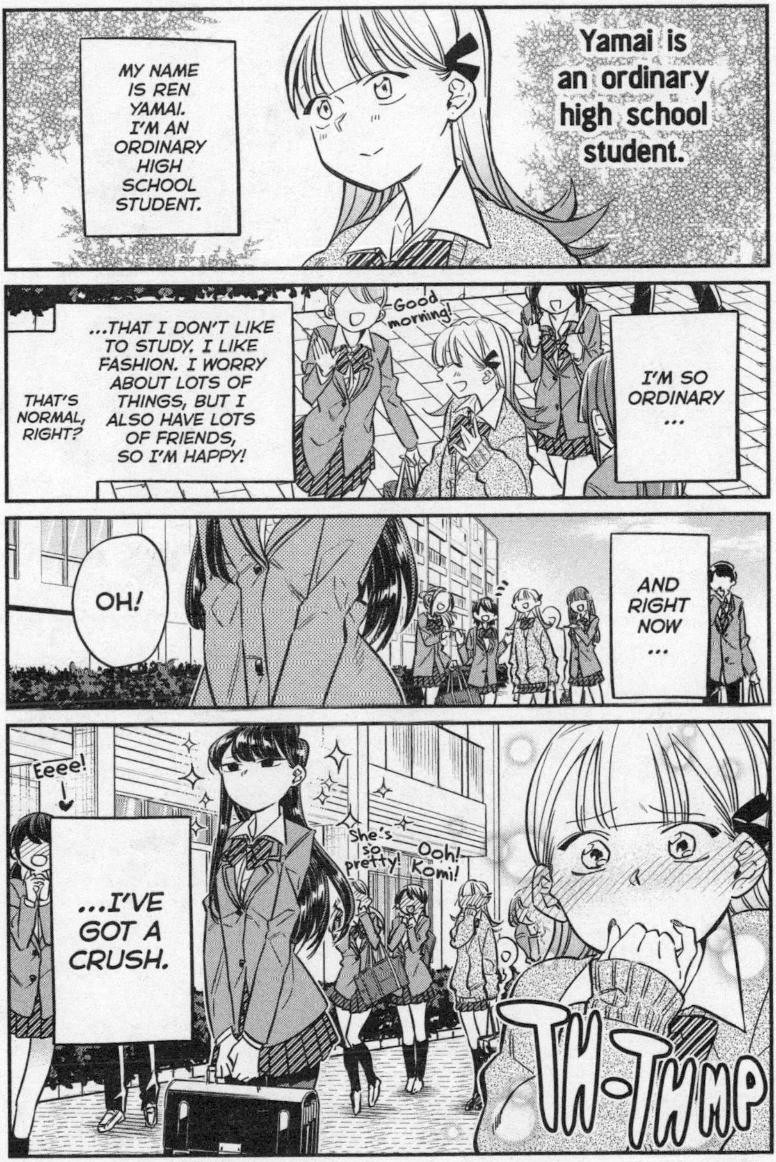
Yamai is an ordinary high school student.
MY NAME IS REN YAMAI. I'M AN ORDINARY HIGH SCHOOL STUDENT.
I'M SO ORDINARY ...
Good morning!
...THAT I DON'T LIKE TO STUDY. I LIKE FASHION. I WORRY ABOUT LOTS OF THINGS, BUT I ALSO HAVE LOTS OF FRIENDS, SO I'M HAPPY!
THAT'S NORMAL, RIGHT?
AND RIGHT NOW ...
OH!
TH-THMP
Ooh! Komi!
She's so pretty!
...I'VE GOT A CRUSH.
Eeee!

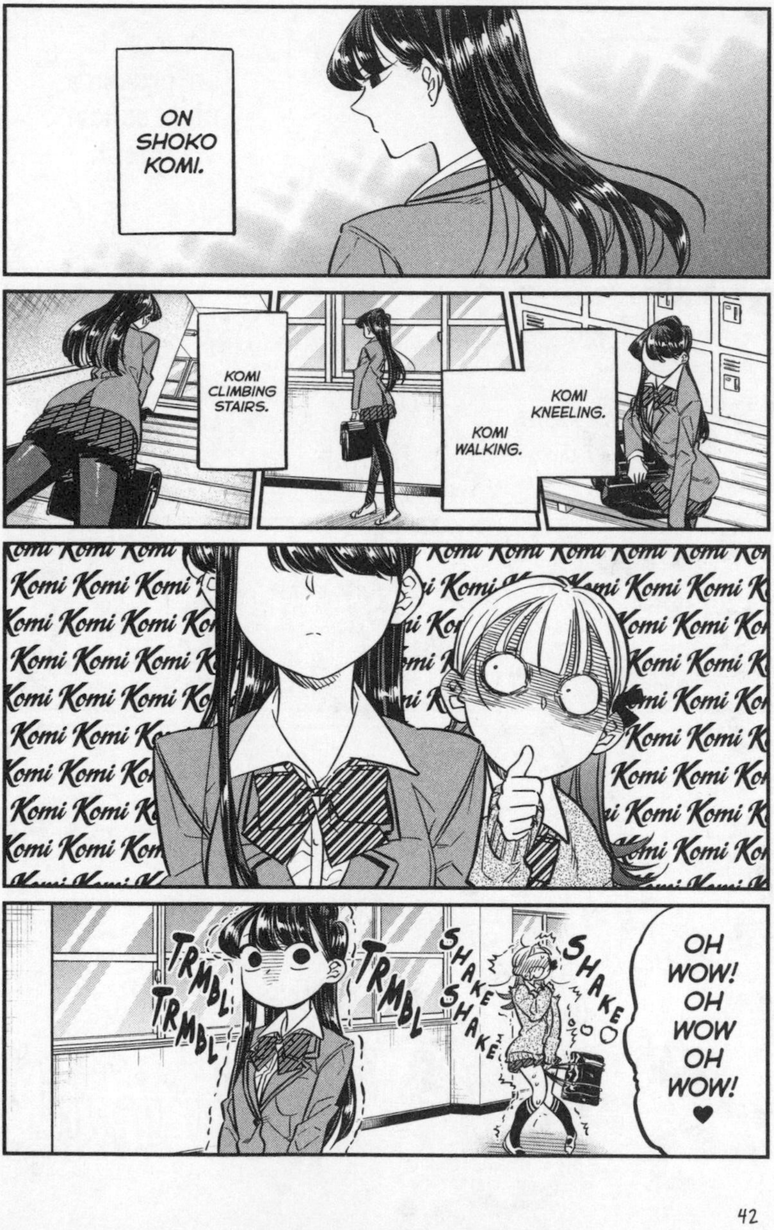
ON SHOKO KOMI.
KOMI KNEELING.
KOMI WALKING.
KOMI CLIMBING STAIRS.
Komi Komi Komi Komi
OH WOW! OH WOW OH WOW! ♥
SHAKE
SHAKE SHAKE SHAKE
TRMBL
TRMBL TRMBL

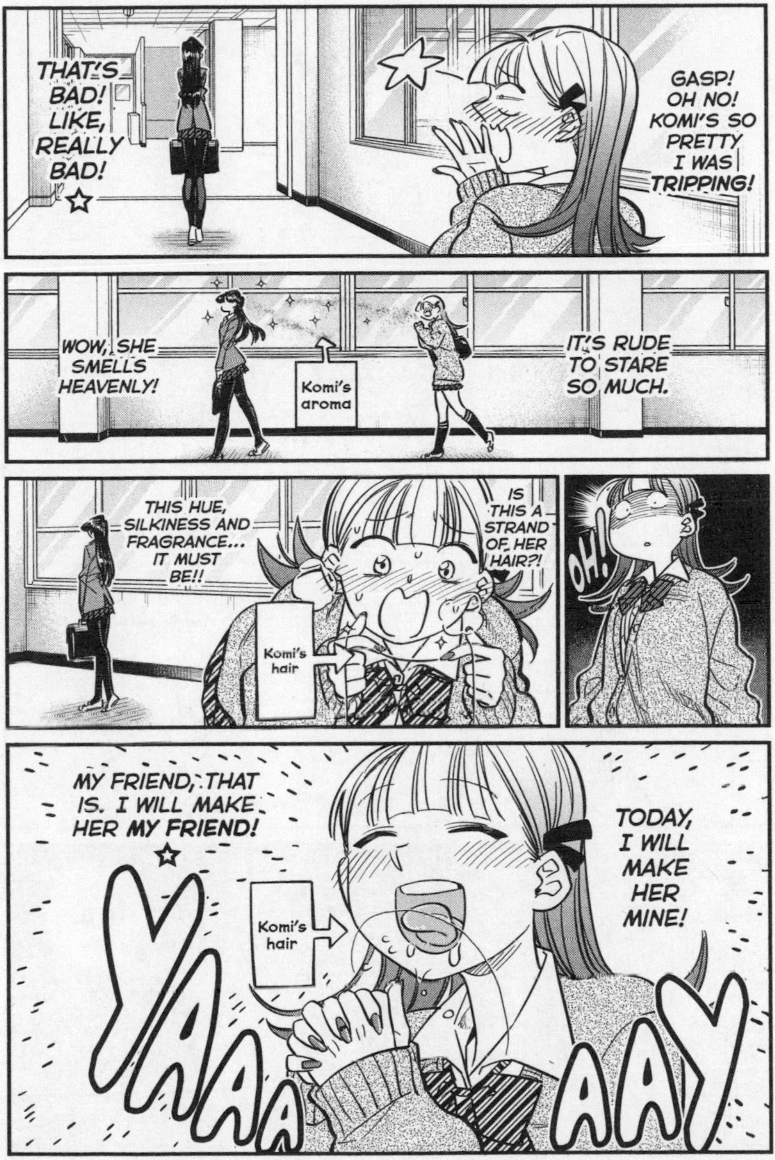
GASP! OH NO! KOMI'S SO PRETTY I WAS TRIPPING!
THAT'S BAD! LIKE, REALLY BAD! ☆
IT'S RUDE TO STARE SO MUCH.
WOW, SHE SMELLS HEAVENLY!
Komi's aroma
OH!
IS THIS A STRAND OF HER HAIR?!
THIS HUE, SILKINESS AND FRAGRANCE... IT MUST BE!!
Komi's hair
TODAY, I WILL MAKE HER MINE!
MY FRIEND, THAT IS. I WILL MAKE HER MY FRIEND! ☆
Komi's hair
YAAAAAY

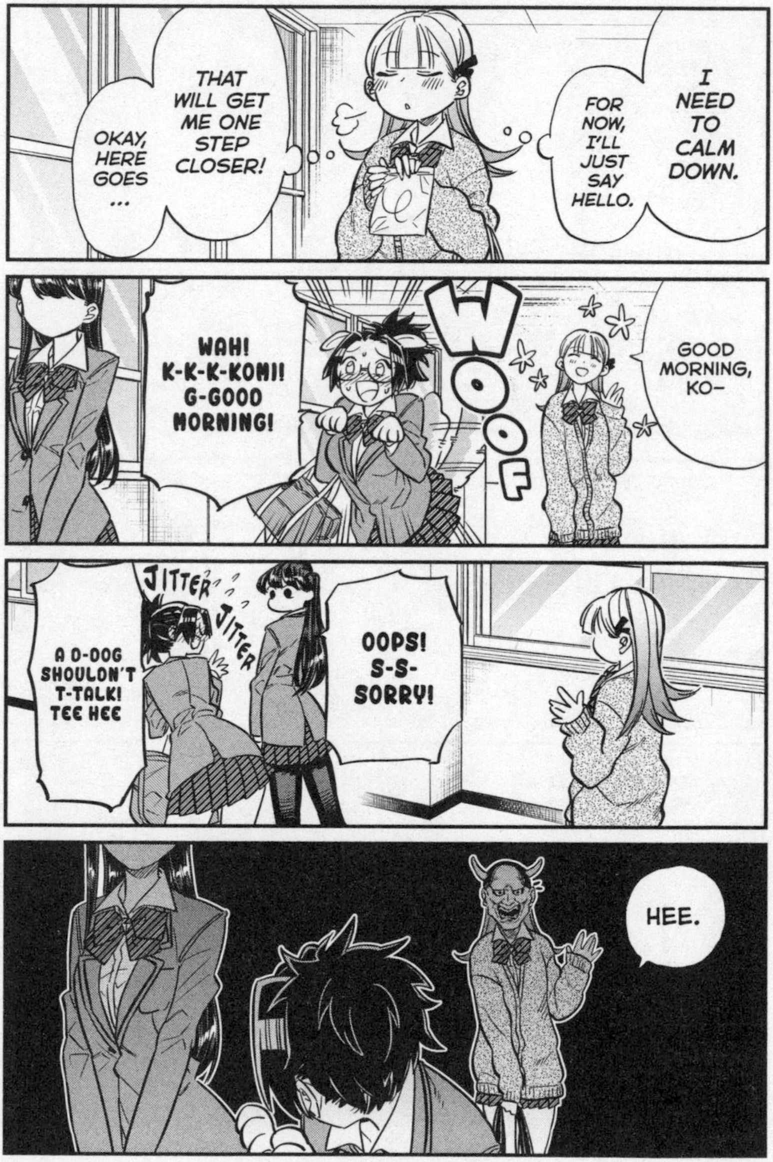
I NEED TO CALM DOWN.
FOR NOW, I'LL JUST SAY HELLO.
THAT WILL GET ME ONE STEP CLOSER!
OKAY, HERE GOES ...
GOOD MORNING, KO–
WOOF
WAH! K-K-K-KOMI! G-GOOD MORNING!
OOPS! S-S-SORRY!
JITTER JITTER
A D-DOG SHOULDN'T T-TALK! TEE HEE
HEE.

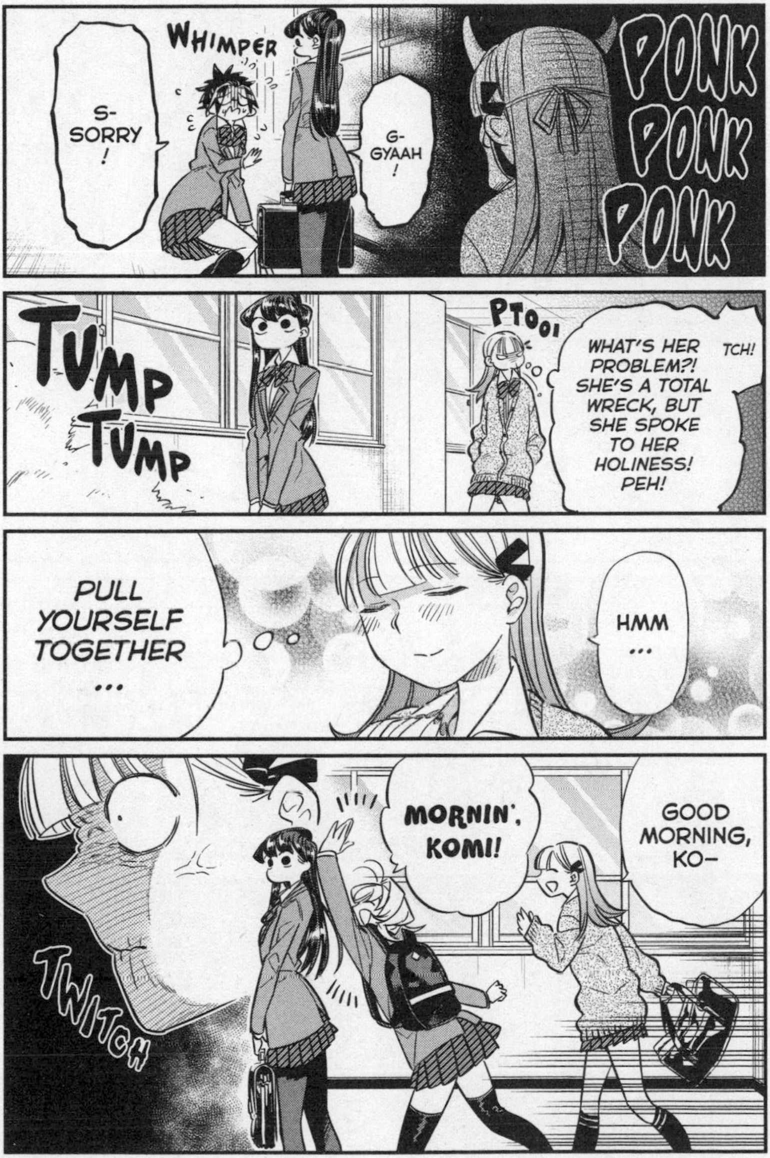
PONK PONK PONK
G-GYAAH!
WHIMPER
S-SORRY!
TCH!
WHAT'S HER PROBLEM?! SHE'S A TOTAL WRECK, BUT SHE SPOKE TO HER HOLINESS! PEH!
PTOOI
TUMP TUMP
HMM...
PULL YOURSELF TOGETHER...
GOOD MORNING, KO–
MORNIN', KOMI!
TWITCH

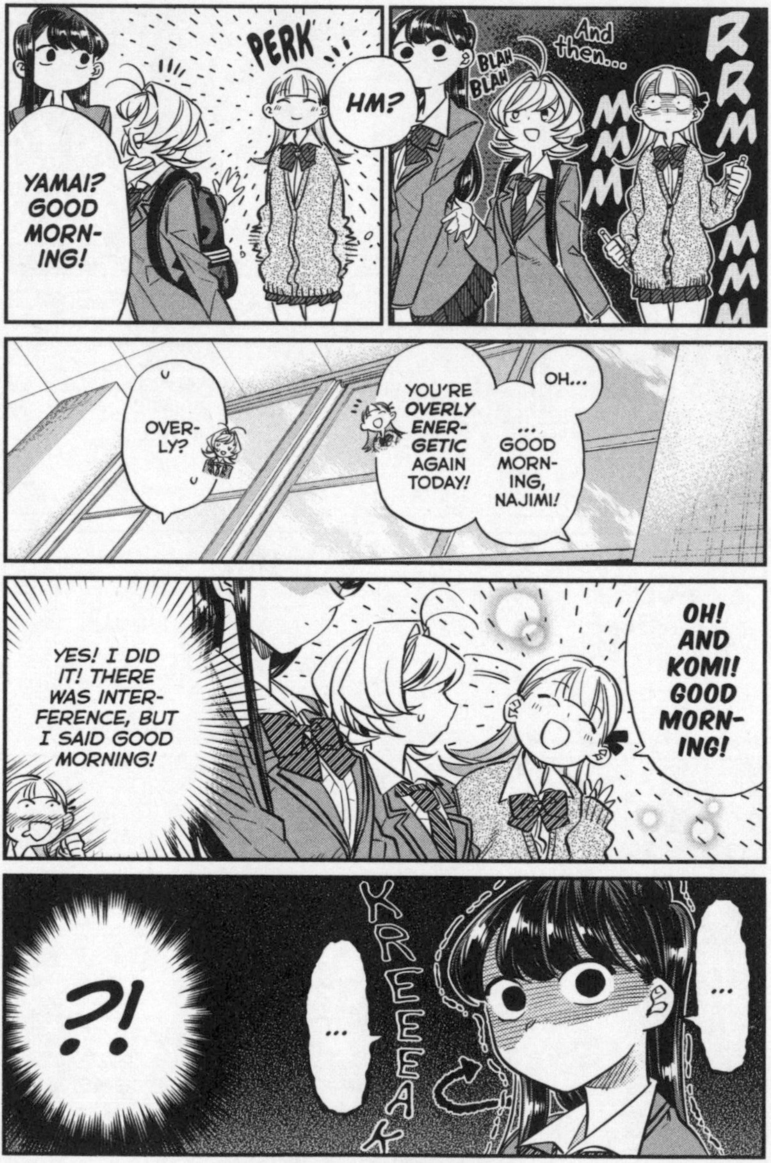
RRMMMM
And then...
BLAH BLAH
MMMM
PERK
HM?
YAMAI? GOOD MORN-ING!
OH... ...GOOD MORN-ING, NAJIMI!
YOU'RE OVERLY ENER-GETIC AGAIN TODAY!
OVER-LY?
OH! AND KOMI! GOOD MORN-ING!
YES! I DID IT! THERE WAS INTER-FERENCE, BUT I SAID GOOD MORNING!
...
KREEEAK
...
?!

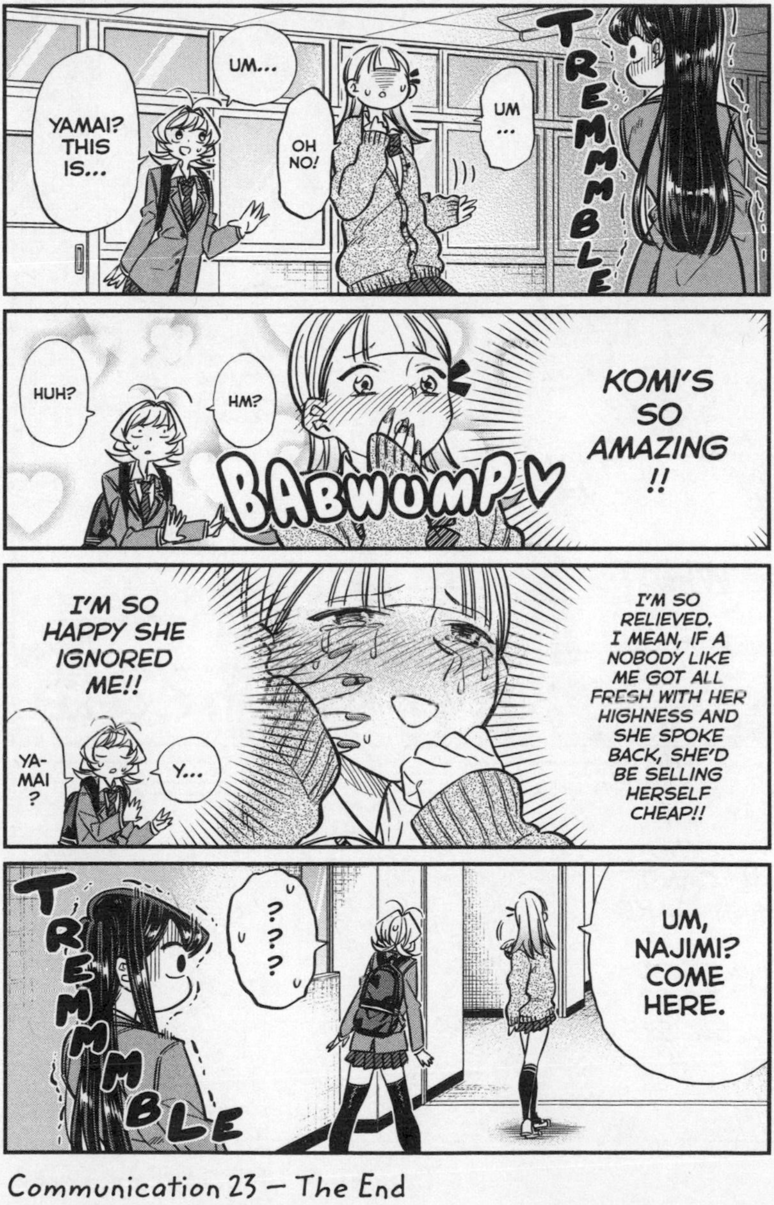
TREMMMBLE
UM ...
OH NO!
UM...
YAMAI? THIS IS...
KOMI'S SO AMAZING !!
BABWUMP♥
HM?
HUH?
I'M SO RELIEVED. I MEAN, IF A NOBODY LIKE ME GOT ALL FRESH WITH HER HIGHNESS AND SHE SPOKE BACK, SHE'D BE SELLING HERSELF CHEAP!!
I'M SO HAPPY SHE IGNORED ME!!
Y...
YA-MAI ?
UM, NAJIMI? COME HERE.
?.?.?.
TREMMMBLE

Communication 23 — The End

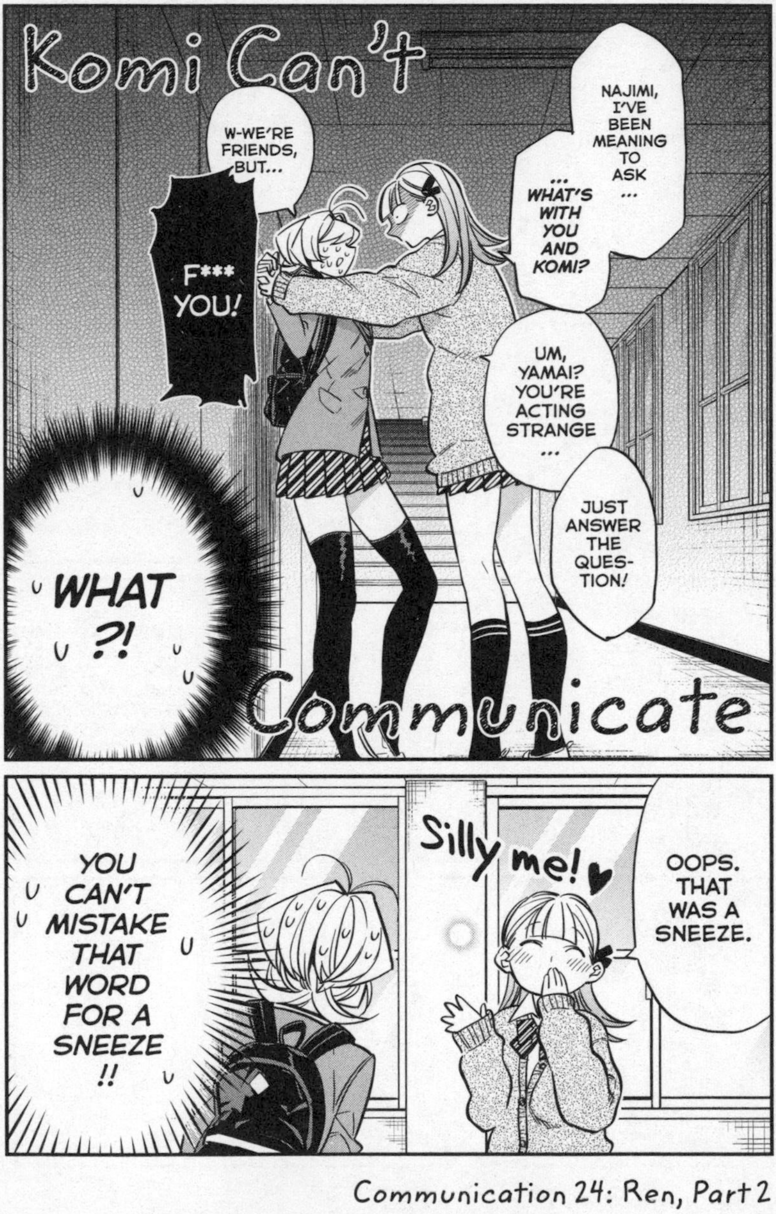
Komi Can't Communicate
NAJIMI, I'VE BEEN MEANING TO ASK...
...WHAT'S WITH YOU AND KOMI?
W-WE'RE FRIENDS, BUT...
F*** YOU!
UM, YAMAI? YOU'RE ACTING STRANGE...
JUST ANSWER THE QUESTION!
WHAT?!
OOPS. THAT WAS A SNEEZE.
Silly me!♥
YOU CAN'T MISTAKE THAT WORD FOR A SNEEZE!!

Communication 24: Ren, Part 2

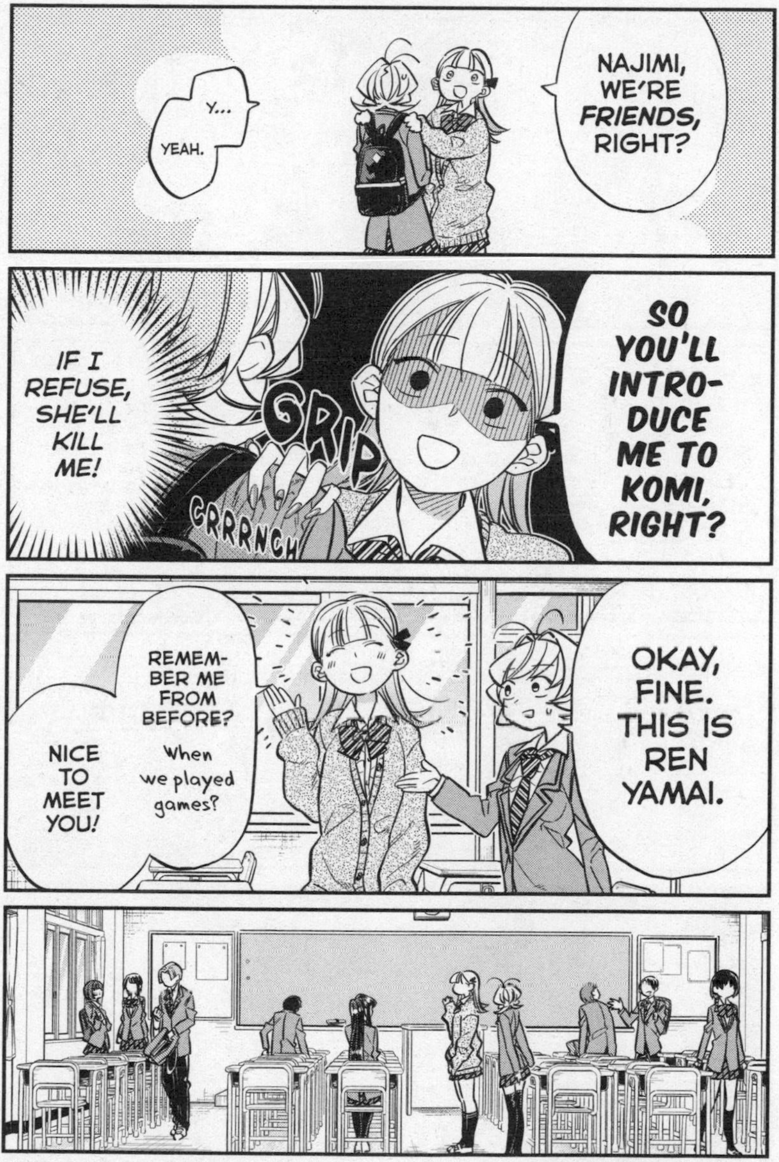
NAJIMI, WE'RE FRIENDS, RIGHT?
Y... YEAH.
SO YOU'LL INTRO-DUCE ME TO KOMI, RIGHT?
GRIP
CRRRNCH
IF I REFUSE, SHE'LL KILL ME!
OKAY, FINE. THIS IS REN YAMAI.
REMEM-BER ME FROM BEFORE? When we played games?
NICE TO MEET YOU!

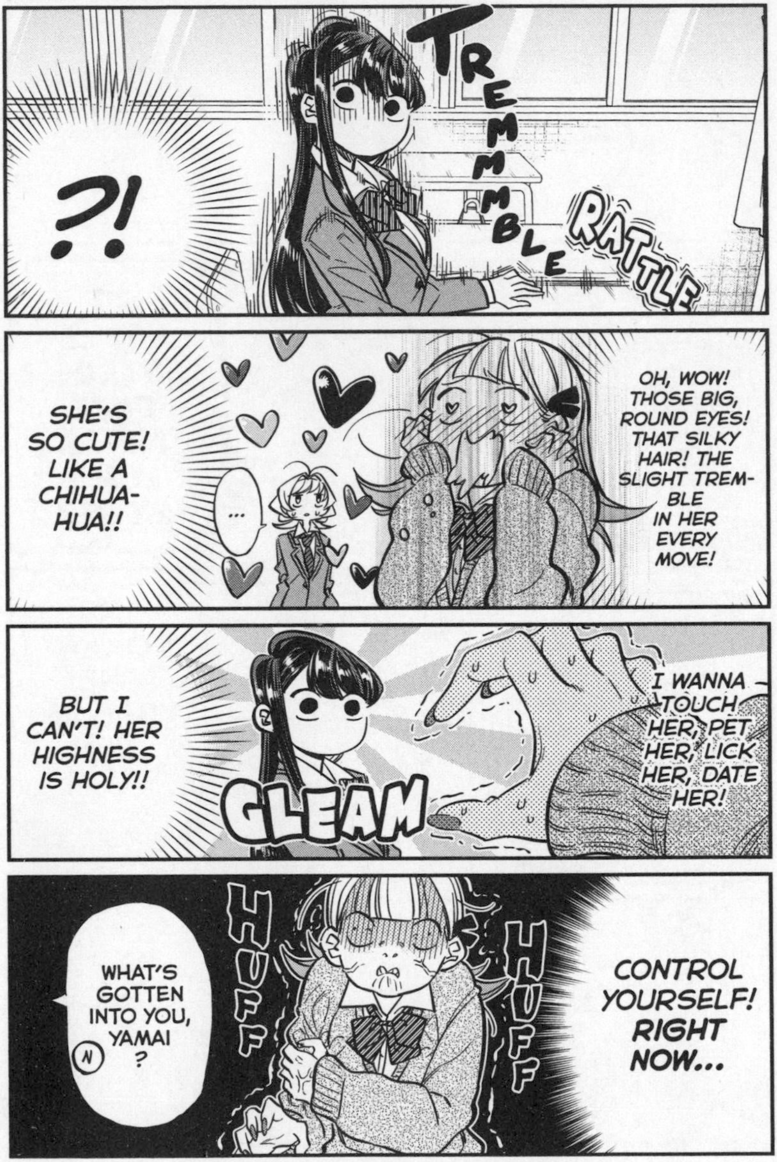
RATTLE
TREMMMBLE
?!
OH, WOW! THOSE BIG, ROUND EYES! THAT SILKY HAIR! THE SLIGHT TREM-BLE IN HER EVERY MOVE!
...
SHE'S SO CUTE! LIKE A CHIHUA-HUA!!
I WANNA TOUCH HER, PET HER, LICK HER, DATE HER!
GLEAM
BUT I CAN'T! HER HIGHNESS IS HOLY!!
CONTROL YOURSELF! RIGHT NOW...
HUFF
HUFF
WHAT'S GOTTEN INTO YOU, YAMAI?

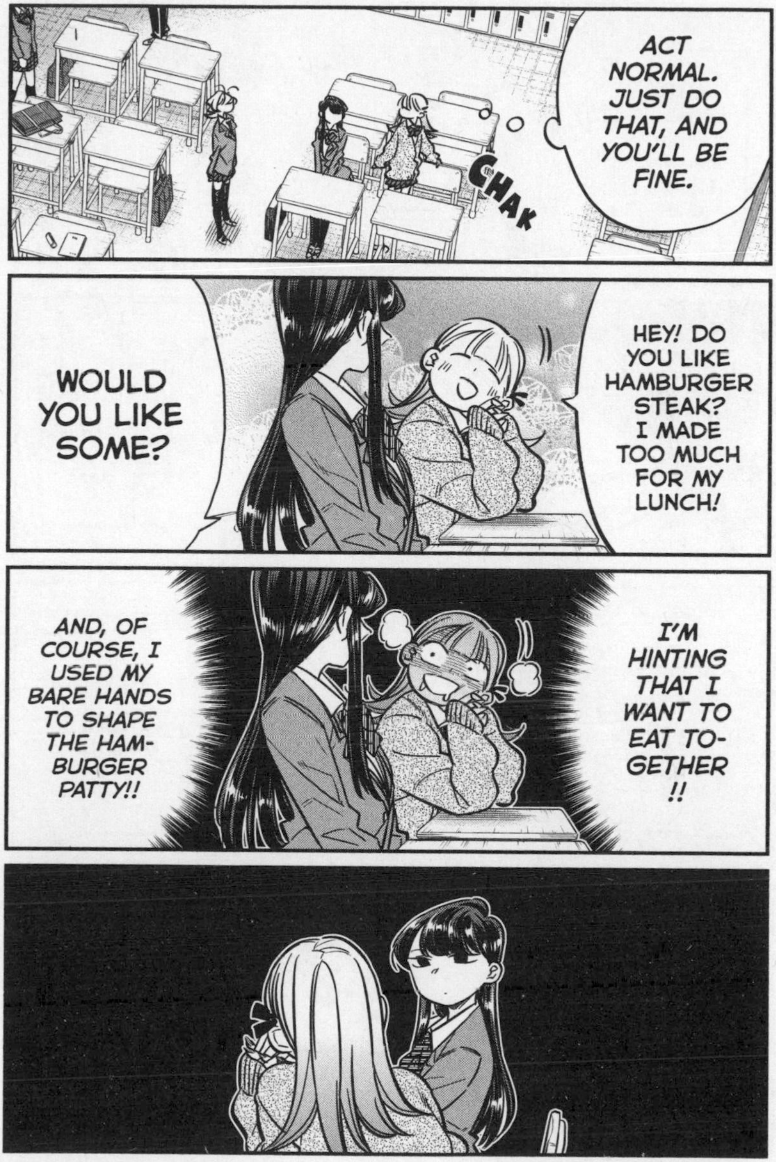
ACT NORMAL. JUST DO THAT, AND YOU'LL BE FINE.
CHAK
HEY! DO YOU LIKE HAMBURGER STEAK? I MADE TOO MUCH FOR MY LUNCH!
WOULD YOU LIKE SOME?
I'M HINTING THAT I WANT TO EAT TO-GETHER!!
AND, OF COURSE, I USED MY BARE HANDS TO SHAPE THE HAM-BURGER PATTY!!

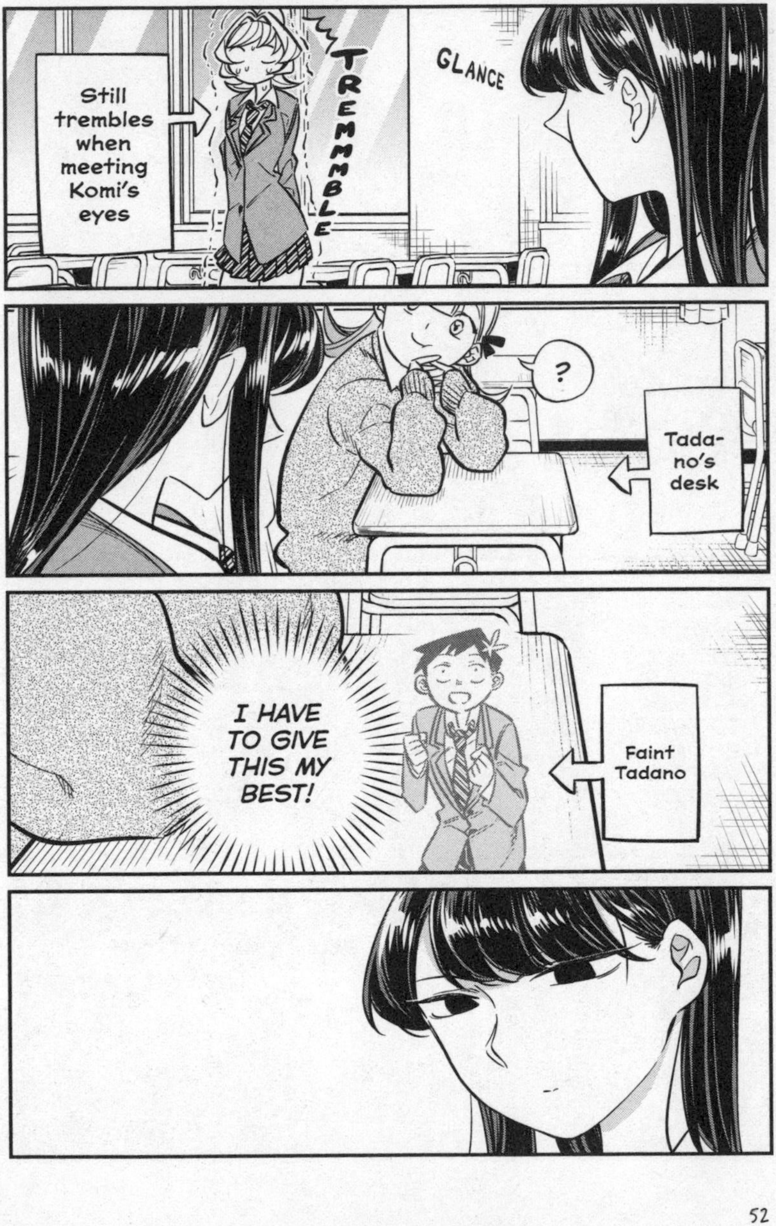
GLANCE
TREMMMBLE
Still trembles when meeting Komi's eyes
?
Tada-no's desk
Faint Tadano
I HAVE TO GIVE THIS MY BEST!

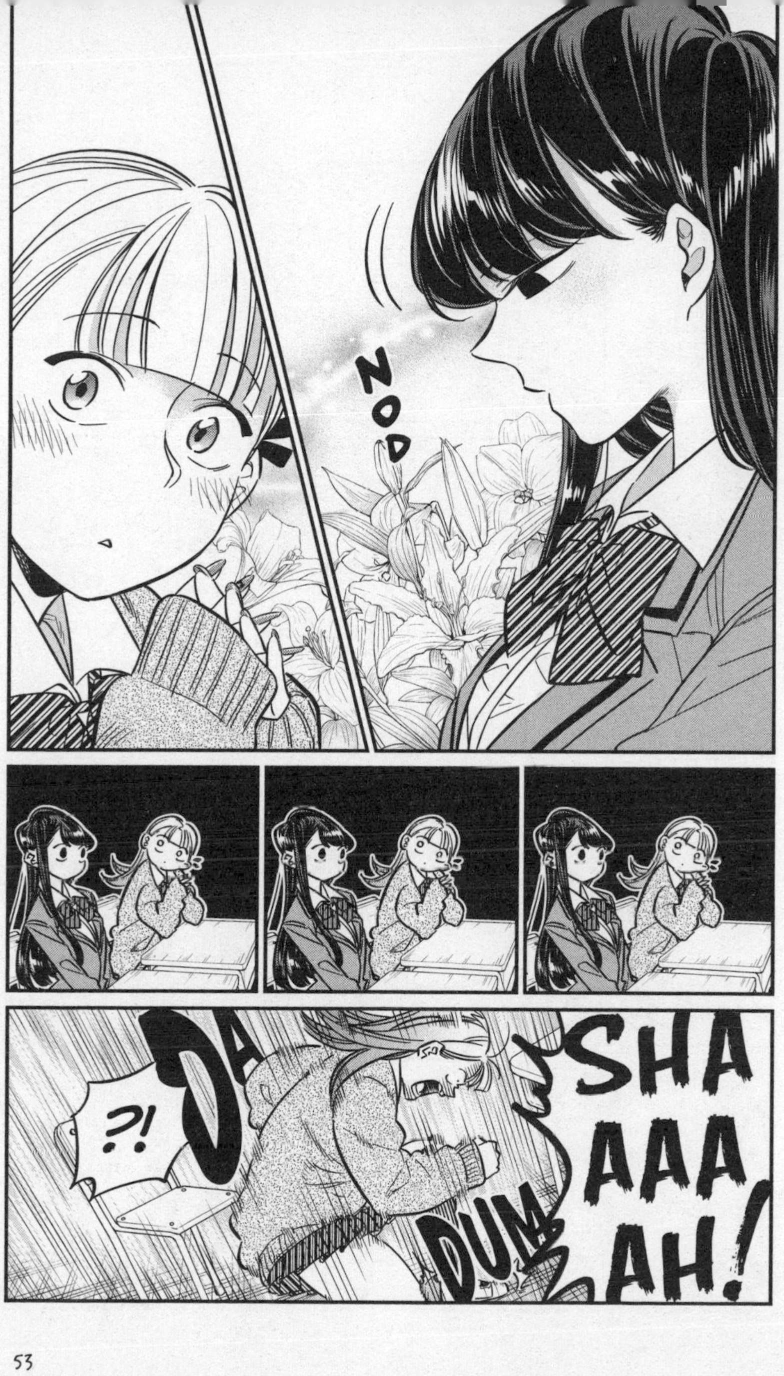
NOD
SHAAAAAAH!
DA
DUM
?!

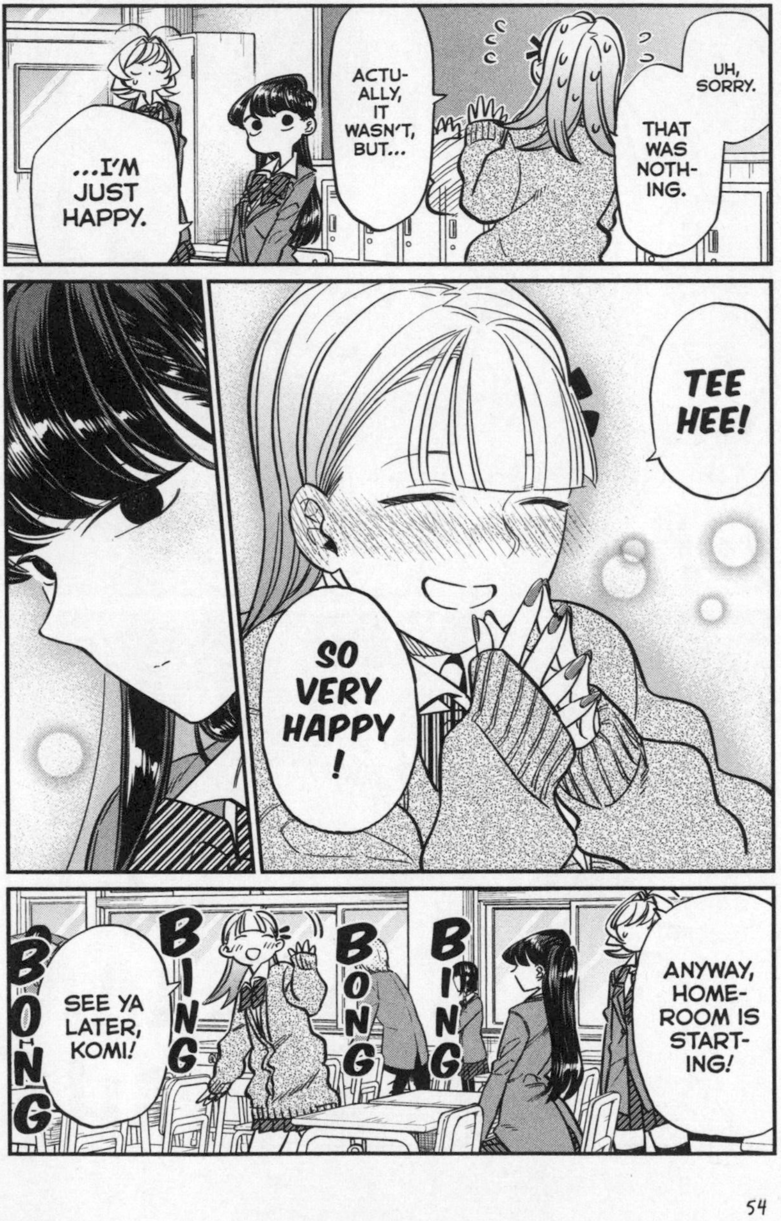
UH, SORRY.
THAT WAS NOTHING.
ACTUALLY, IT WASN'T, BUT...
...I'M JUST HAPPY.
TEE HEE!
SO VERY HAPPY!
ANYWAY, HOMEROOM IS STARTING!
BING
BONG
BING
SEE YA LATER, KOMI!
BONG

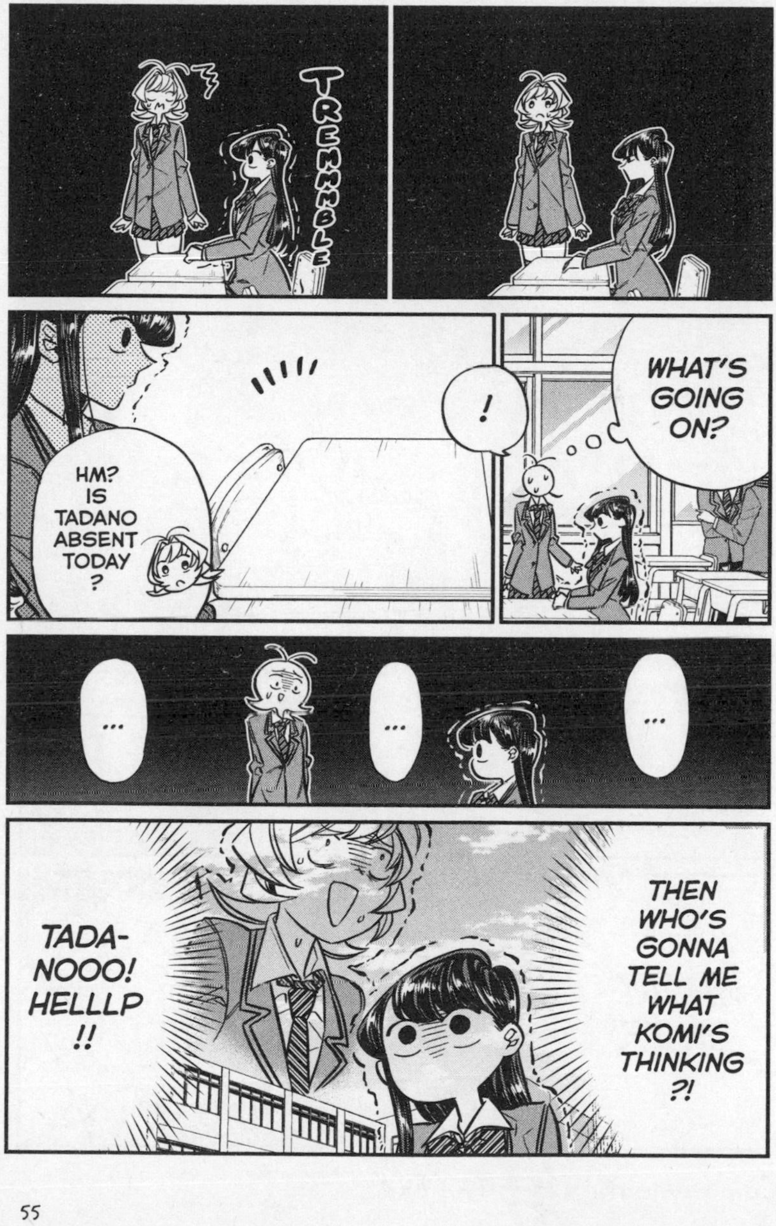
TREMMMBLE
!
WHAT'S GOING ON?
HM? IS TADANO ABSENT TODAY?
...
...
...
THEN WHO'S GONNA TELL ME WHAT KOMI'S THINKING?!
TADA-NOOO! HELLLP!!

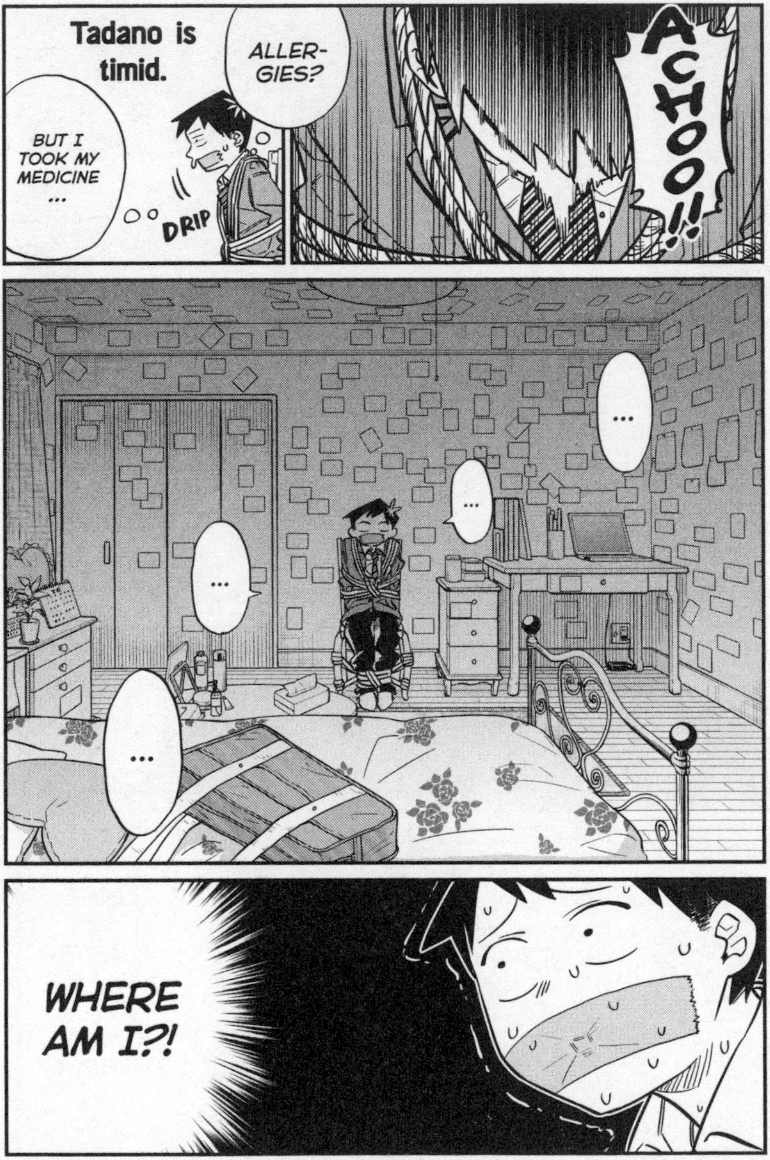
ACHOO!!
ALLER-GIES?
Tadano is timid.
BUT I TOOK MY MEDICINE ...
DRIP
...
...
...
...
WHERE AM I?!

Communication 24 – The End

Komi Can't Communicate

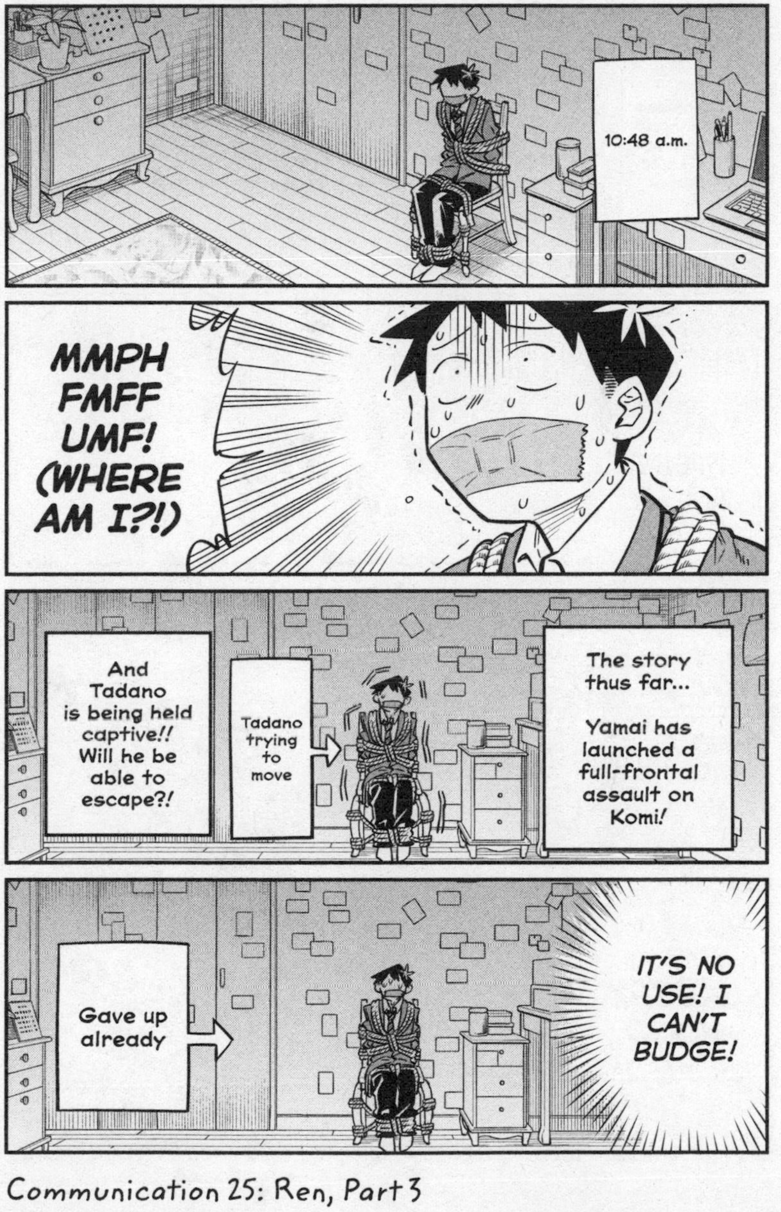
10:48 a.m.
MMPH FMFF UMF! (WHERE AM I?!)
The story thus far...
Yamai has launched a full-frontal assault on Komi!
Tadano trying to move
And Tadano is being held captive!! Will he be able to escape?!
IT'S NO USE! I CAN'T BUDGE!
Gave up already

Communication 25: Ren, Part 3

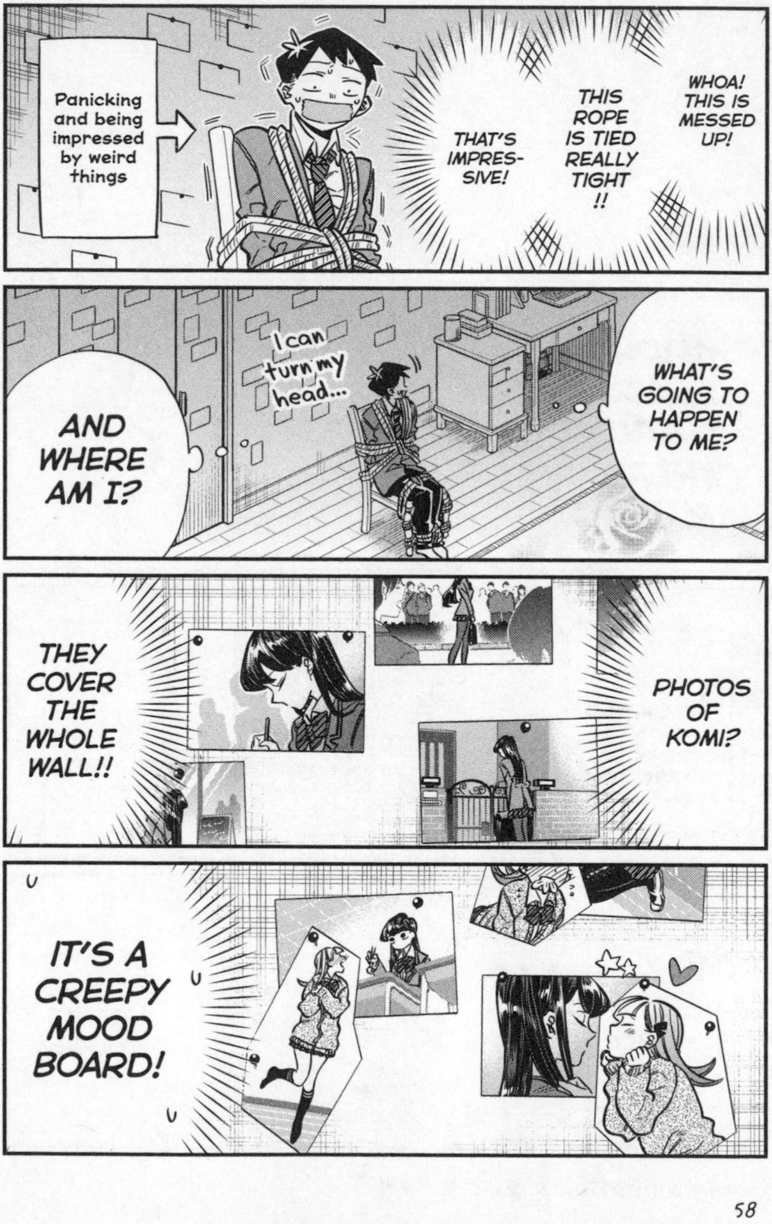
WHOA! THIS IS MESSED UP!
THIS ROPE IS TIED REALLY TIGHT !!
THAT'S IMPRES-SIVE!
Panicking and being impressed by weird things
WHAT'S GOING TO HAPPEN TO ME?
I can turn my head...
AND WHERE AM I?
PHOTOS OF KOMI?
THEY COVER THE WHOLE WALL!!
IT'S A CREEPY MOOD BOARD!

I THINK THIS IS YAMAI'S ROOM!
THERE ARE EVEN PHOTOS ON THE CEILING!
TIK
...
TOK
TIK
TOK
TIK
TOK
...
TOK
TIK
WHAT'S GONNA HAPPEN TO ME?!
S-SOME-ONE HELLLP!!

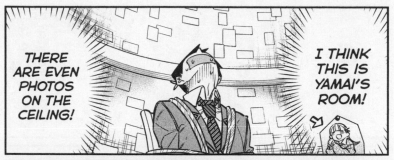

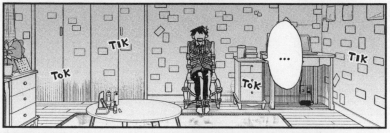

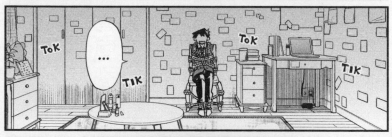

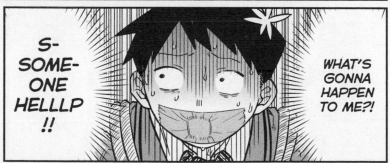

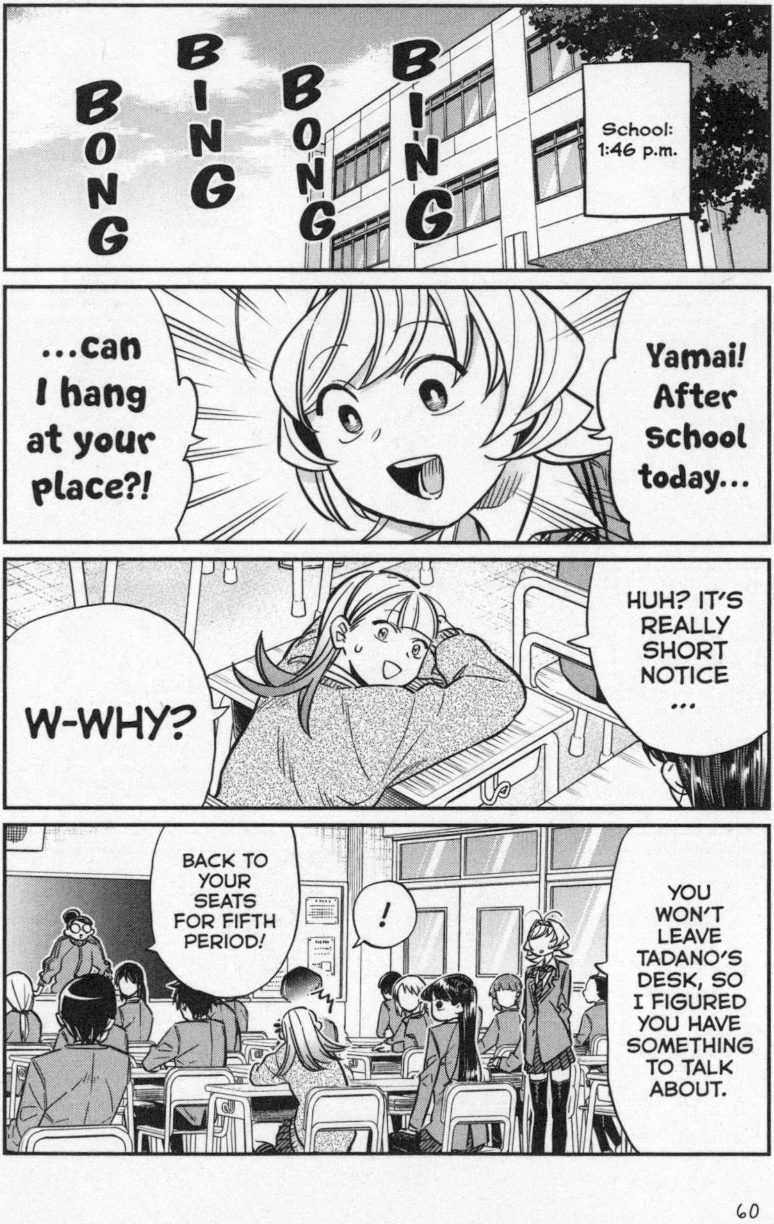
School: 1:46 p.m.
BING
BONG
BING
BONG
Yamai! After School today...
...can I hang at your place?!
HUH? IT'S REALLY SHORT NOTICE ...
W-WHY?
YOU WON'T LEAVE TADANO'S DESK, SO I FIGURED YOU HAVE SOMETHING TO TALK ABOUT.
!
BACK TO YOUR SEATS FOR FIFTH PERIOD!

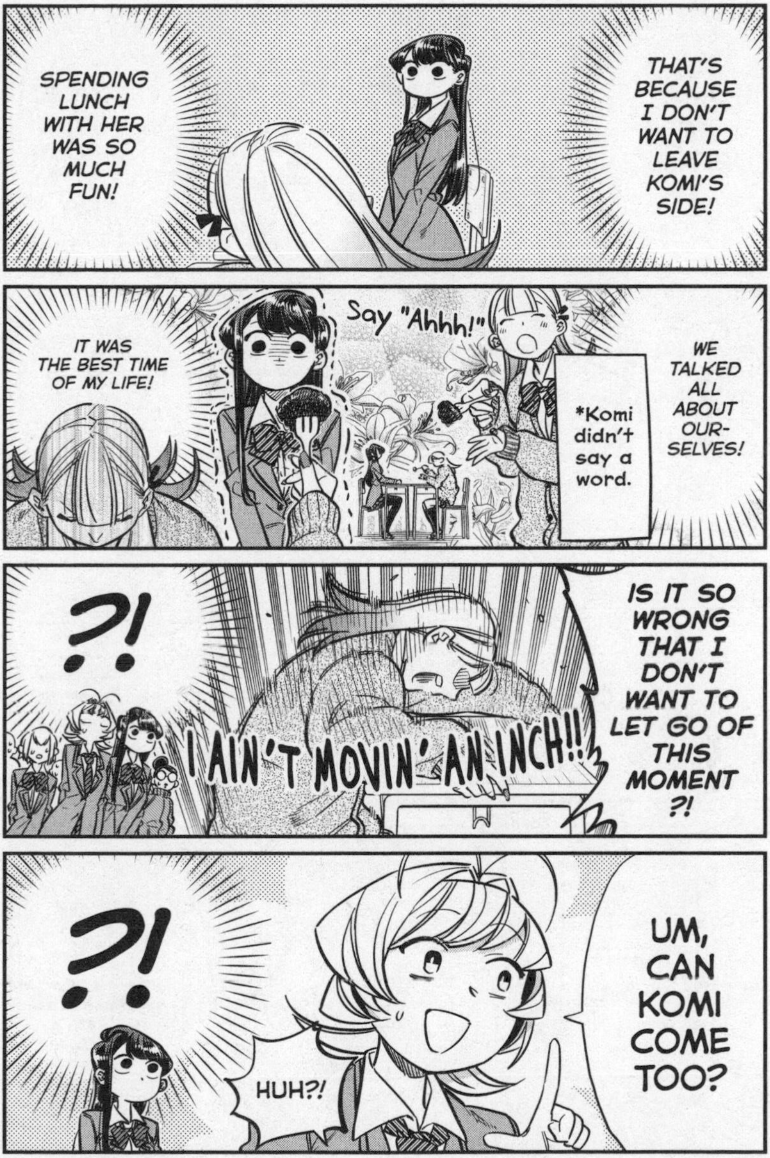
THAT'S BECAUSE I DON'T WANT TO LEAVE KOMI'S SIDE!
SPENDING LUNCH WITH HER WAS SO MUCH FUN!
WE TALKED ALL ABOUT OURSELVES!
*Komi didn't say a word.
Say "Ahhh!"
IT WAS THE BEST TIME OF MY LIFE!
IS IT SO WRONG THAT I DON'T WANT TO LET GO OF THIS MOMENT ?!
I AIN'T MOVIN' AN INCH!!
?!
UM, CAN KOMI COME TOO?
?!
HUH?!

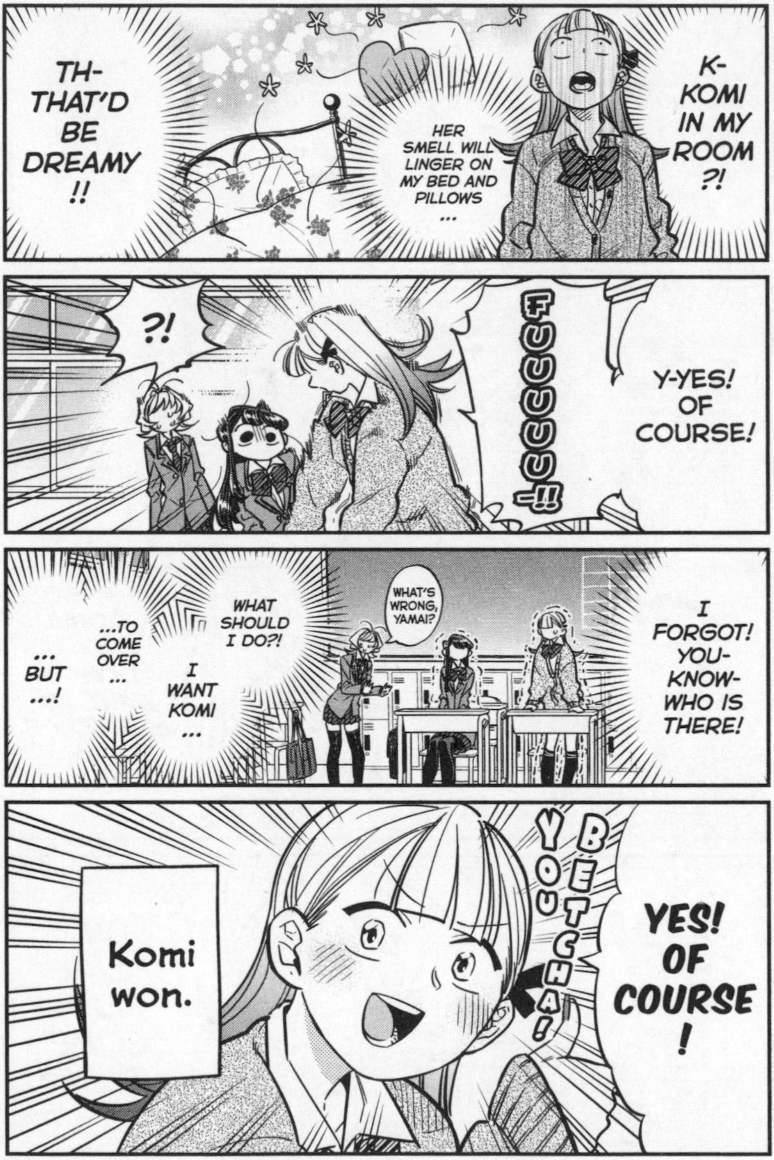
K-KOMI IN MY ROOM?!
HER SMELL WILL LINGER ON MY BED AND PILLOWS ...
TH-THAT'D BE DREAMY!!
Y-YES! OF COURSE!
FUUUUUU—!!
?!
I FORGOT! YOU-KNOW-WHO IS THERE!
WHAT'S WRONG, YAMAI?
WHAT SHOULD I DO?!
I WANT KOMI ...
...TO COME OVER ...
... BUT ...!
YES! OF COURSE!
YOU BETCHA!
Komi won.

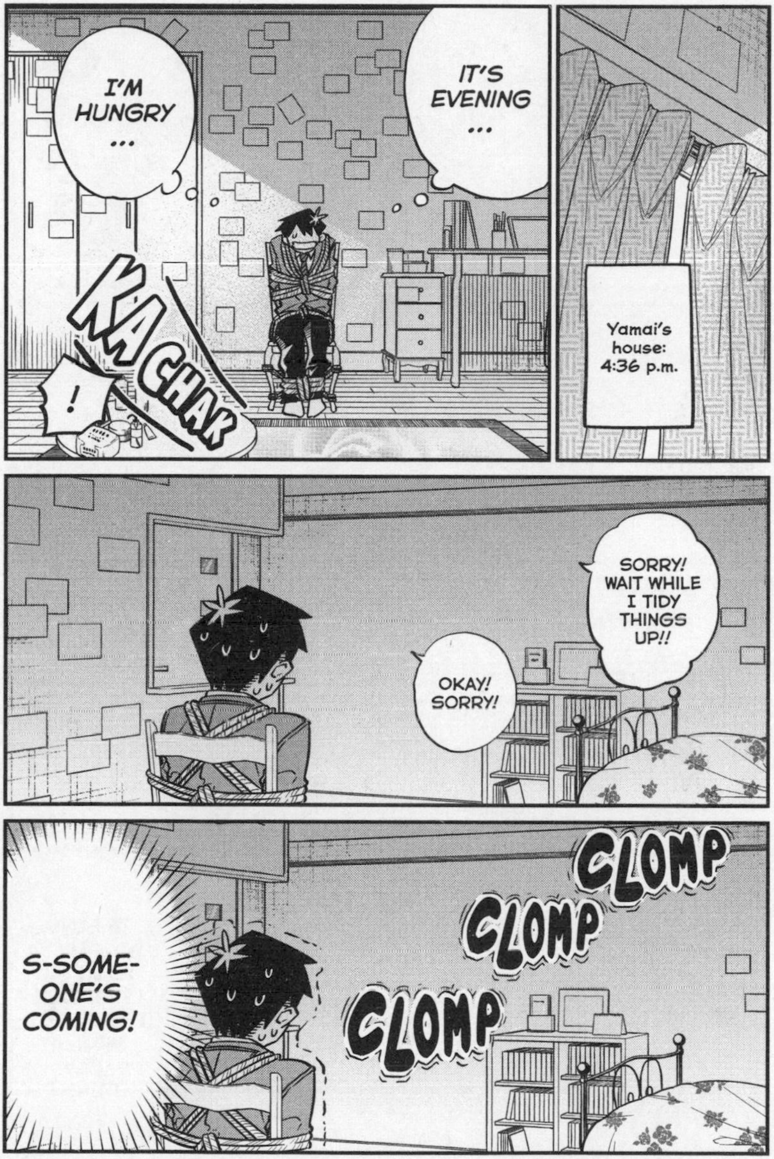
Yamai's house: 4:36 p.m.
IT'S EVENING ...
I'M HUNGRY ...
KA CHAK
!
SORRY! WAIT WHILE I TIDY THINGS UP!!
OKAY! SORRY!
CLOMP
CLOMP
CLOMP
S-SOME-ONE'S COMING!

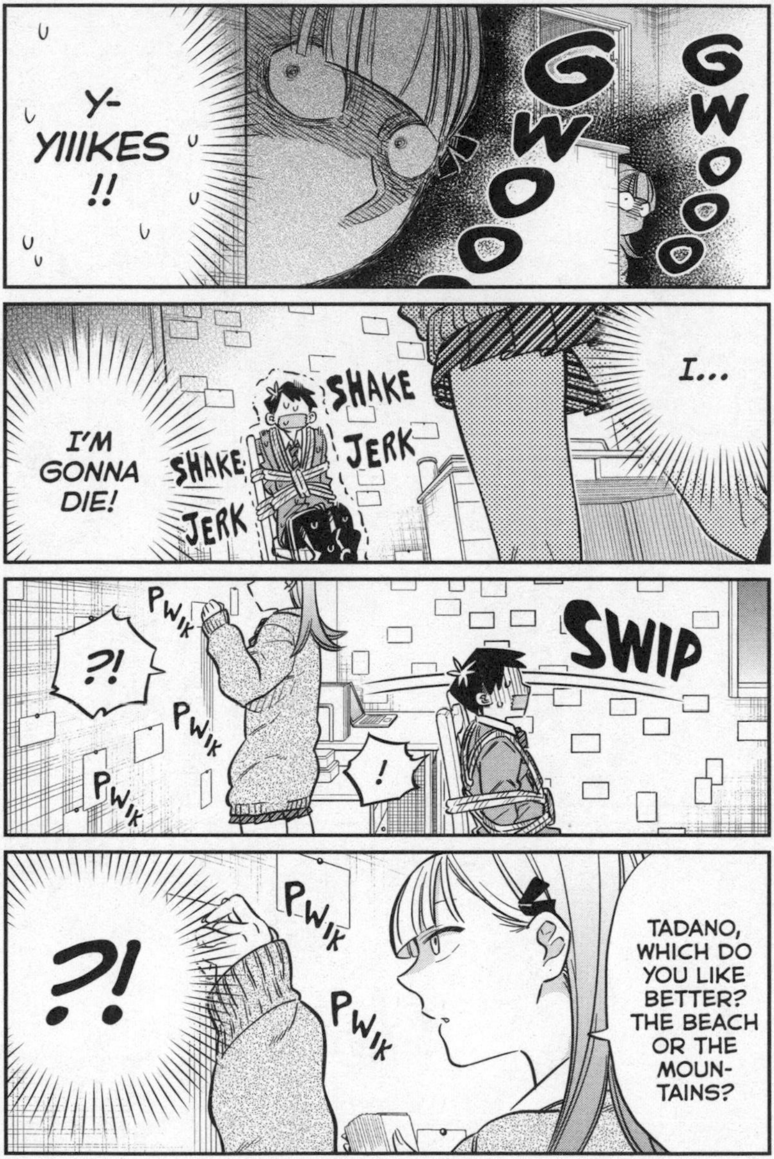
GWOOOO
GWOOO
Y-YIIIKES!!
I...
SHAKE
JERK
SHAKE
JERK
I'M GONNA DIE!
SWIP
!
PWIK
?!
PWIK
PWIK
TADANO, WHICH DO YOU LIKE BETTER? THE BEACH OR THE MOUN-TAINS?
PWIK
PWIK
?!

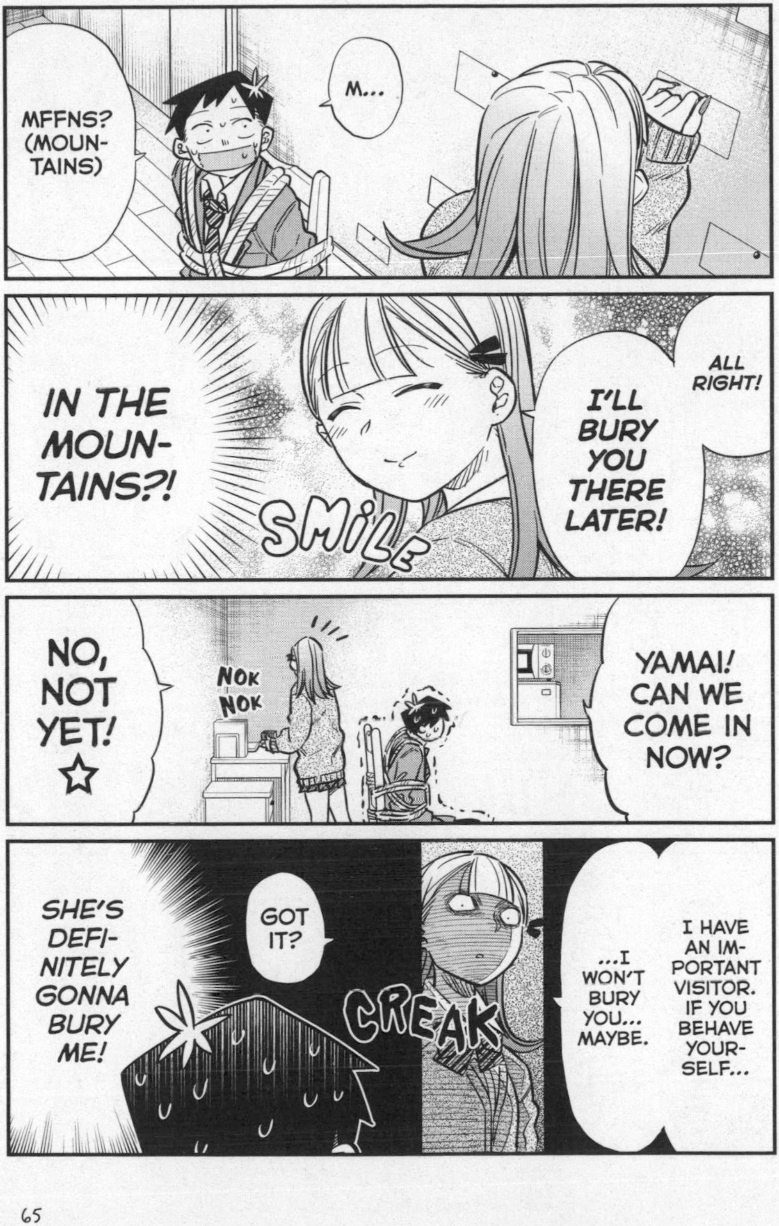
M...
MFFNS? (MOUNTAINS)
ALL RIGHT!
I'LL BURY YOU THERE LATER!
SMILE
IN THE MOUNTAINS?!
YAMAI! CAN WE COME IN NOW?
NOK NOK
NO, NOT YET! ☆
I HAVE AN IMPORTANT VISITOR. IF YOU BEHAVE YOURSELF...
...I WON'T BURY YOU... MAYBE.
CREAK
GOT IT?
SHE'S DEFINITELY GONNA BURY ME!

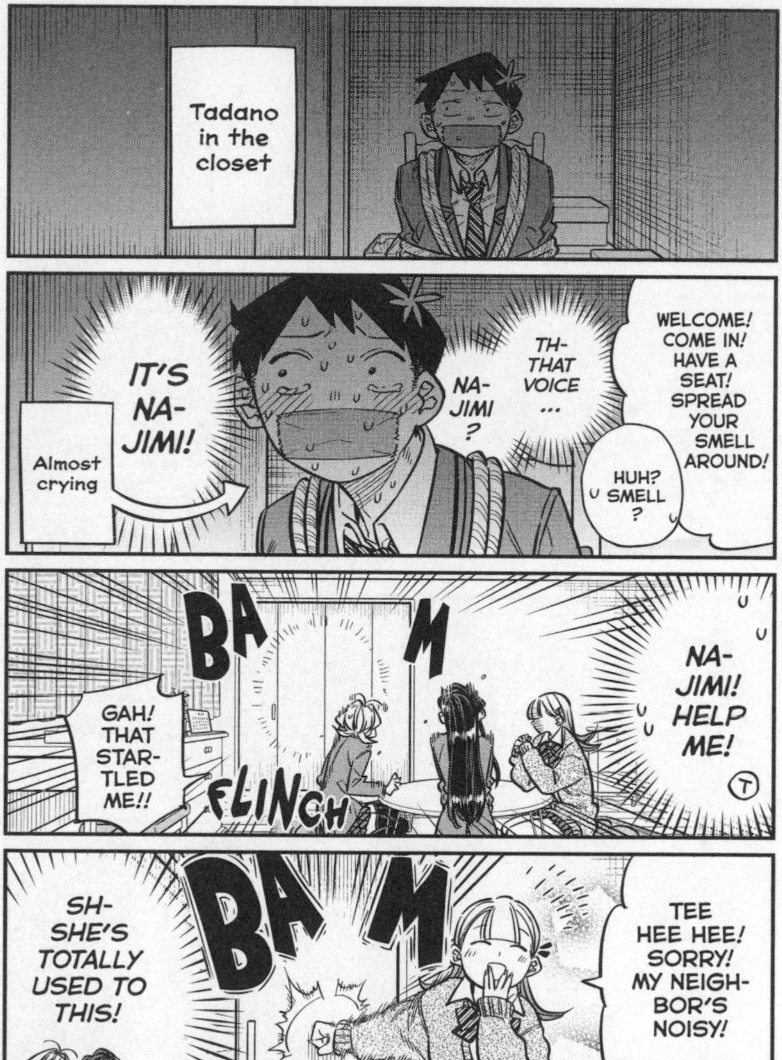

Tadano in the closet
WELCOME! COME IN! HAVE A SEAT! SPREAD YOUR SMELL AROUND!
HUH? SMELL?
TH-THAT VOICE...
NA-JIMI?
IT'S NA-JIMI!
Almost crying
NA-JIMI! HELP ME!
BAM
GAH! THAT STARTLED ME!!
FLINCH
TEE HEE HEE! SORRY! MY NEIGHBOR'S NOISY!
I'm just renting!
BAM
SH-SHE'S TOTALLY USED TO THIS!
HITTING THE WALL BACK TO SUPPORT HER STORY

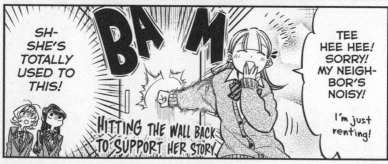

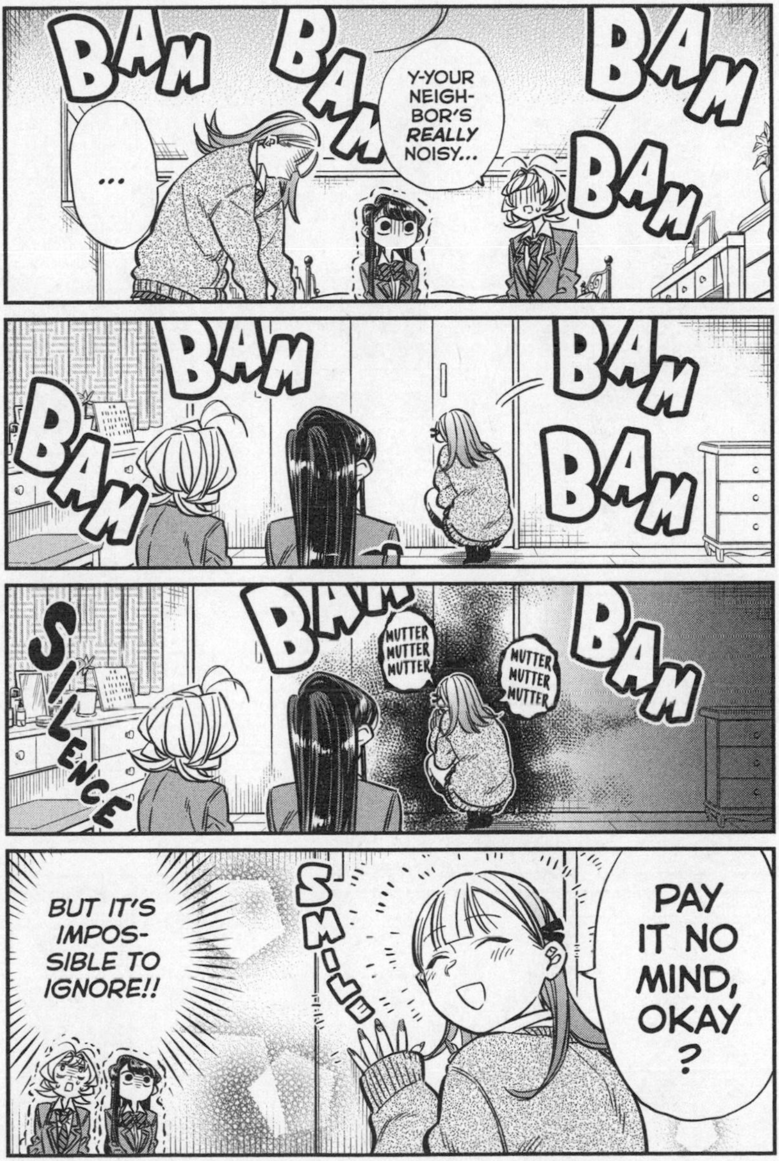
BAM
BAM
Y-YOUR NEIGH-BOR'S REALLY NOISY...
BAM
BAM
...
BAM
BAM
BAM
BAM
BAM
MUTTER MUTTER MUTTER
MUTTER MUTTER MUTTER
BAM
SILENCE
PAY IT NO MIND, OKAY?
SMILE
BUT IT'S IMPOS-SIBLE TO IGNORE!!

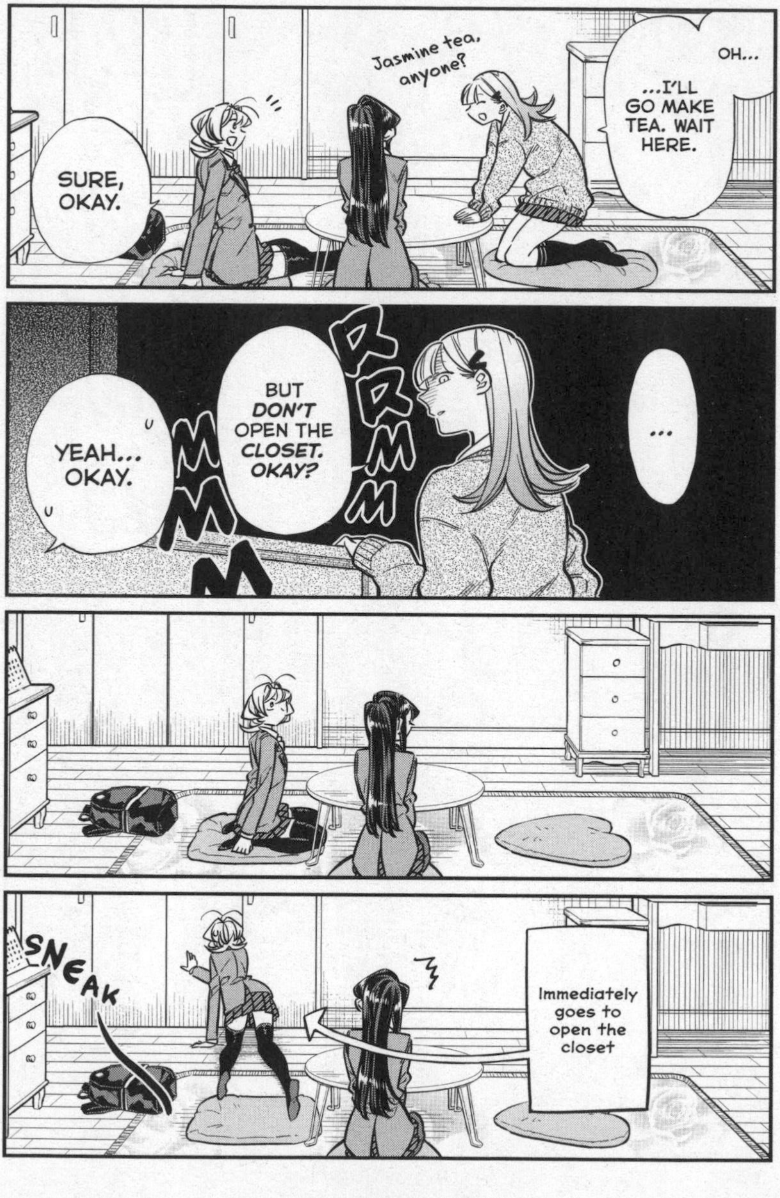
OH... ...I'LL GO MAKE TEA. WAIT HERE.
Jasmine tea, anyone?
SURE, OKAY.
...
RRMMMMMM
BUT DON'T OPEN THE CLOSET. OKAY?
YEAH... OKAY.
Immediately goes to open the closet
SNEAK

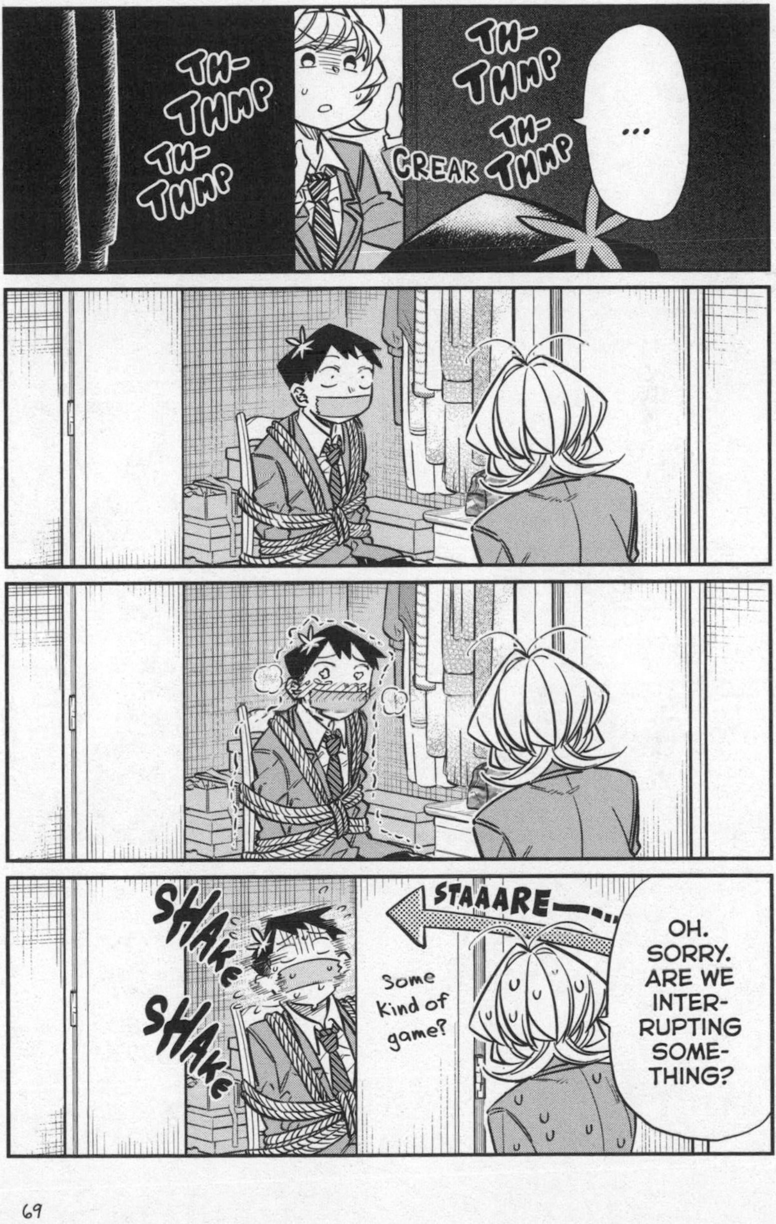
...
TH-THMP
TH-THMP
CREAK
TH-THMP
TH-THMP
OH. SORRY. ARE WE INTER-RUPTING SOME-THING?
STAAARE—
Some kind of game?
SHAKE
SHAKE

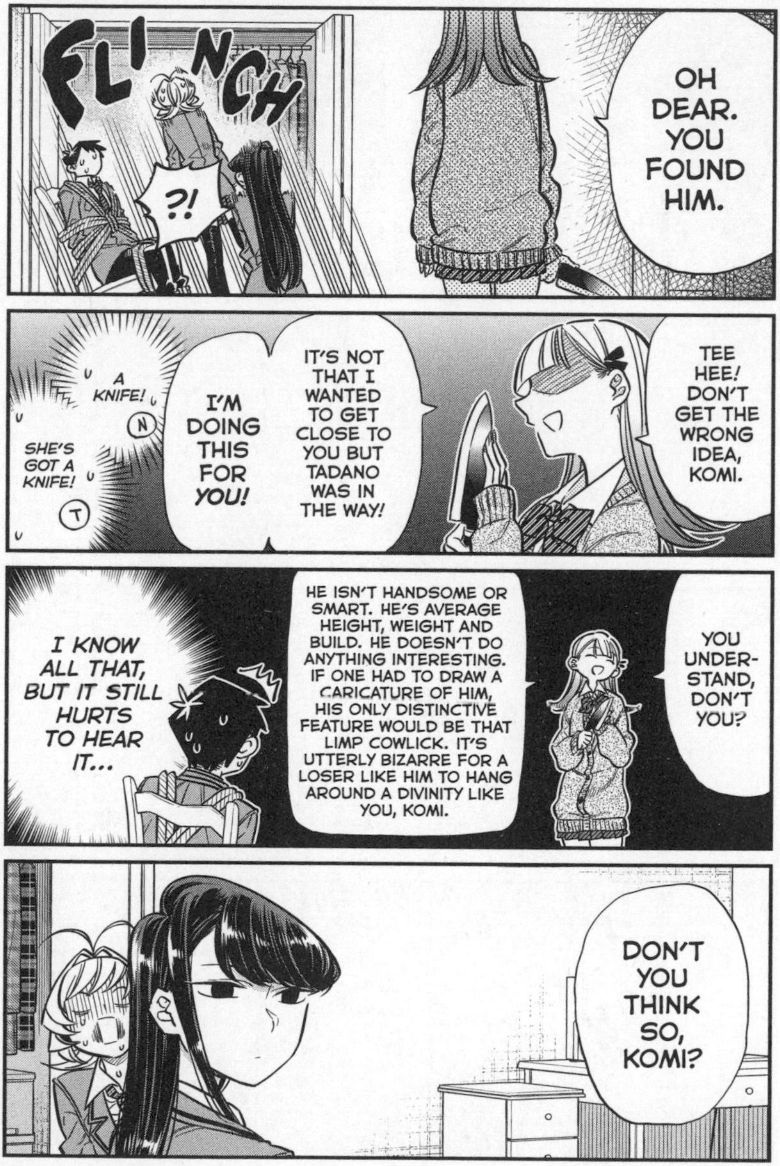
OH DEAR. YOU FOUND HIM.
FLINCH
?!
TEE HEE! DON'T GET THE WRONG IDEA, KOMI.
IT'S NOT THAT I WANTED TO GET CLOSE TO YOU BUT TADANO WAS IN THE WAY!
I'M DOING THIS FOR YOU!
A KNIFE!
N
SHE'S GOT A KNIFE!
T
YOU UNDER-STAND, DON'T YOU?
HE ISN'T HANDSOME OR SMART. HE'S AVERAGE HEIGHT, WEIGHT AND BUILD. HE DOESN'T DO ANYTHING INTERESTING. IF ONE HAD TO DRAW A CARICATURE OF HIM, HIS ONLY DISTINCTIVE FEATURE WOULD BE THAT LIMP COWLICK. IT'S UTTERLY BIZARRE FOR A LOSER LIKE HIM TO HANG AROUND A DIVINITY LIKE YOU, KOMI.
I KNOW ALL THAT, BUT IT STILL HURTS TO HEAR IT...
DON'T YOU THINK SO, KOMI?

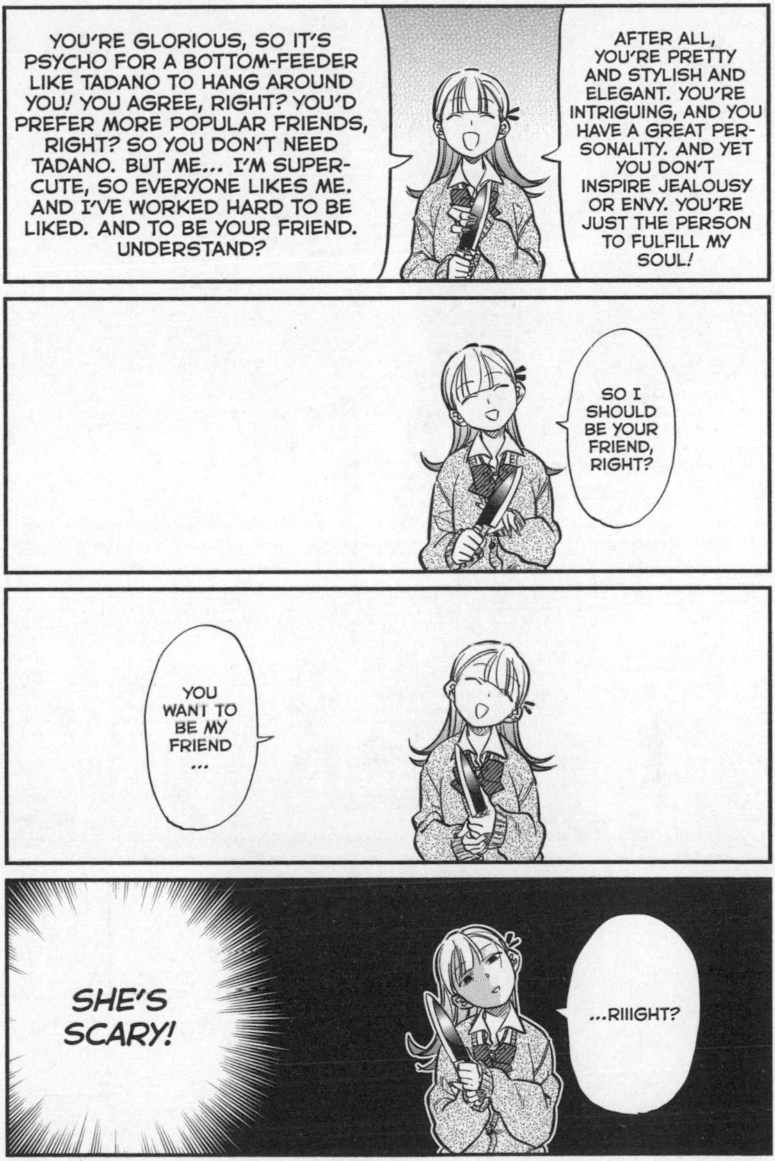
AFTER ALL, YOU'RE PRETTY AND STYLISH AND ELEGANT. YOU'RE INTRIGUING, AND YOU HAVE A GREAT PERSONALITY. AND YET YOU DON'T INSPIRE JEALOUSY OR ENVY. YOU'RE JUST THE PERSON TO FULFILL MY SOUL!
YOU'RE GLORIOUS, SO IT'S PSYCHO FOR A BOTTOM-FEEDER LIKE TADANO TO HANG AROUND YOU! YOU AGREE, RIGHT? YOU'D PREFER MORE POPULAR FRIENDS, RIGHT? SO YOU DON'T NEED TADANO. BUT ME... I'M SUPER-CUTE, SO EVERYONE LIKES ME. AND I'VE WORKED HARD TO BE LIKED. AND TO BE YOUR FRIEND. UNDERSTAND?
SO I SHOULD BE YOUR FRIEND, RIGHT?
YOU WANT TO BE MY FRIEND ...
...RIIIGHT?
SHE'S SCARY!

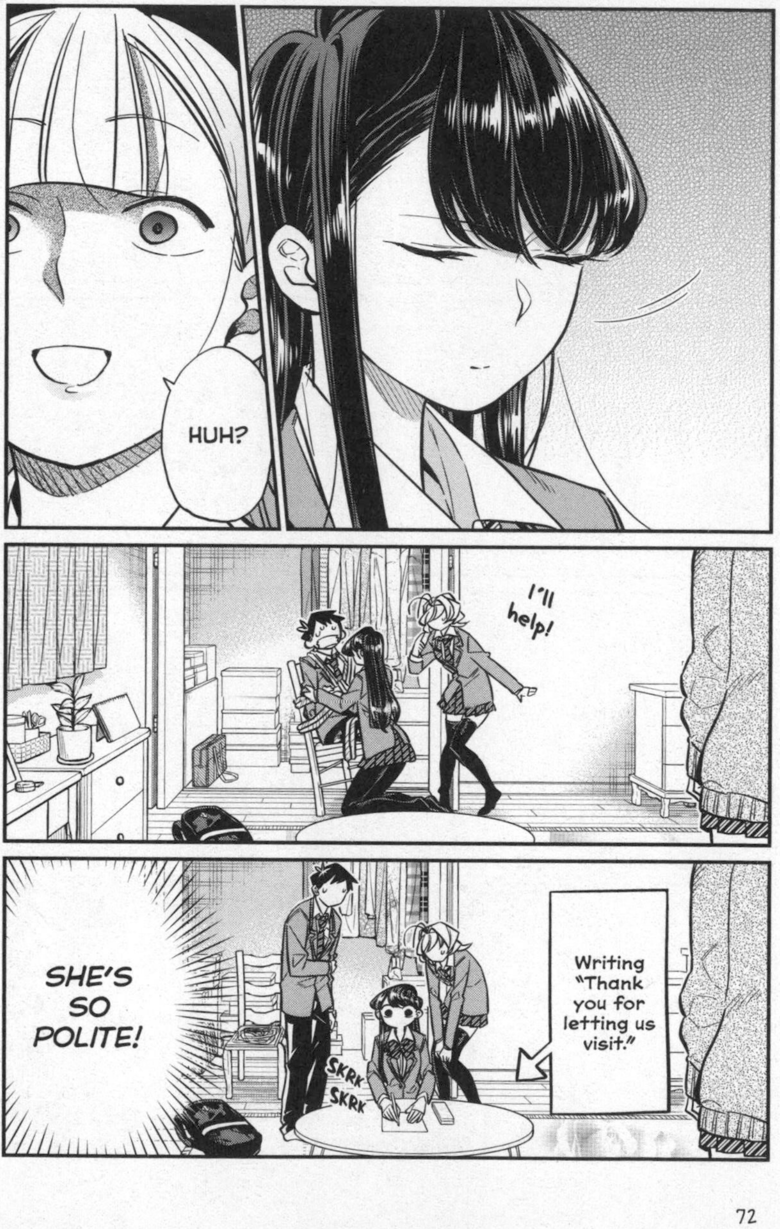
HUH?
I'll help!
Writing "Thank you for letting us visit."
SKRK SKRK
SHE'S SO POLITE!

...
W-WAIT, KOMI!
WHSH
I...
I DID THIS FOR YOU!

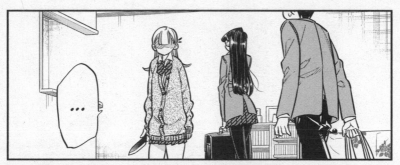

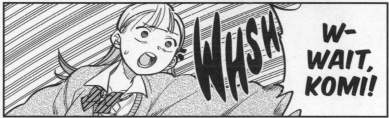

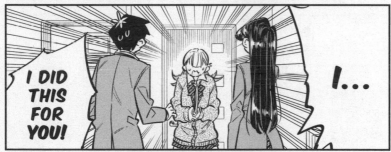

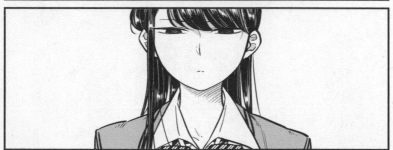

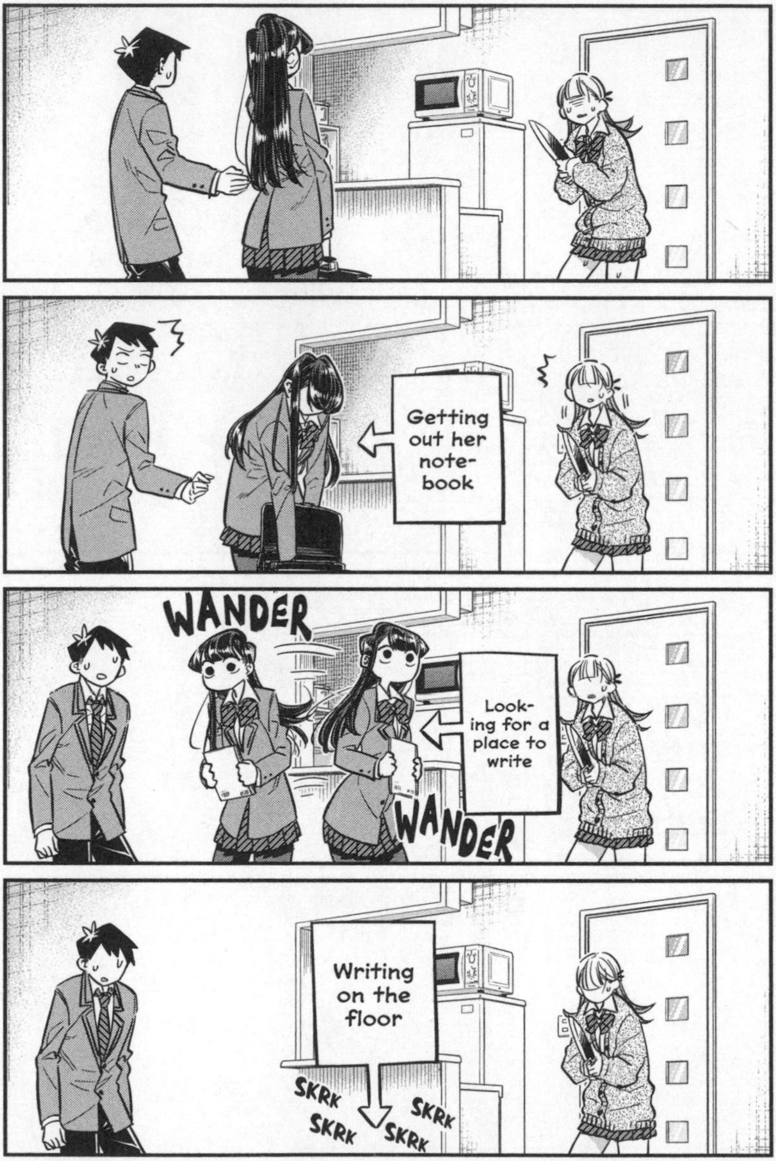

Getting out her notebook
Looking for a place to write
WANDER
WANDER
Writing on the floor
SKRK
SKRK
SKRK
SKRK

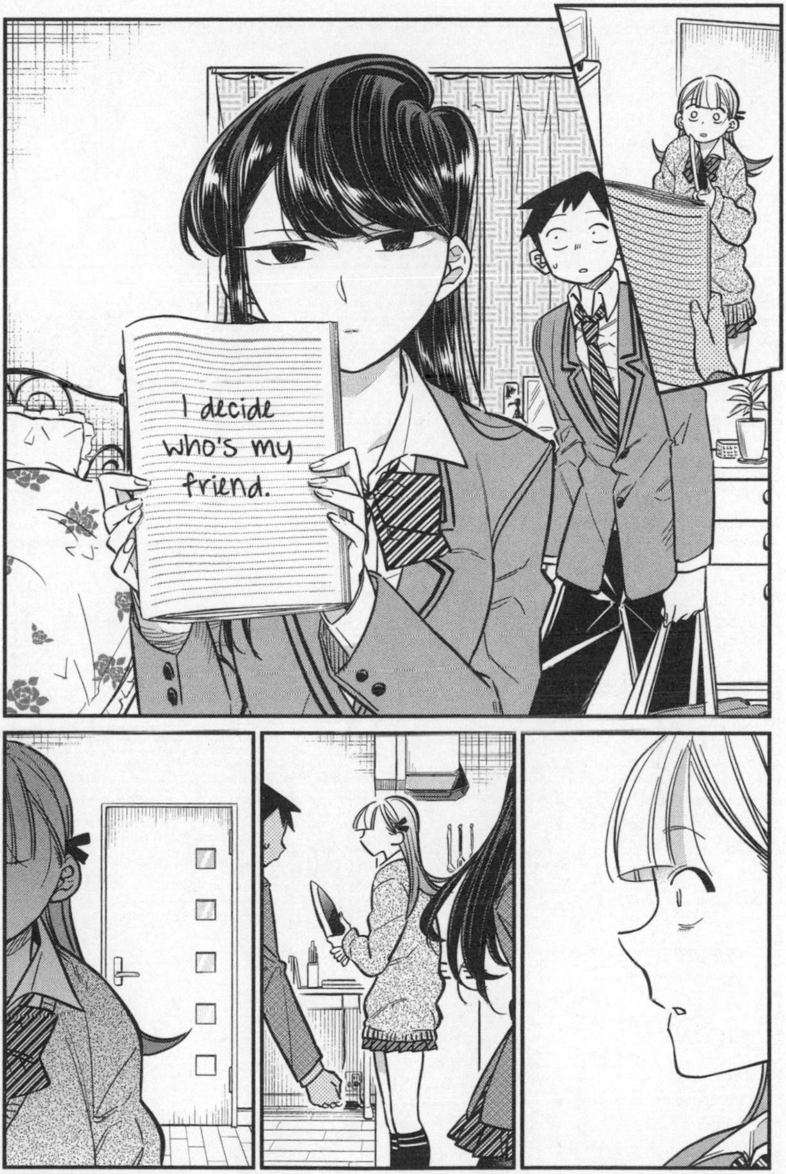
I decide who's my friend.

...
SHE WON'T EVEN SPEAK TO ME, HUH?
HA HA... SHE MUST HATE ME.
AH HA... AH HA HA...
... HA... SOB ...
W...
SOB
WHAT SHOULD I DO, TADANO?!
SOB

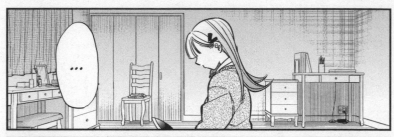

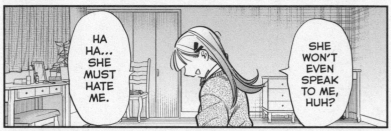

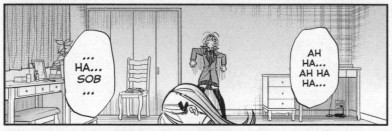

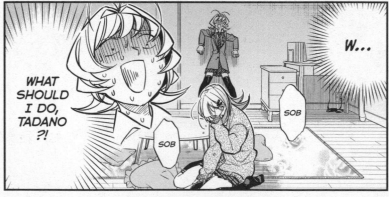

Communication 25 – The End

Komi Can't Communicate

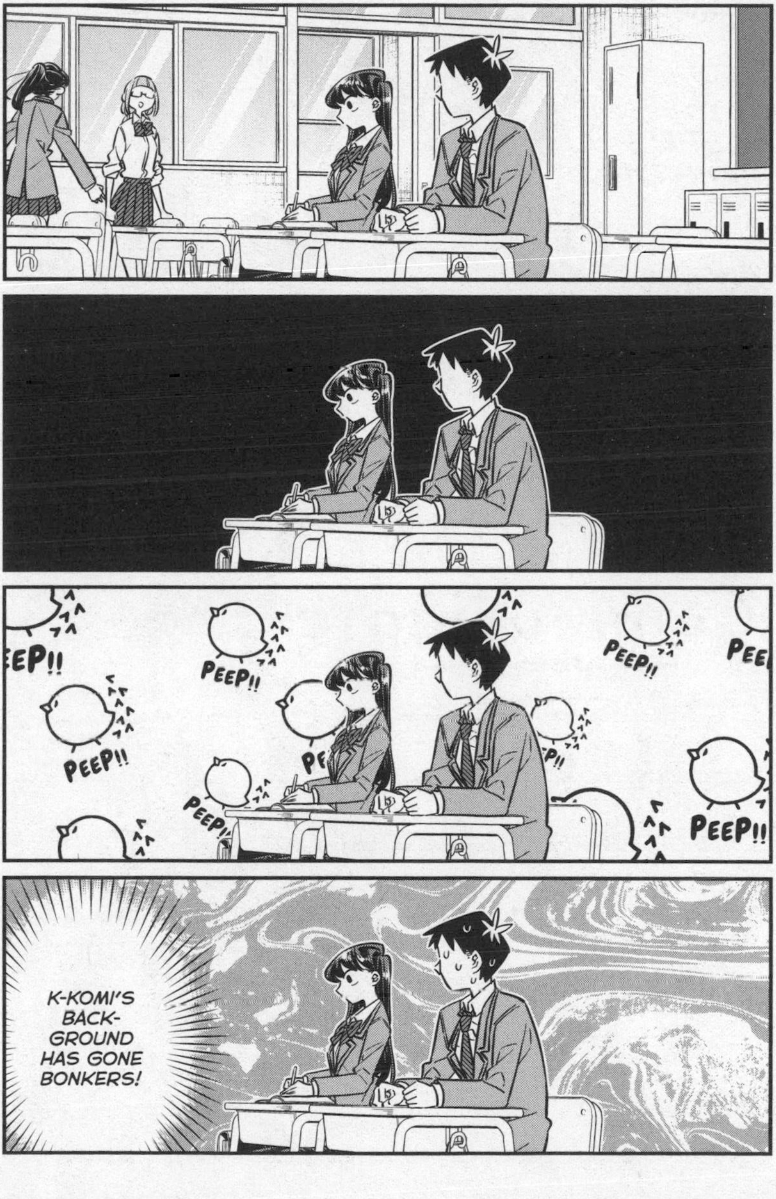
PEEP!!
PEEP!!
PEEP!!
PEEP!!
PEEP!!
PEEP!!
K-KOMI'S BACK-GROUND HAS GONE BONKERS!

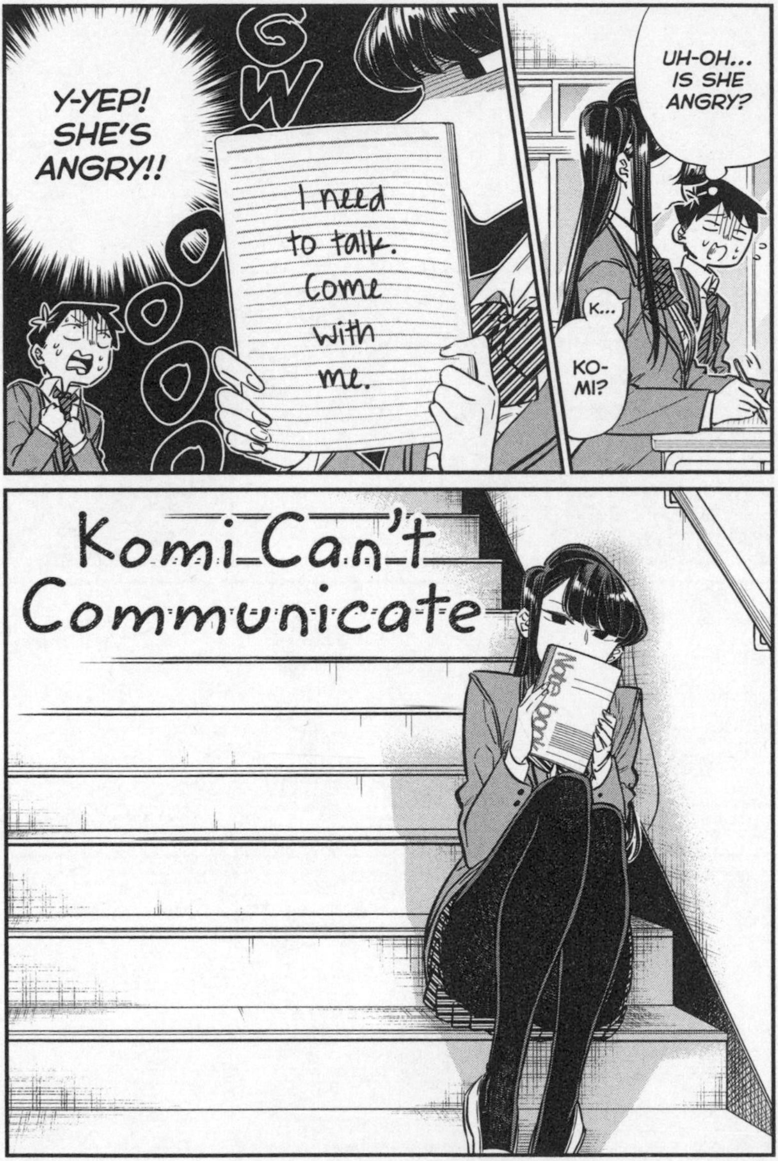
UH-OH... IS SHE ANGRY?
K...
KO-MI?
I need to talk. Come with me.
Y-YEP! SHE'S ANGRY!!
Komi Can't Communicate

Communication 26: Ren, Part 4

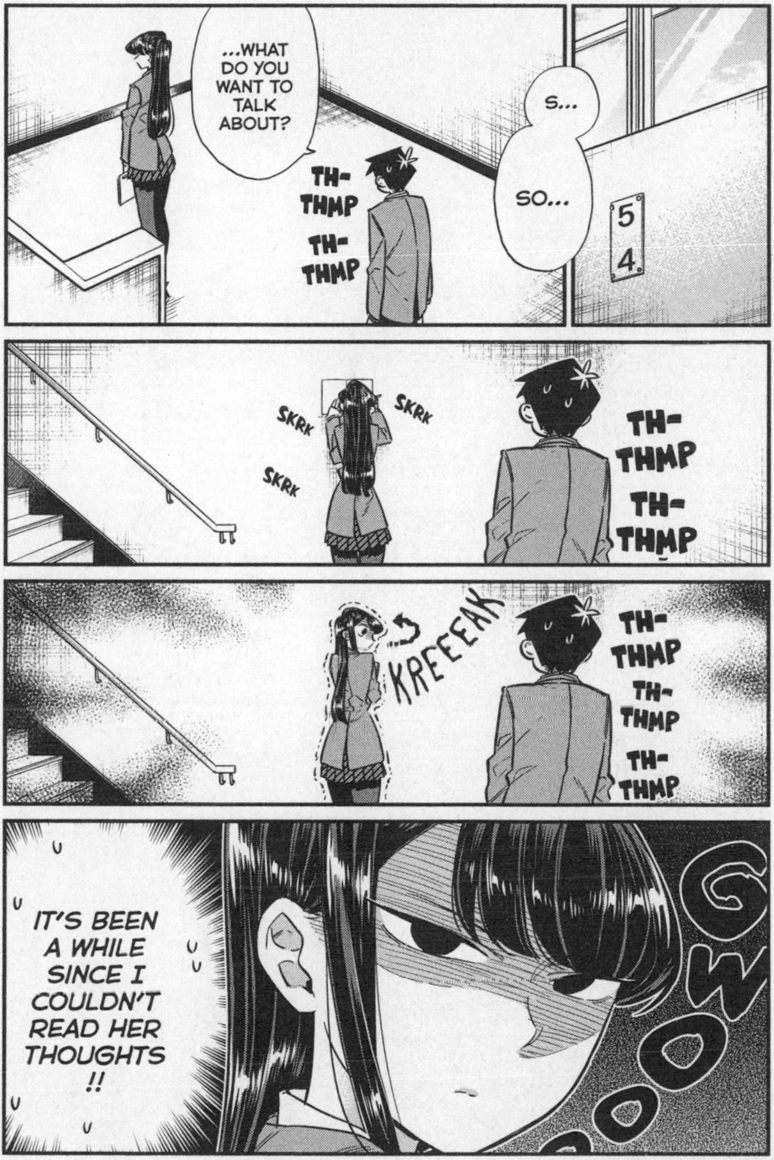
S...
SO...
5
4
...WHAT DO YOU WANT TO TALK ABOUT?
TH-THMP
TH-THMP
TH-THMP
TH-THMP
SKRK
SKRK
SKRK
TH-THMP
TH-THMP
TH-THMP
KREEEAK
GWOOO
IT'S BEEN A WHILE SINCE I COULDN'T READ HER THOUGHTS!!

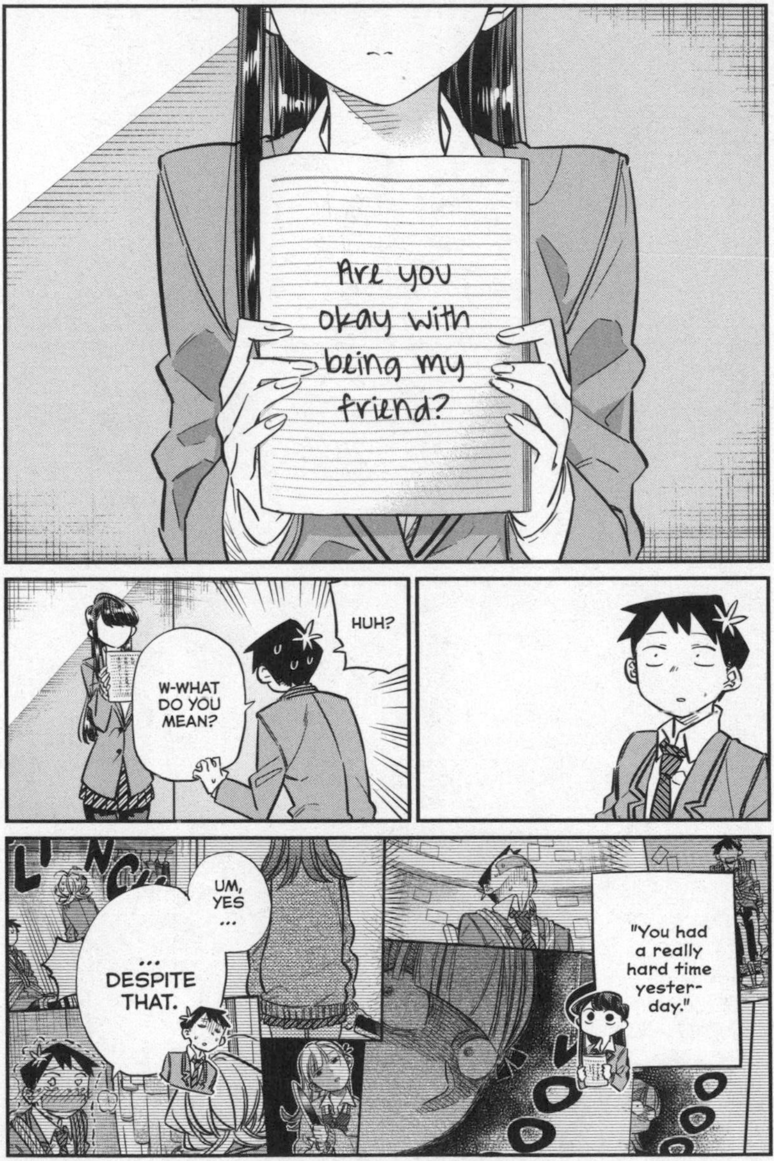
Are you okay with being my friend?
HUH?
W-WHAT DO YOU MEAN?
"You had a really hard time yester-day."
UM, YES ...
... DESPITE THAT.

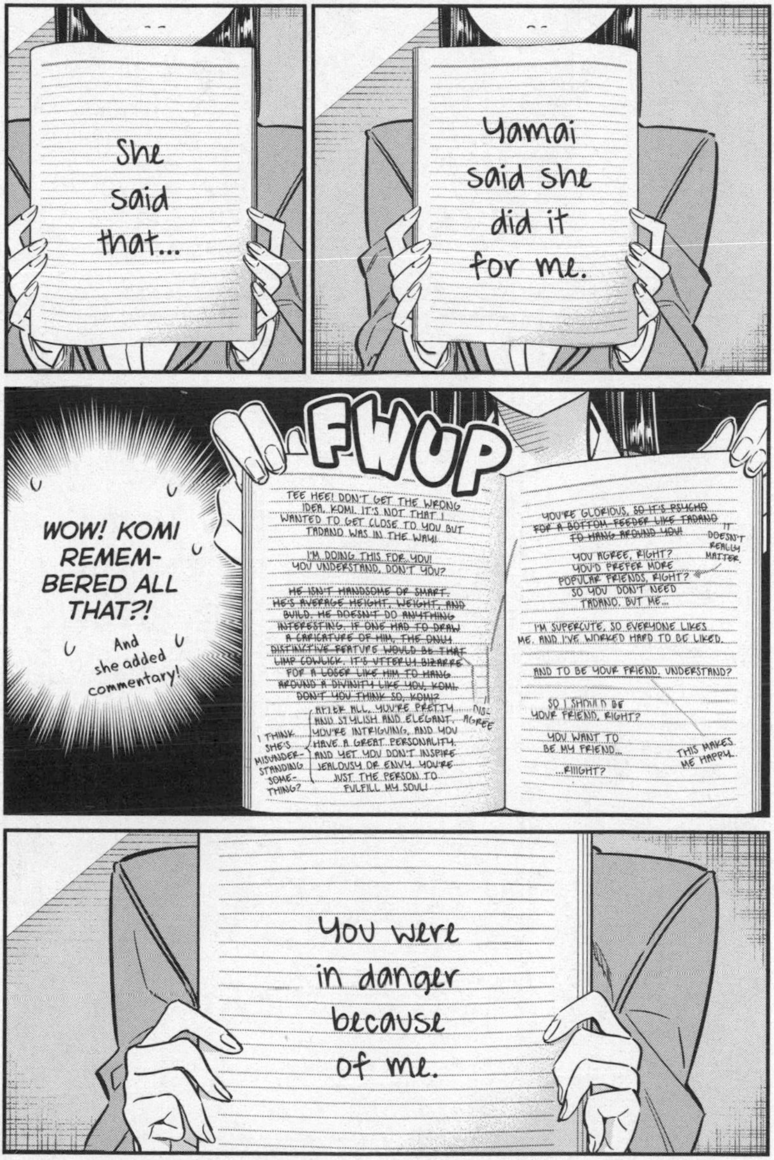
Yamai said she did it for me.
She said that...
FWUP
TEE HEE! DON'T GET THE WRONG IDEA, KOMI. IT'S NOT THAT I WANTED TO GET CLOSE TO YOU BUT TADANO WAS IN THE WAY!
I'M DOING THIS FOR YOU! YOU UNDERSTAND, DON'T YOU?
HE ISN'T HANDSOME OR SMART. HE'S AVERAGE HEIGHT, WEIGHT, AND BUILD. HE DOESN'T DO ANYTHING INTERESTING. IF ONE HAD TO DRAW A CARICATURE OF HIM, THE ONLY DISTINCTIVE FEATURE WOULD BE THAT LIMP COWLICK. IT'S UTTERLY BIZARRE FOR A LOSER LIKE HIM TO HANG AROUND A DIVINITY LIKE YOU, KOMI. DON'T YOU THINK SO, KOMI?
I DISAGREE
AFTER ALL, YOU'RE PRETTY AND STYLISH AND ELEGANT. YOU'RE INTRIGUING, AND YOU HAVE A GREAT PERSONALITY. AND YET YOU DON'T INSPIRE JEALOUSY OR ENVY. YOU'RE JUST THE PERSON TO FULFILL MY SOUL!
I THINK SHE'S MISUNDERSTANDING SOMETHING?
YOU'RE GLORIOUS, SO IT'S PSYCHO FOR A BOTTOM FEEDER LIKE TADANO TO HANG AROUND YOU!
YOU AGREE, RIGHT? YOU'D PREFER MORE POPULAR FRIENDS, RIGHT? SO YOU DON'T NEED TADANO. BUT ME...
IT DOESN'T REALLY MATTER.
I'M SUPERCUTE, SO EVERYONE LIKES ME. AND I'VE WORKED HARD TO BE LIKED.
AND TO BE YOUR FRIEND. UNDERSTAND?
SO I SHOULD BE YOUR FRIEND, RIGHT?
YOU WANT TO BE MY FRIEND...
...RIIIGHT?
THIS MAKES ME HAPPY.
WOW! KOMI REMEMBERED ALL THAT?!
And she added commentary!
You were in danger because of me.

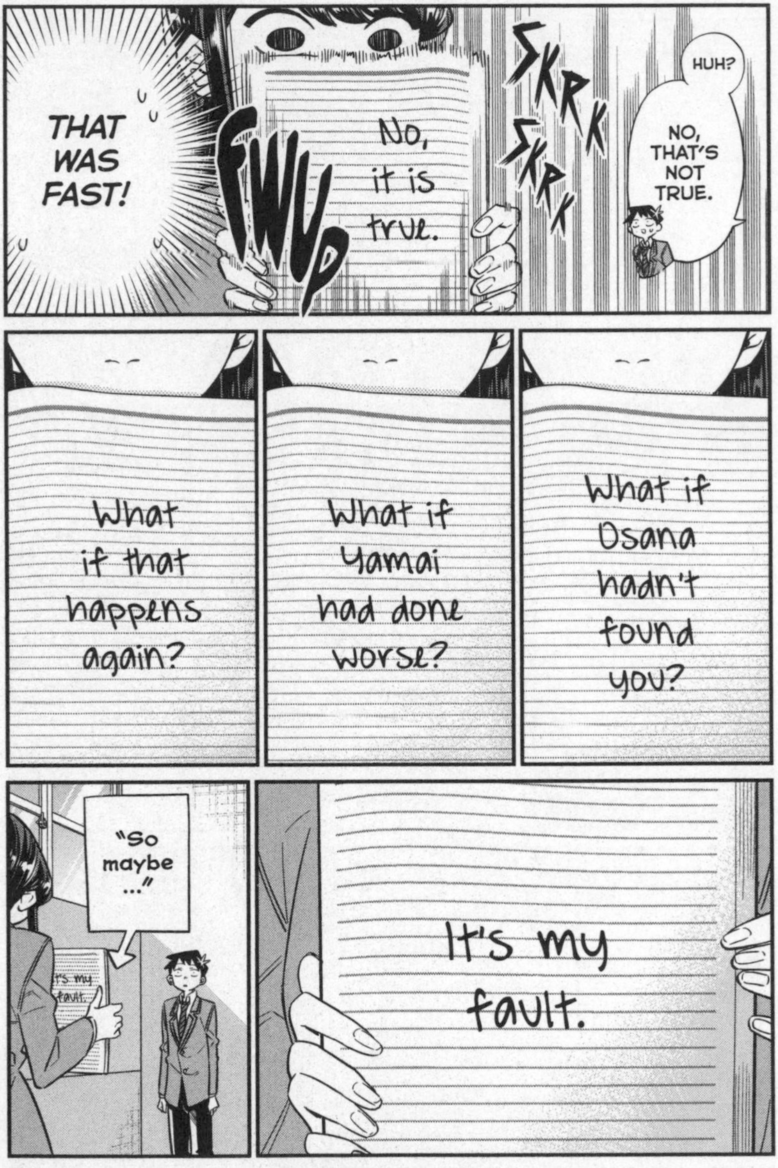
HUH?
NO, THAT'S NOT TRUE.
SKRK SKRK
No, it is true.
FWUP
THAT WAS FAST!
What if Osana hadn't found you?
What if Yamai had done worse?
What if that happens again?
It's my fault.
"So maybe ..."

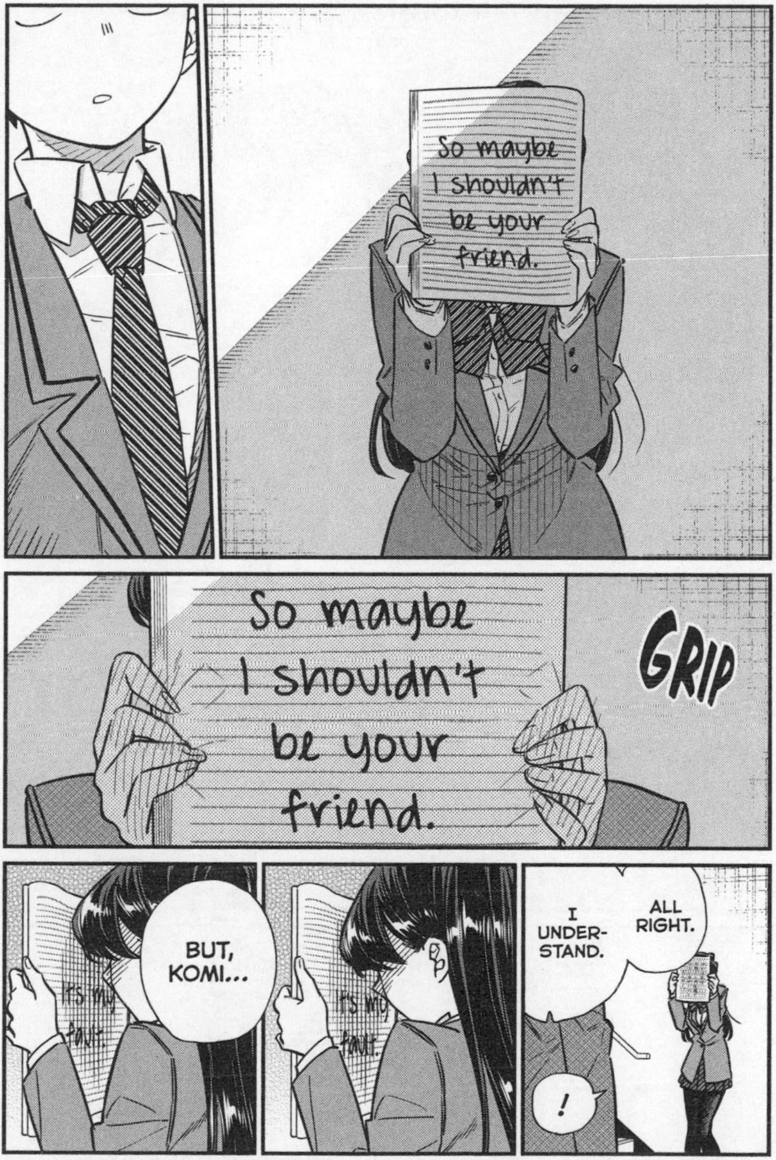
So maybe I shouldn't be your friend.
So maybe I shouldn't be your friend.
GRIP
ALL RIGHT.
I UNDER-STAND.
!
It's my fault.
BUT, KOMI...
It's my fault.

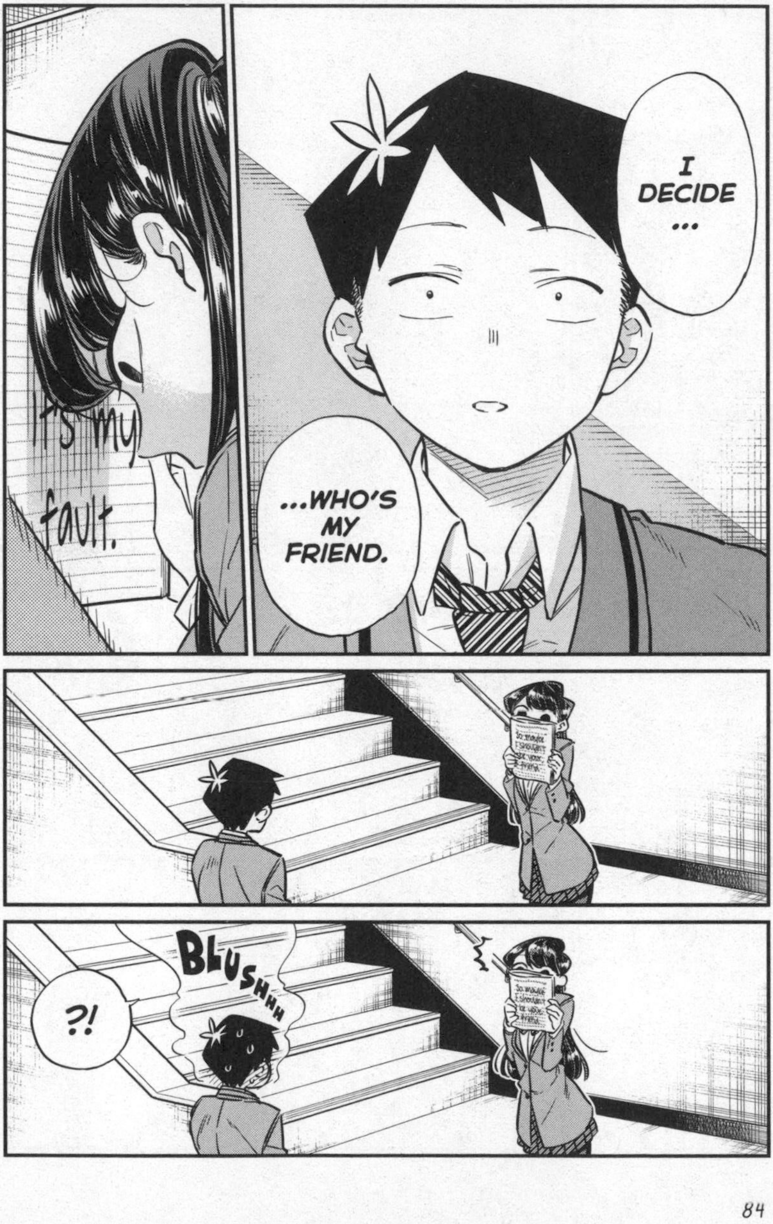
I DECIDE ...
...WHO'S MY FRIEND.
It's my fault.
BLUSHHH
?!

N-NO! I DIDN'T MEAN IT THAT WAY!! I WAS JUST... YOU KNOW! REPEATING WHAT YOU SAID! LIKE A CATCH-PHRASE!
IT JUST POPPED OUT! SO DON'T LOOK SO WOUNDED!
F-FORGET I SAID IT!
STAGGER
Add another page to Tadano's dark history ...
I'm sorry.
HUH?! W-WHAT FOR?!
I'm sorry.
B-BUT...

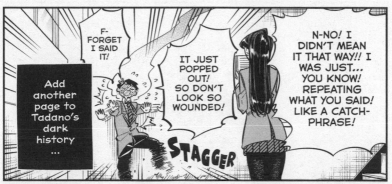

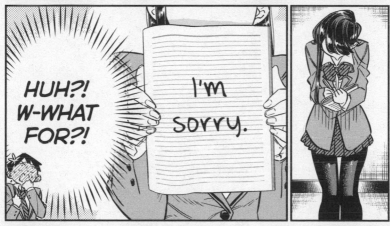

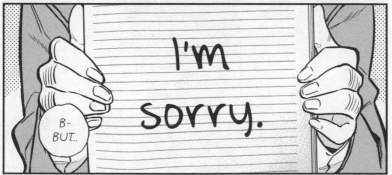

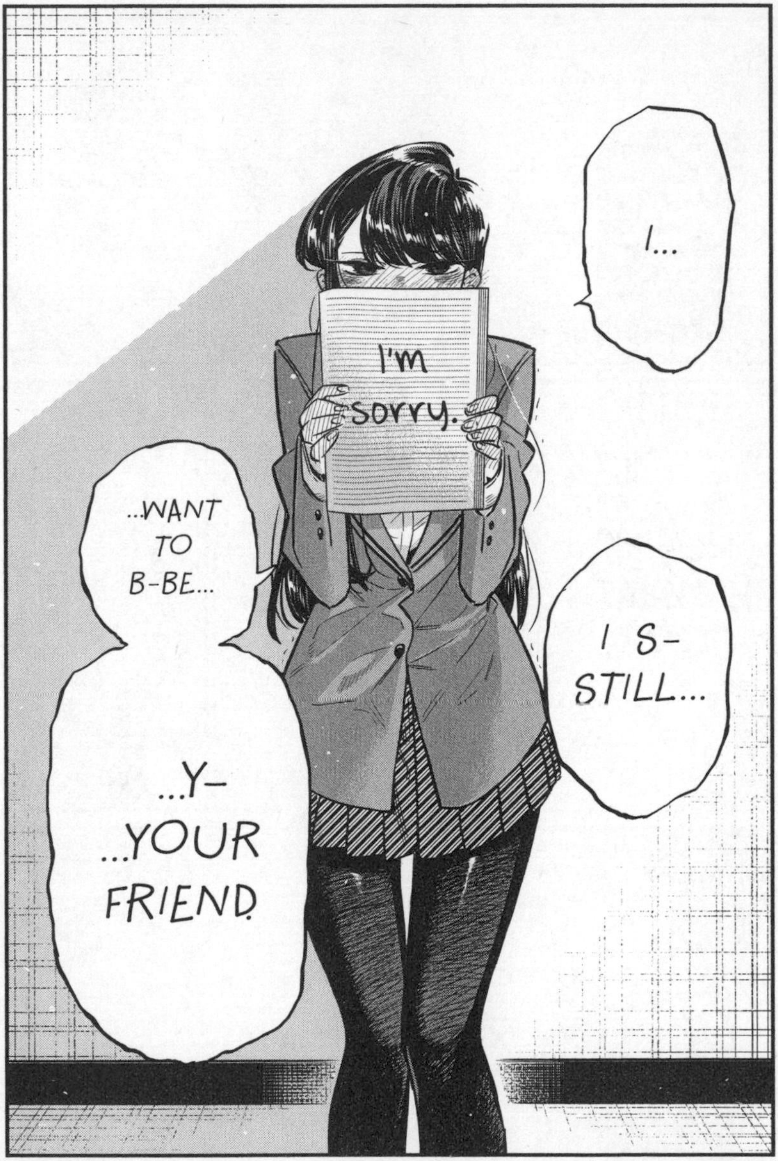
I...
I'm sorry.
I S-STILL...
...WANT TO B-BE...
...Y- ...YOUR FRIEND.

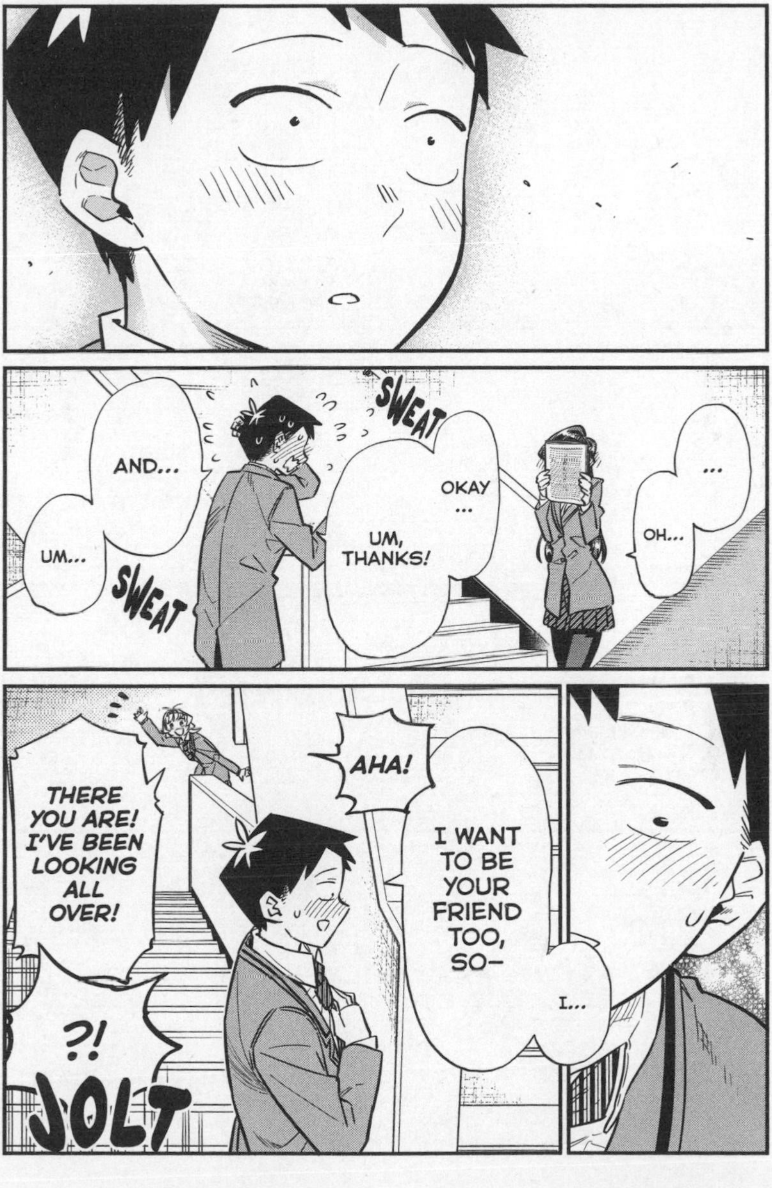

...
OH...
SWEAT
OKAY ...
UM, THANKS!
AND...
UM...
SWEAT
I...
AHA!
I WANT TO BE YOUR FRIEND TOO, SO-
THERE YOU ARE! I'VE BEEN LOOKING ALL OVER!
?!
JOLT

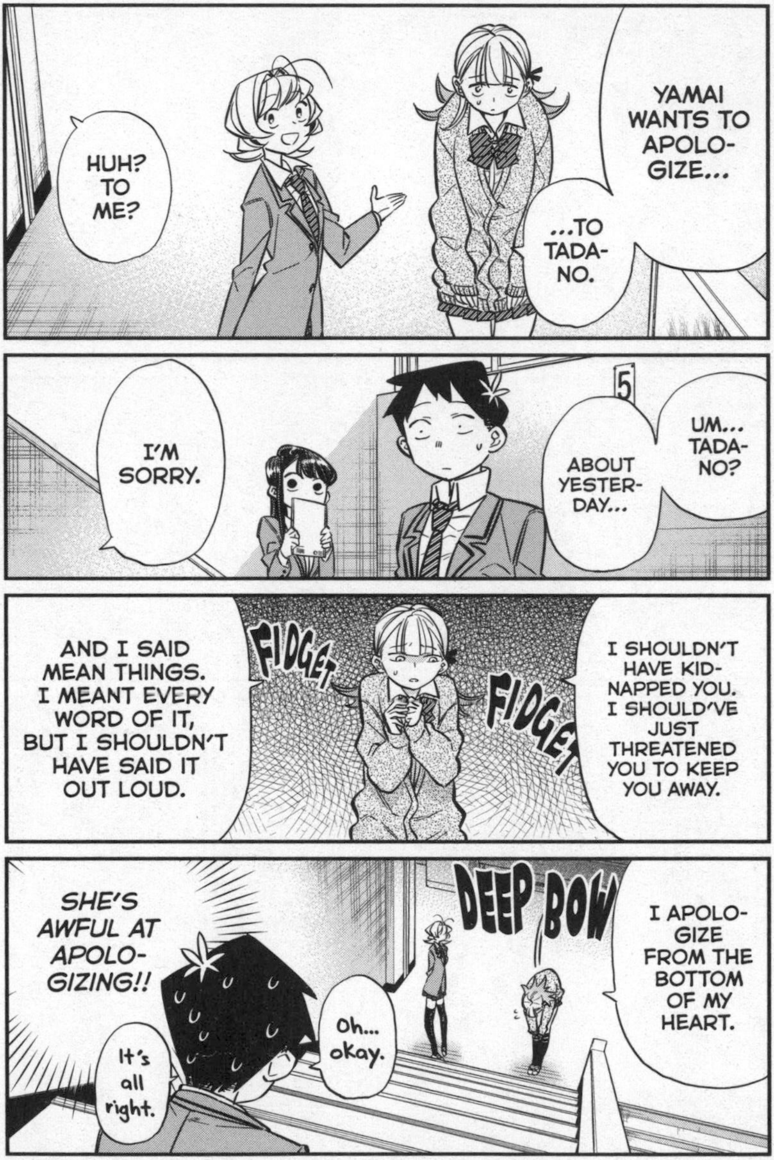
YAMAI WANTS TO APOLO-GIZE...
...TO TADA-NO.
HUH? TO ME?
UM... TADA-NO?
ABOUT YESTER-DAY...
I'M SORRY.
I SHOULDN'T HAVE KID-NAPPED YOU. I SHOULD'VE JUST THREATENED YOU TO KEEP YOU AWAY.
FIDGET
FIDGET
AND I SAID MEAN THINGS. I MEANT EVERY WORD OF IT, BUT I SHOULDN'T HAVE SAID IT OUT LOUD.
I APOLO-GIZE FROM THE BOTTOM OF MY HEART.
DEEP BOW
Oh... okay.
SHE'S AWFUL AT APOLO-GIZING!!
It's all right.

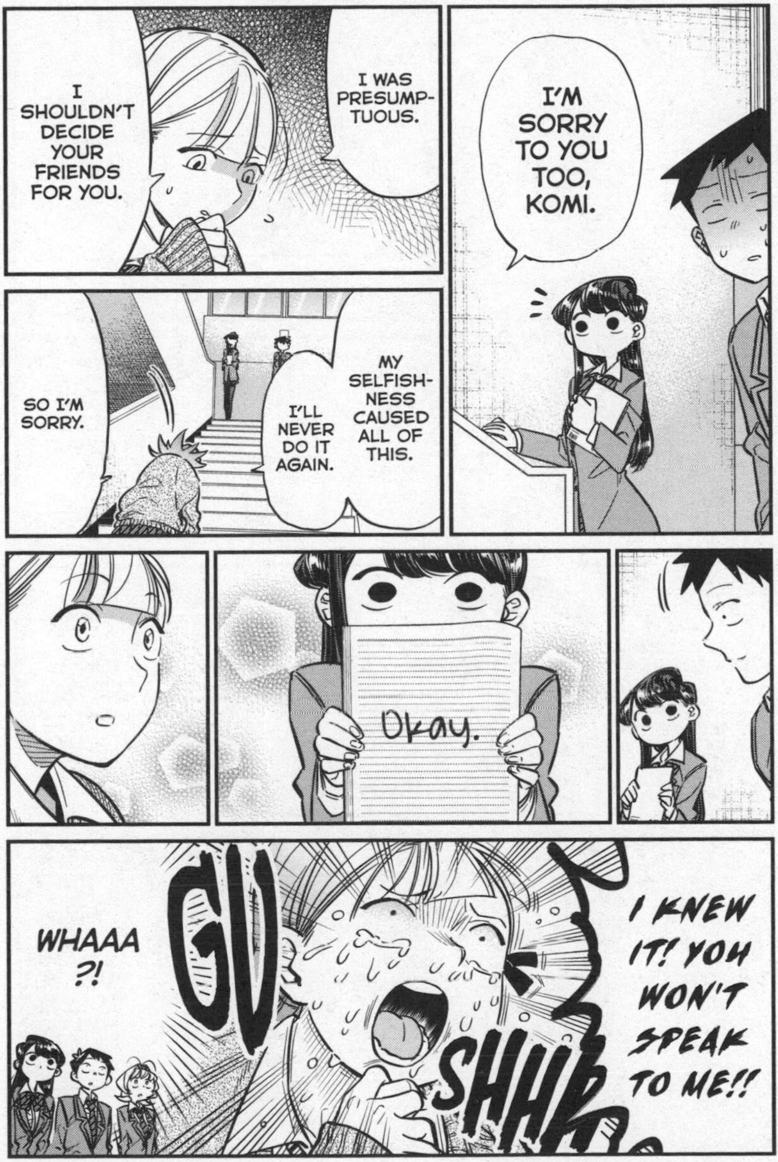
I'M SORRY TO YOU TOO, KOMI.
I WAS PRESUMPTUOUS.
I SHOULDN'T DECIDE YOUR FRIENDS FOR YOU.
MY SELFISHNESS CAUSED ALL OF THIS.
I'LL NEVER DO IT AGAIN.
SO I'M SORRY.
Okay.
I KNEW IT! YOU WON'T SPEAK TO ME!!
GUSHH
WHAAA ?!

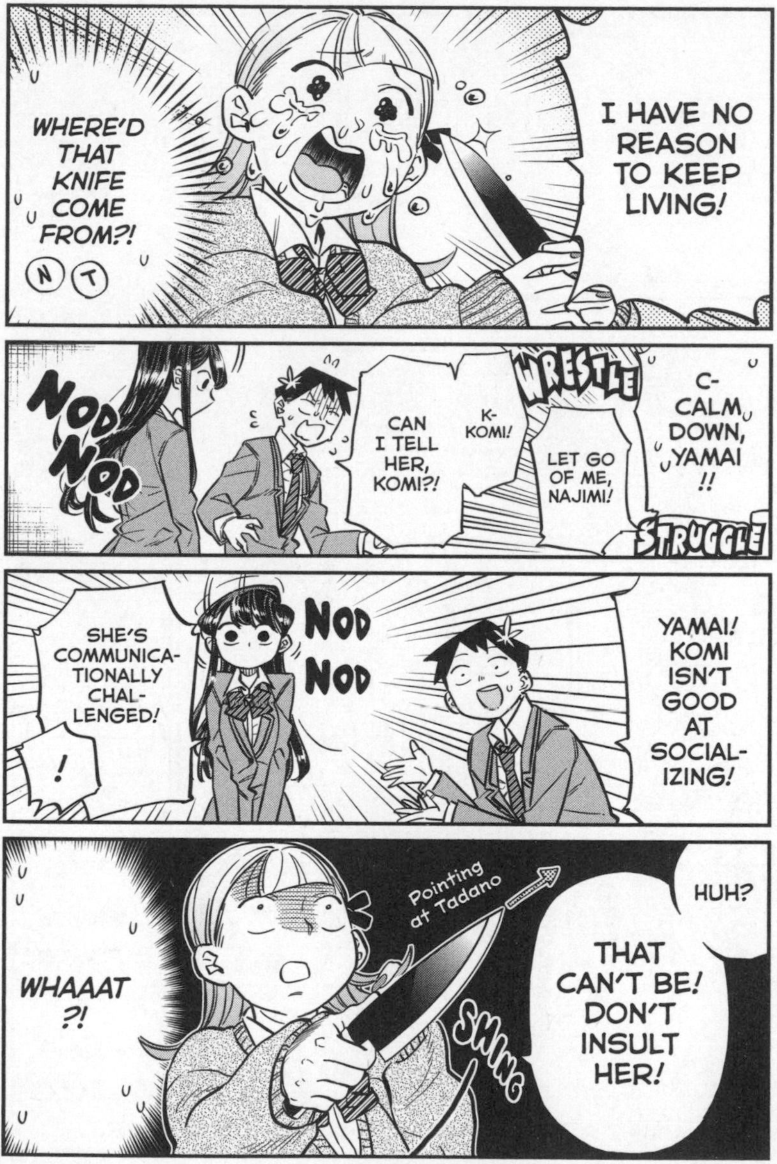
I HAVE NO REASON TO KEEP LIVING!
WHERE'D THAT KNIFE COME FROM?!
C-CALM DOWN, YAMAI!!
WRESTLE
STRUGGLE
LET GO OF ME, NAJIMI!
K-KOMI!
CAN I TELL HER, KOMI?!
NOD NOD
YAMAI! KOMI ISN'T GOOD AT SOCIALIZING!
NOD NOD
SHE'S COMMUNICATIONALLY CHALLENGED!
!
HUH?
THAT CAN'T BE! DON'T INSULT HER!
Pointing at Tadano
SHING
WHAAAT?!

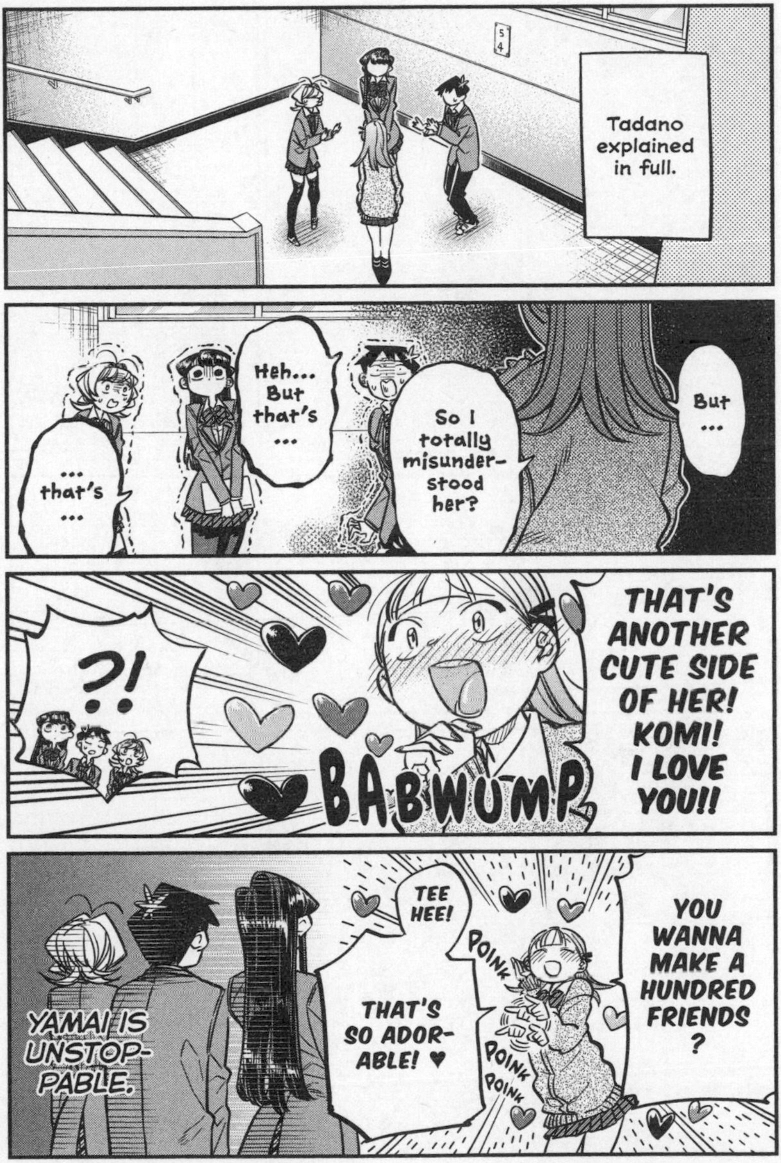
Tadano explained in full.
But ...
So I totally misunder-stood her?
Heh... But that's ...
... that's ...
THAT'S ANOTHER CUTE SIDE OF HER! KOMI! I LOVE YOU!!
BABWUMP
?!
YOU WANNA MAKE A HUNDRED FRIENDS ?
POINK
POINK
POINK
TEE HEE!
THAT'S SO ADOR-ABLE! ♥
YAMAI IS UNSTOP-PABLE.

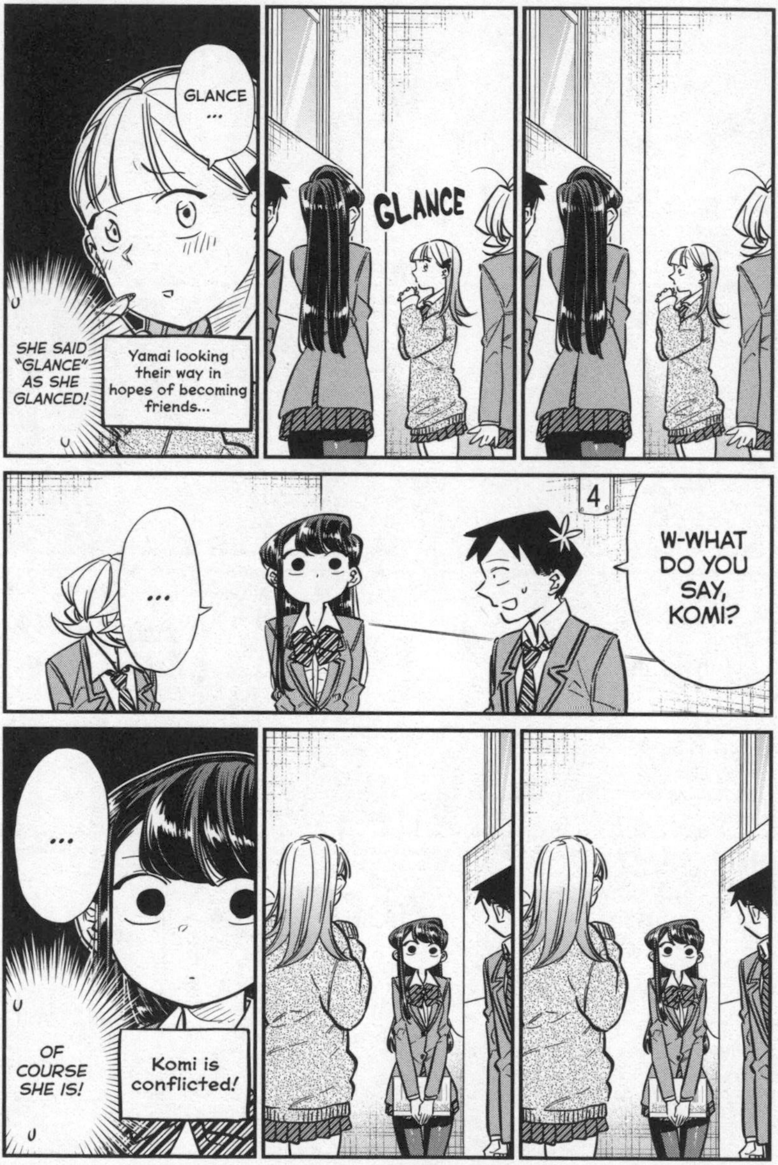
GLANCE
GLANCE ...
Yamai looking their way in hopes of becoming friends...
SHE SAID "GLANCE" AS SHE GLANCED!
W-WHAT DO YOU SAY, KOMI?
...
...
Komi is conflicted!
OF COURSE SHE IS!

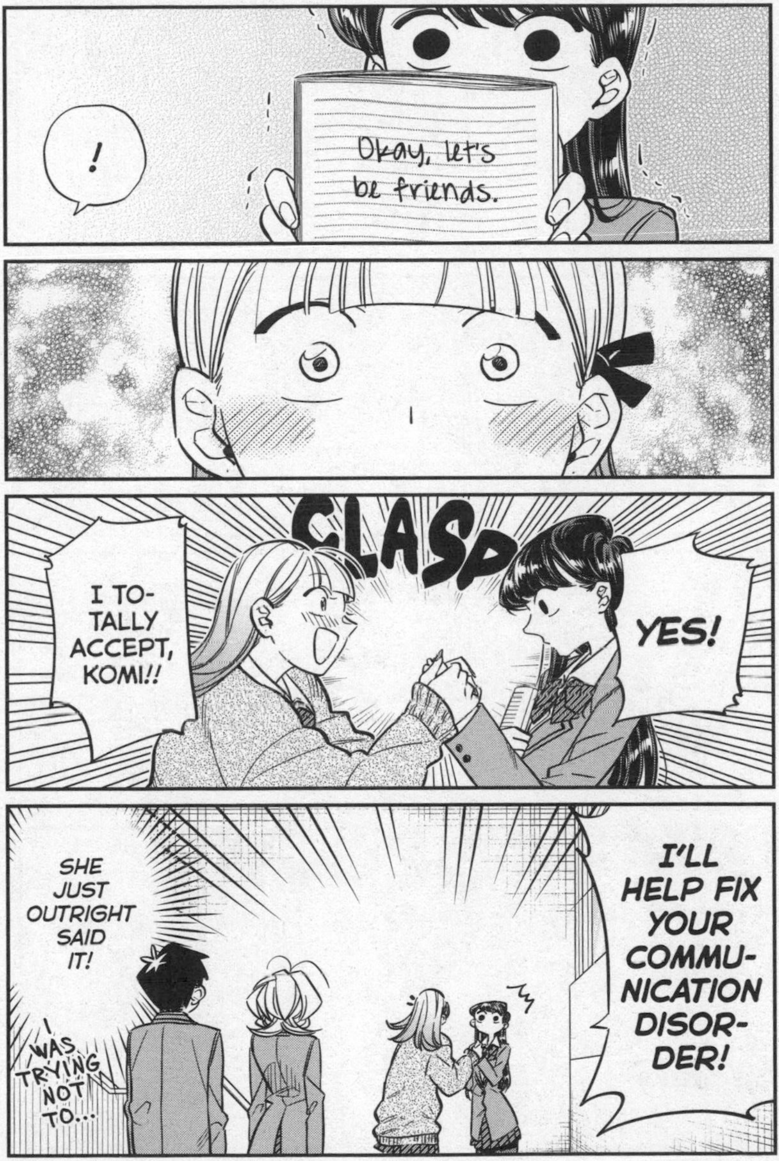
Okay, let's be friends.
!
CLASP
YES!
I TO-TALLY ACCEPT, KOMI!!
I'LL HELP FIX YOUR COMMUNICATION DISORDER!
SHE JUST OUTRIGHT SAID IT!
I WAS TRYING NOT TO...

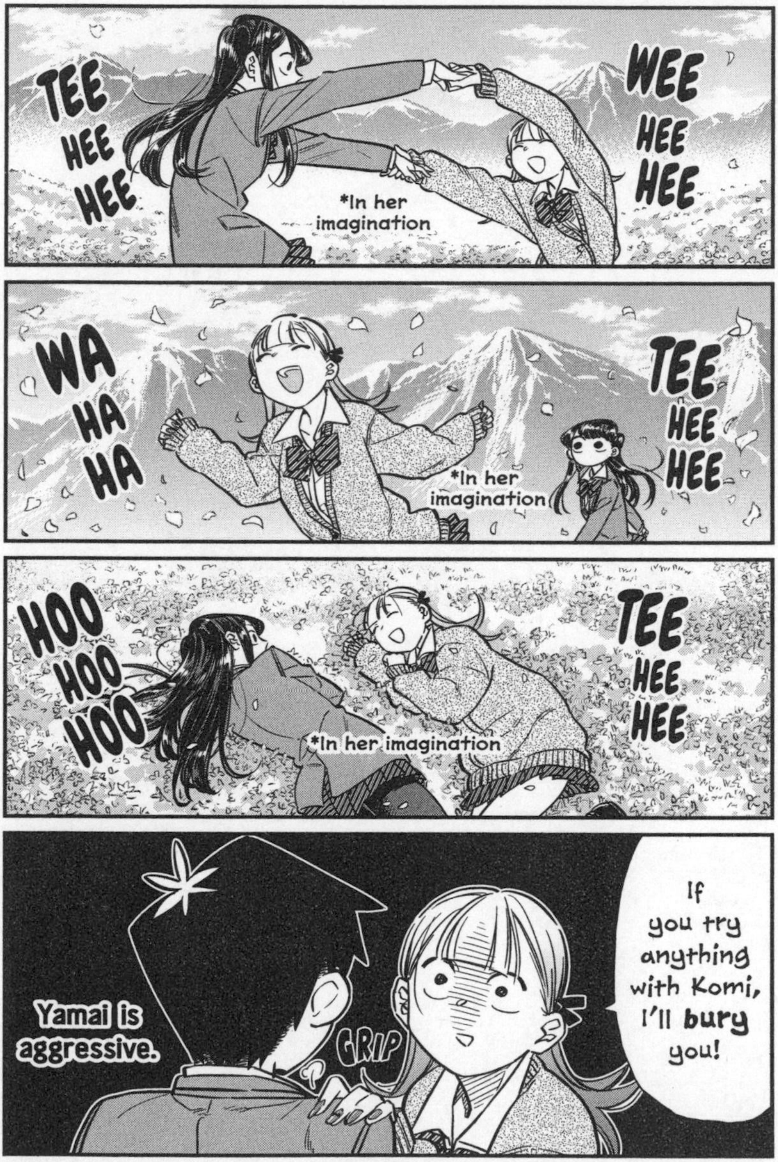
WEE HEE HEE
TEE HEE HEE
*In her imagination
TEE HEE HEE
WA HA HA
*In her imagination
TEE HEE HEE
HOO HOO HOO
*In her imagination
If you try anything with Komi, I'll **bury** you!
GRIP
Yamai is aggressive.

Communication 26 – The End

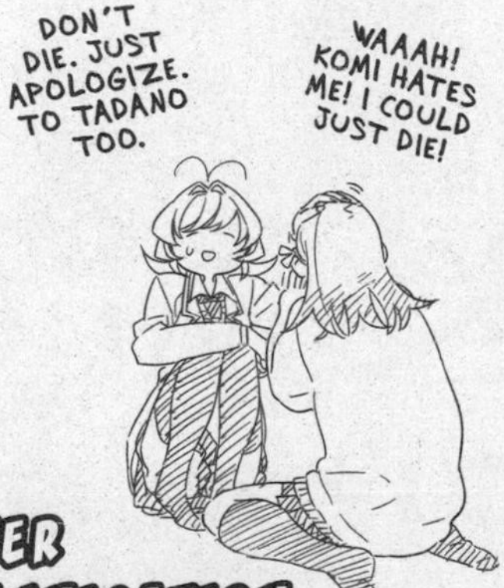
WAAAH! KOMI HATES ME! I COULD JUST DIE!
DON'T DIE. JUST APOLOGIZE. TO TADANO TOO.

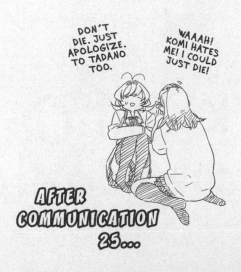

AFTER COMMUNICATION 25...

Komi Can't
Communicate

Komi Can't Communicate

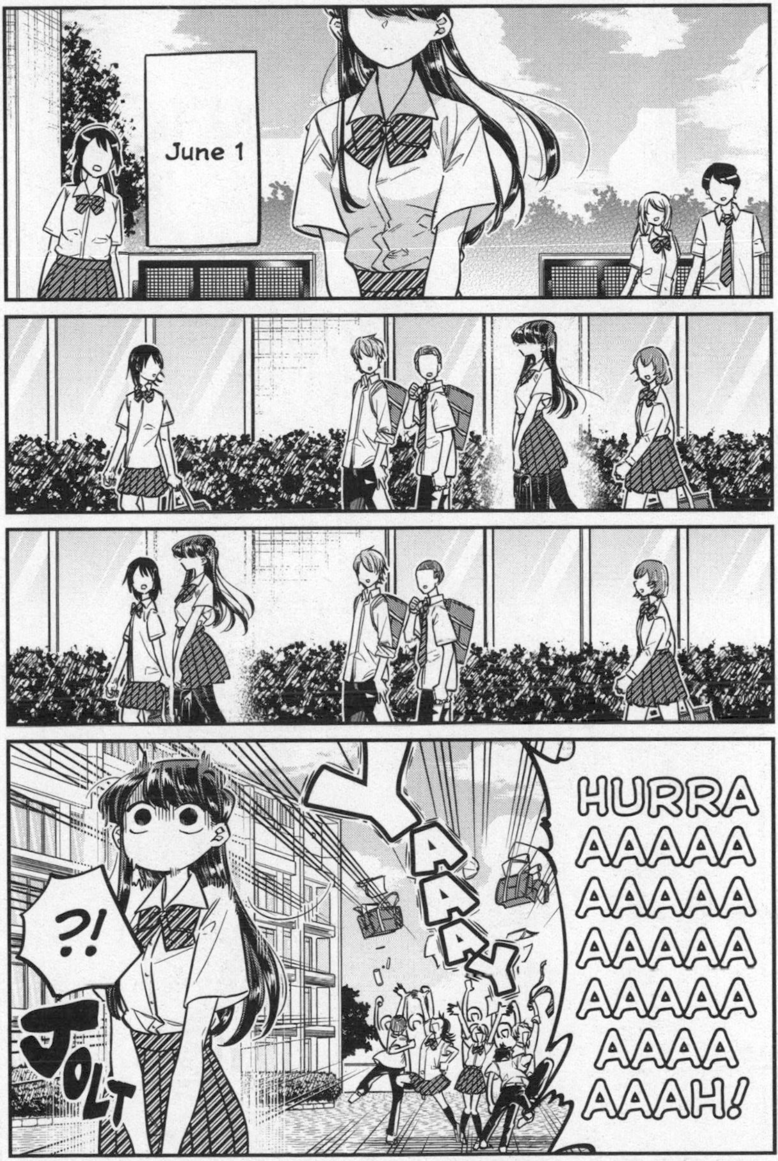
June 1
HURRAAAAAAAAAAAAAAAAAAAAAAAAAAAAH!
YAAAY
?!
JOLT

Komi Can't Communicate

Communication 27: Summer Uniform

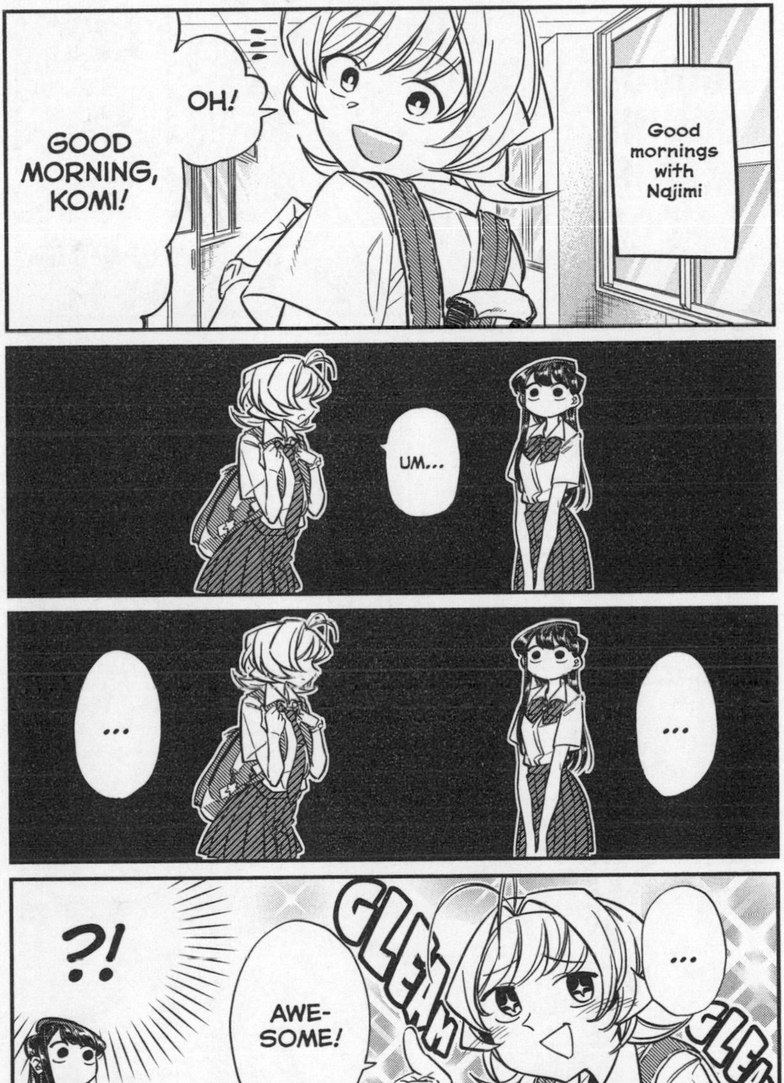
Good mornings with Najimi
OH!
GOOD MORNING, KOMI!
UM...
...
...
...
GLEAM
GLEAM
AWE-SOME!
?!

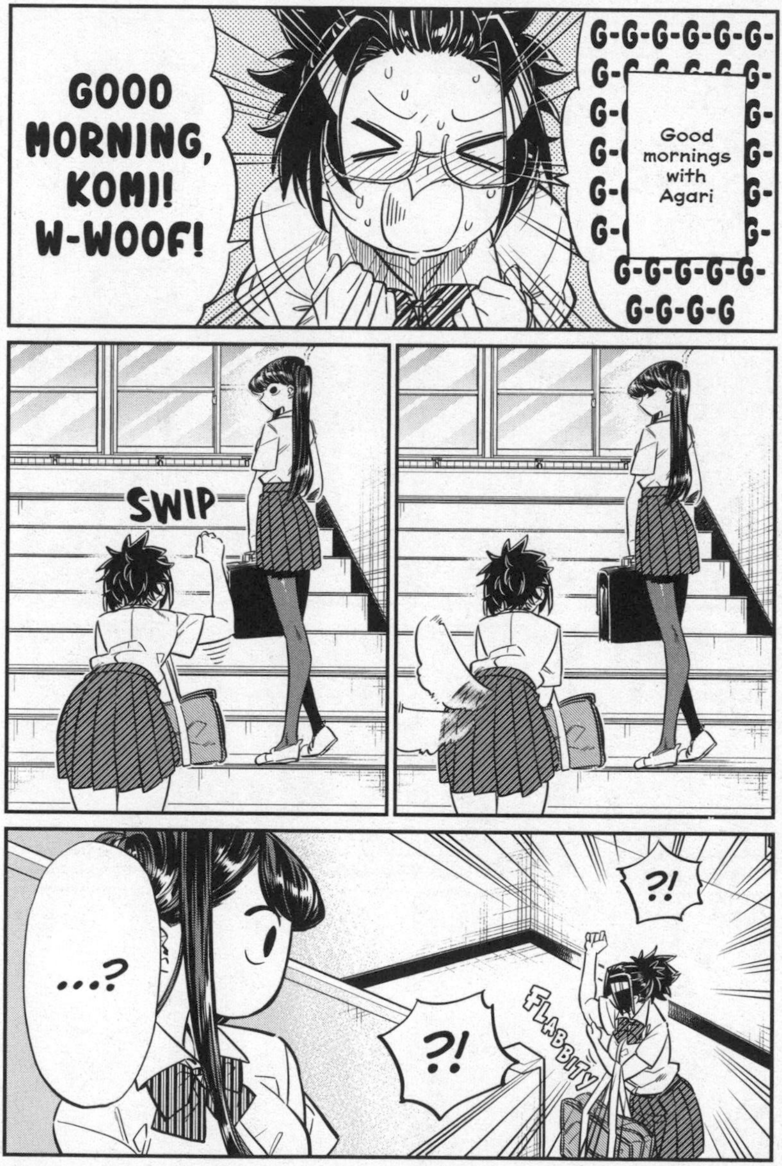
G-G-G-G-G-G-
G-G-G-G-G-
G-G-G-G
Good mornings with Agari
GOOD MORNING, KOMI! W-WOOF!
SWIP
?!
FLABBITY
?!
...?

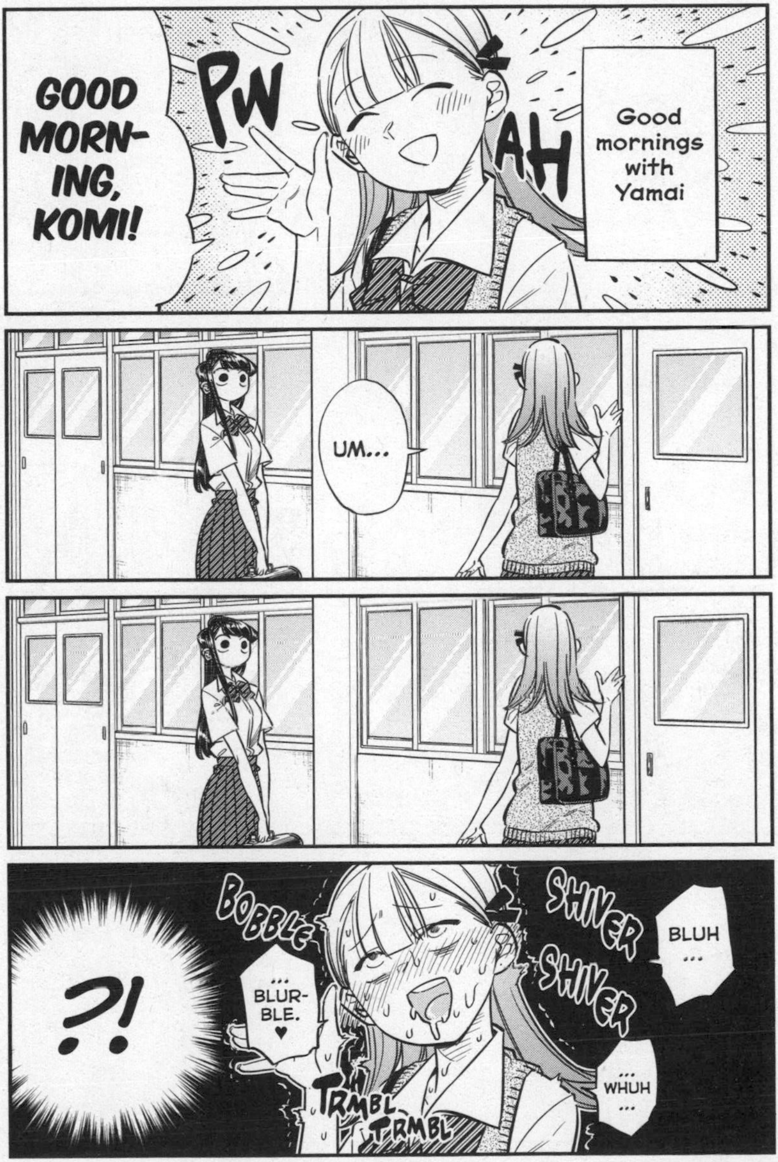
Good mornings with Yamai
PWAH
GOOD MORNING, KOMI!
UM...
BLUH ...
SHIVER SHIVER
... WHUH ...
BOBBLE
... BLURBLE. ♥
TRMBL TRMBL
?!

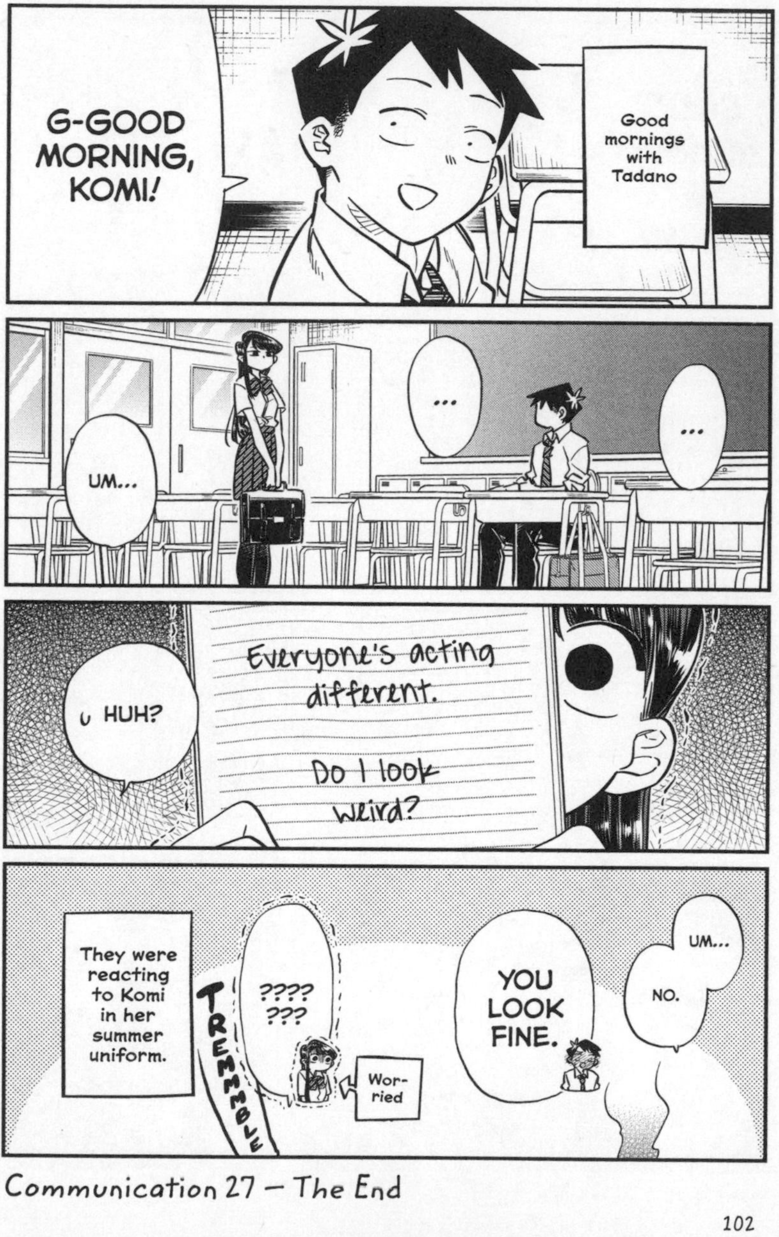
Good mornings with Tadano
G-GOOD MORNING, KOMI!
...
...
UM...
Everyone's acting different.
Do I look weird?
HUH?
UM...
NO.
YOU LOOK FINE.
Wor-ried
????
???
TREMMBLE
They were reacting to Komi in her summer uniform.

Communication 27 – The End

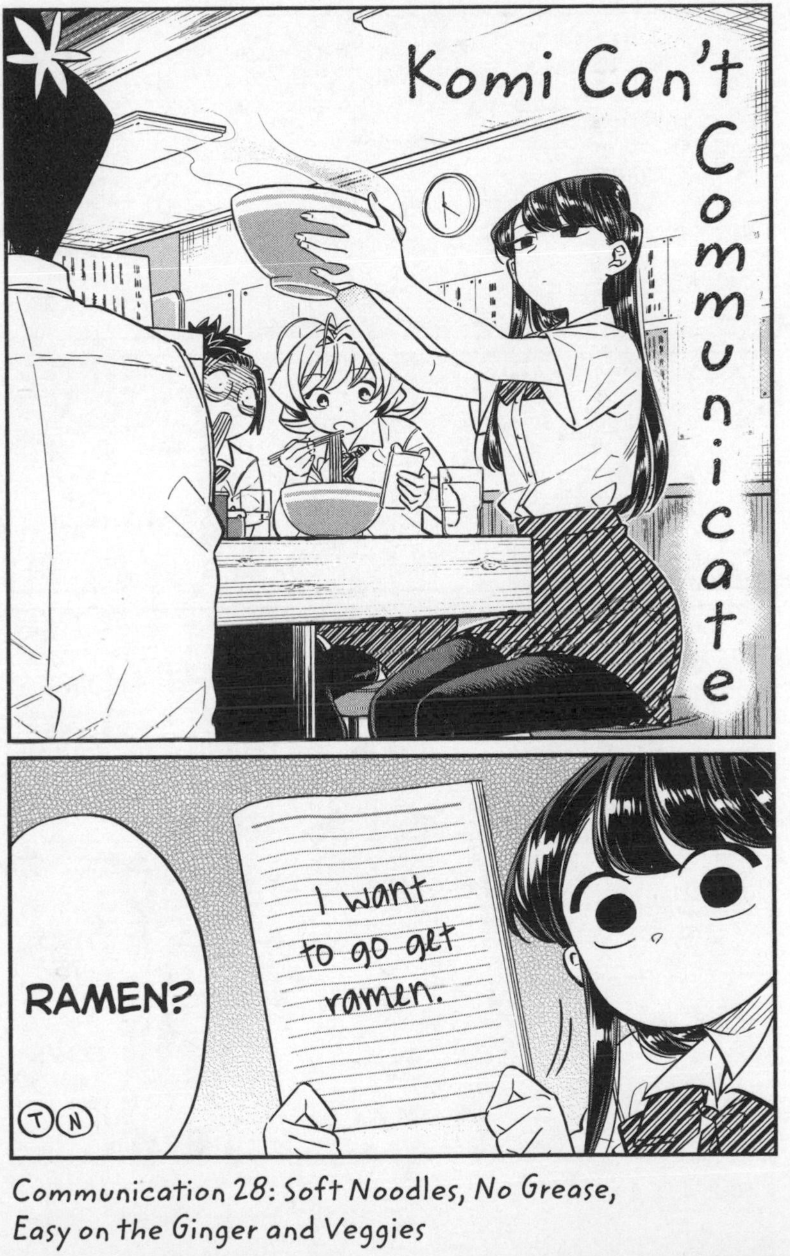
Komi Can't Communicate
I want to go get ramen.
RAMEN?
TN

Communication 28: Soft Noodles, No Grease, Easy on the Ginger and Veggies

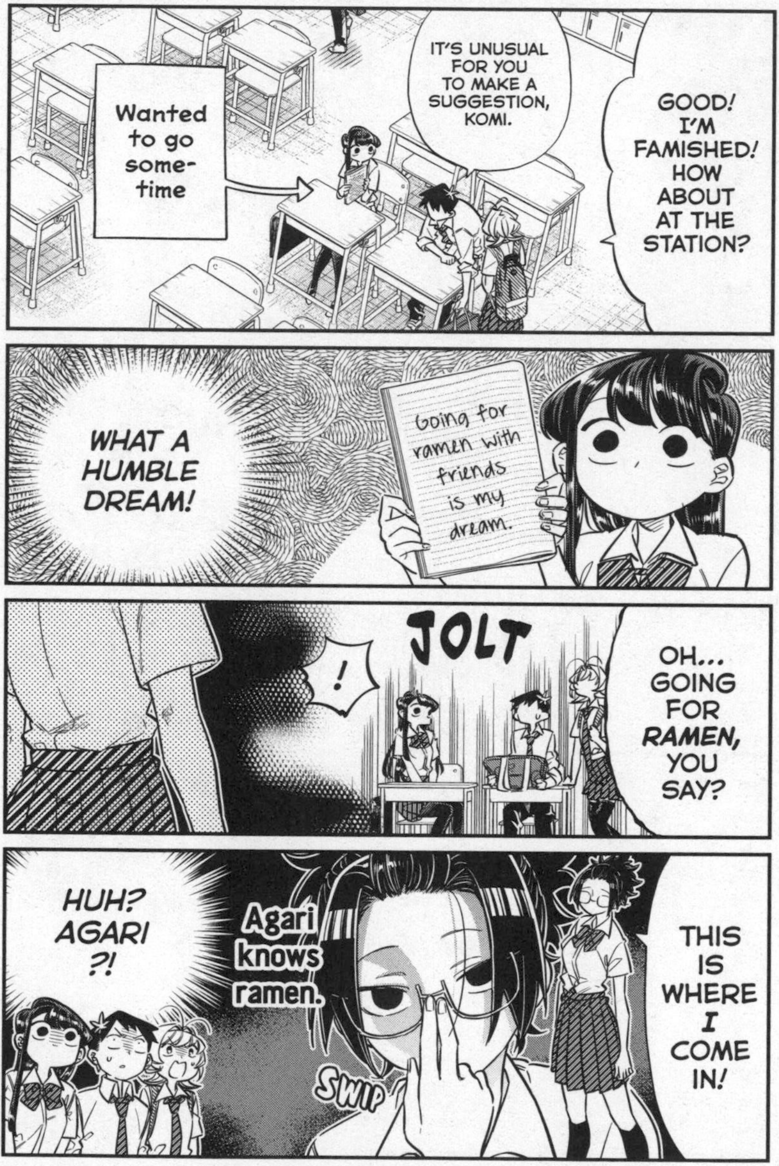
GOOD! I'M FAMISHED! HOW ABOUT AT THE STATION?
IT'S UNUSUAL FOR YOU TO MAKE A SUGGESTION, KOMI.
Wanted to go some-time
Going for ramen with friends is my dream.
WHAT A HUMBLE DREAM!
OH... GOING FOR RAMEN, YOU SAY?
JOLT
!
THIS IS WHERE I COME IN!
SWIP
Agari knows ramen.
HUH? AGARI ?!

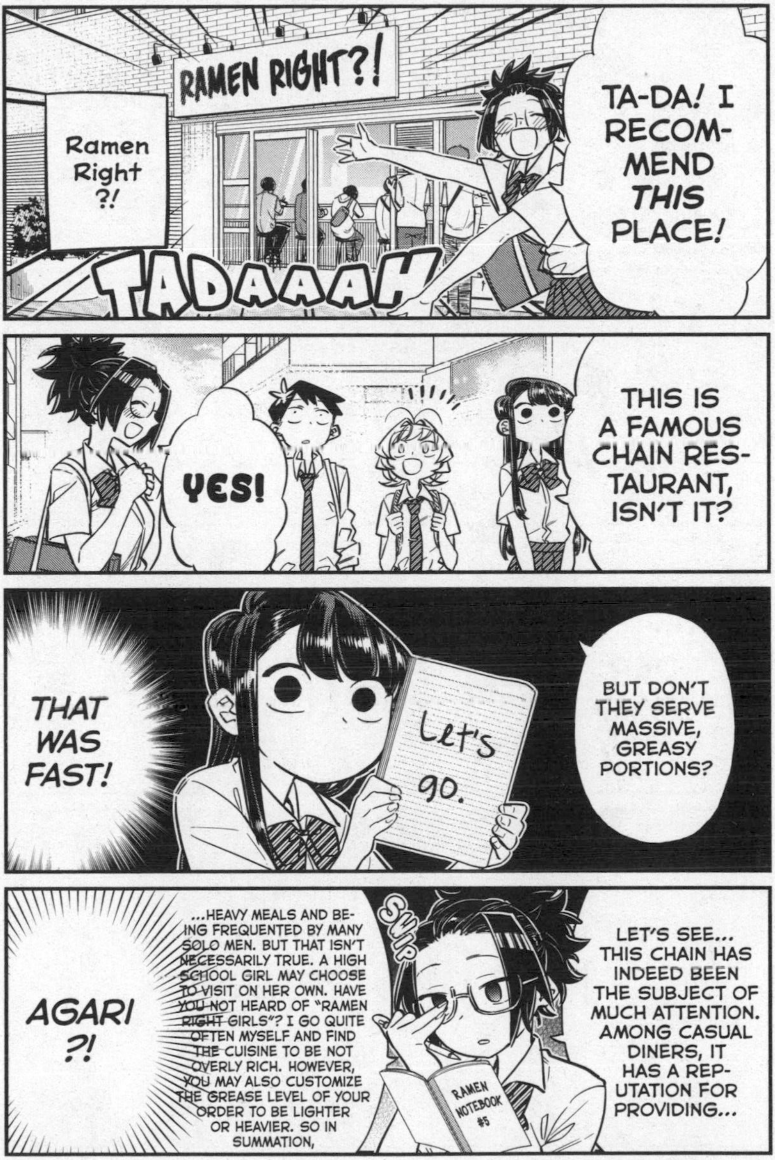
TA-DA! I RECOMMEND THIS PLACE!
RAMEN RIGHT?!
Ramen Right ?!
TADAAAH
THIS IS A FAMOUS CHAIN RESTAURANT, ISN'T IT?
YES!
BUT DON'T THEY SERVE MASSIVE, GREASY PORTIONS?
Let's go.
THAT WAS FAST!
LET'S SEE... THIS CHAIN HAS INDEED BEEN THE SUBJECT OF MUCH ATTENTION. AMONG CASUAL DINERS, IT HAS A REPUTATION FOR PROVIDING...
SWIP
...HEAVY MEALS AND BEING FREQUENTED BY MANY SOLO MEN. BUT THAT ISN'T NECESSARILY TRUE. A HIGH SCHOOL GIRL MAY CHOOSE TO VISIT ON HER OWN. HAVE YOU NOT HEARD OF "RAMEN RIGHT GIRLS"? I GO QUITE OFTEN MYSELF AND FIND THE CUISINE TO BE NOT OVERLY RICH. HOWEVER, YOU MAY ALSO CUSTOMIZE THE GREASE LEVEL OF YOUR ORDER TO BE LIGHTER OR HEAVIER. SO IN SUMMATION,
RAMEN NOTEBOOK #5
AGARI ?!

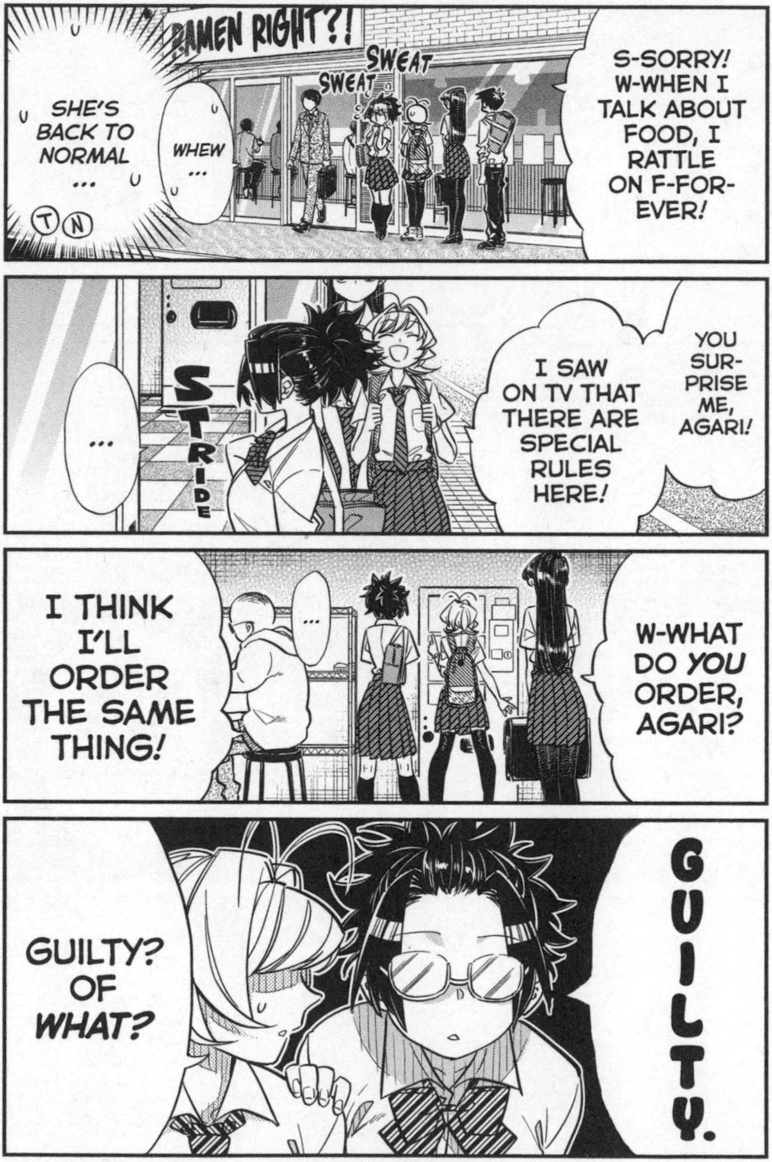
S-SORRY! W-WHEN I TALK ABOUT FOOD, I RATTLE ON F-FOR-EVER!
RAMEN RIGHT?!
SWEAT
SWEAT
WHEW ...
SHE'S BACK TO NORMAL ...
TN
YOU SURPRISE ME, AGARI!
I SAW ON TV THAT THERE ARE SPECIAL RULES HERE!
STRIDE
...
W-WHAT DO YOU ORDER, AGARI?
...
I THINK I'LL ORDER THE SAME THING!
GUILTY.
GUILTY? OF WHAT?

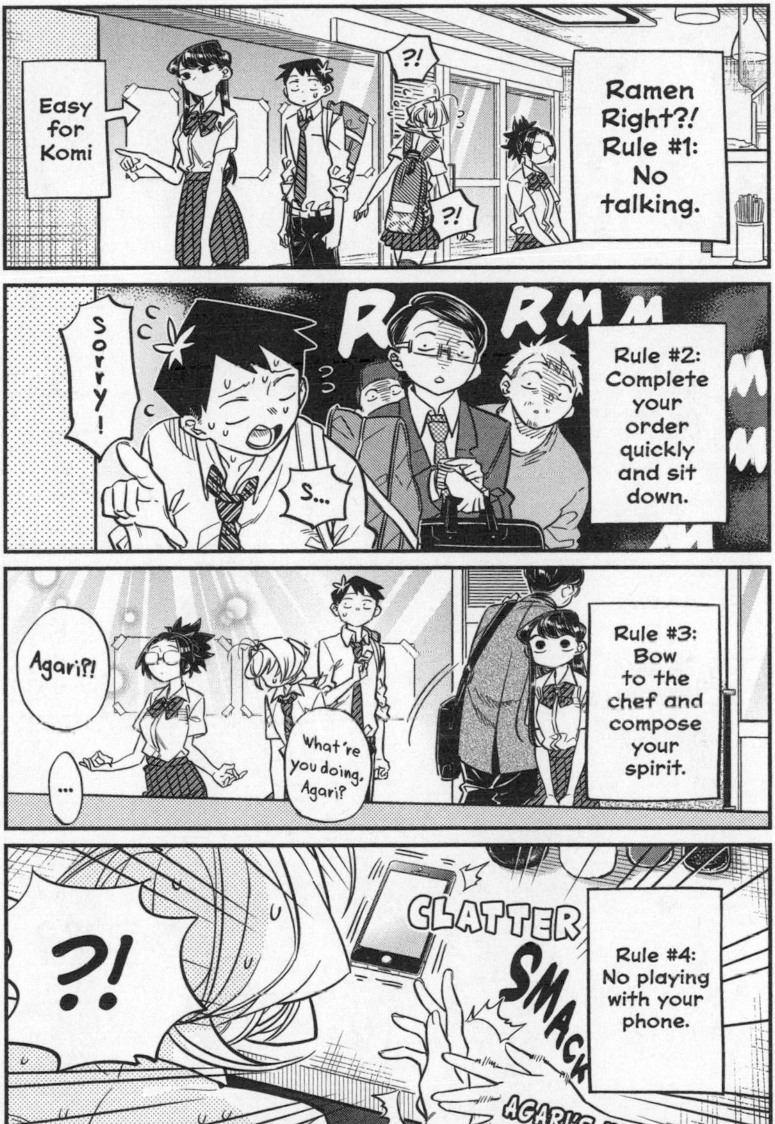
Ramen Right?! Rule #1: No talking.
?!
?!
Easy for Komi
Rule #2: Complete your order quickly and sit down.
RRMM
S...
Sorry!
Rule #3: Bow to the chef and compose your spirit.
What're you doing, Agari?
Agari?!
...
Rule #4: No playing with your phone.
CLATTER
SMACK
AGARI'S HAND
?!

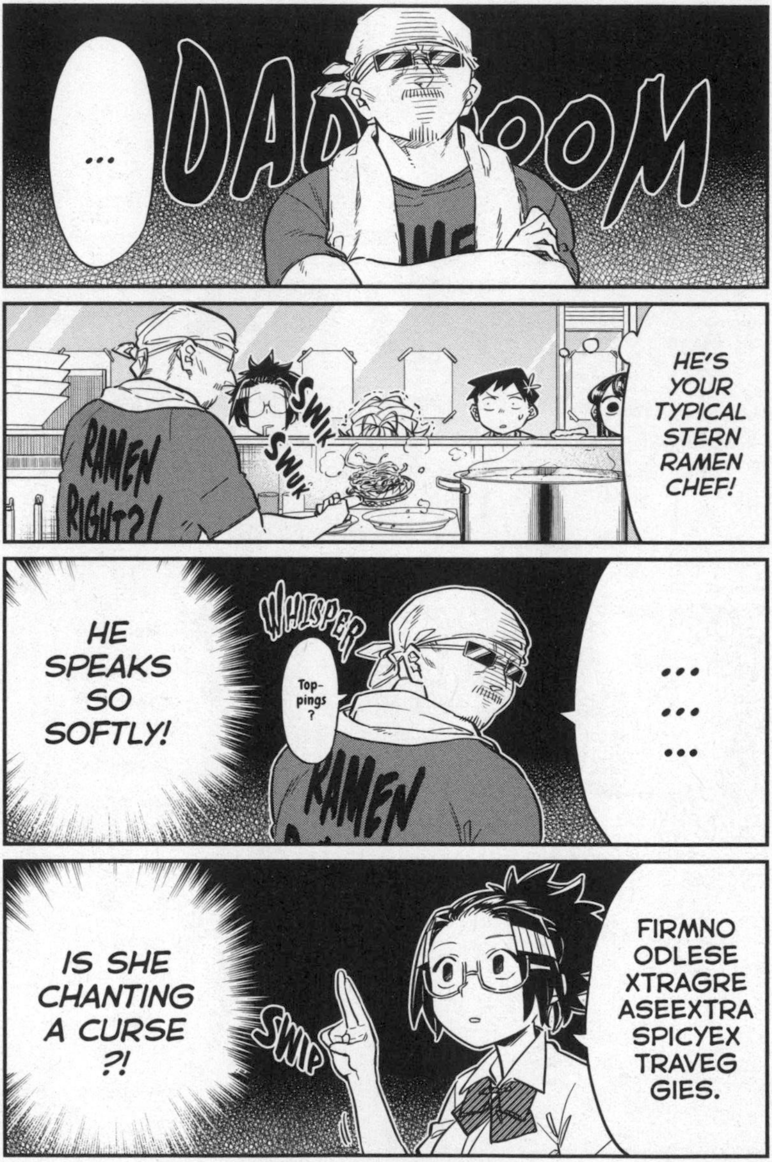
DAD OOM
...
HE'S YOUR TYPICAL STERN RAMEN CHEF!
SWIK SWUK
RAMEN RIGHT?!
... ...
WHISPER
Top-pings?
HE SPEAKS SO SOFTLY!
RAMEN
FIRMNOODLESEXTRAGREASEEXTRASPICYEXTRAVEGGIES.
SWIP
IS SHE CHANTING A CURSE?!

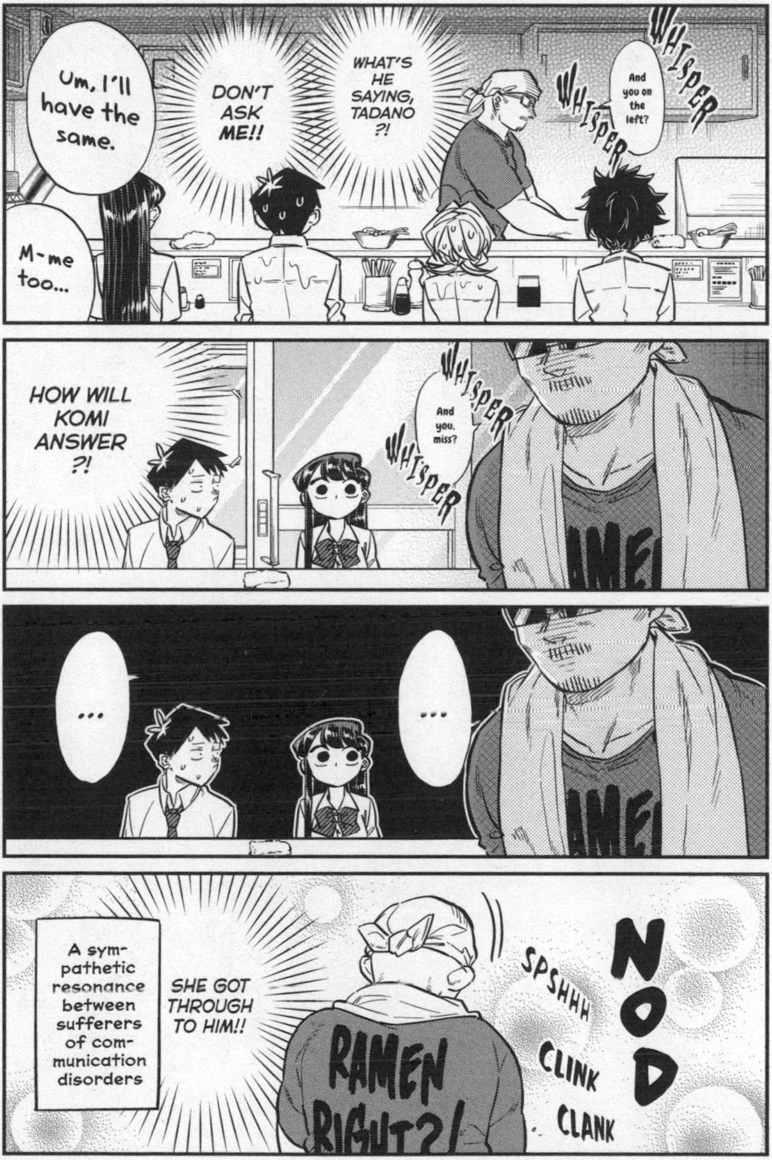
WHISPER
WHISPER
WHISPER
And you on the left?
WHAT'S HE SAYING, TADANO?!
DON'T ASK ME!!
Um, I'll have the same.
M-me too...
WHISPER
And you, miss?
WHISPER
HOW WILL KOMI ANSWER?!
...
...
NOD
SPSHHH
CLINK
CLANK
RAMEN RIGHT?!
SHE GOT THROUGH TO HIM!!
A sym-pathetic resonance between sufferers of com-munication disorders

Agari's, Najimi's and Tadano's ramen
BA
GW !!
OOO
OOOOO
N
W-WHAT A HUGE SERVING ...
Time to dig in!!
GWOO
GWOO
GWOO
Komi's ramen
SWIP
SPARKLE
Beautiful presen-tation
GLEAM
WHAT THE HECK, CHEF?!
SWUF

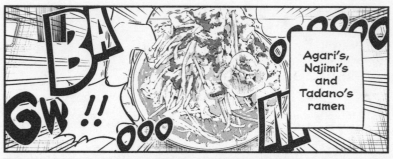

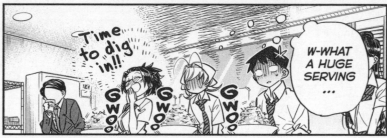

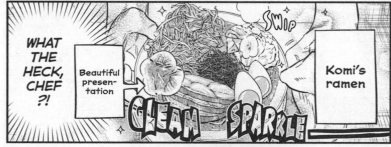

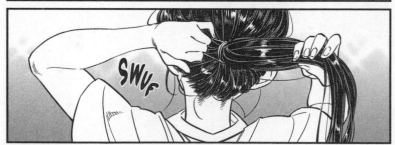

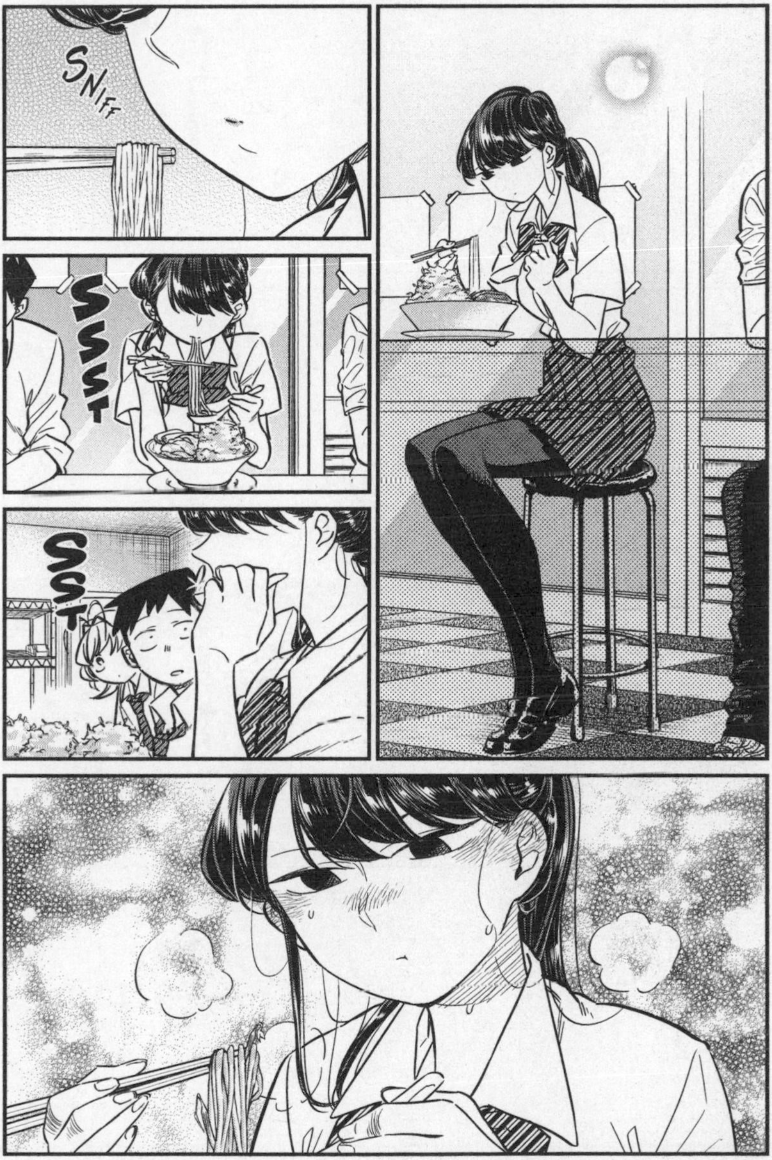
SNIFF
SSSST
SSST

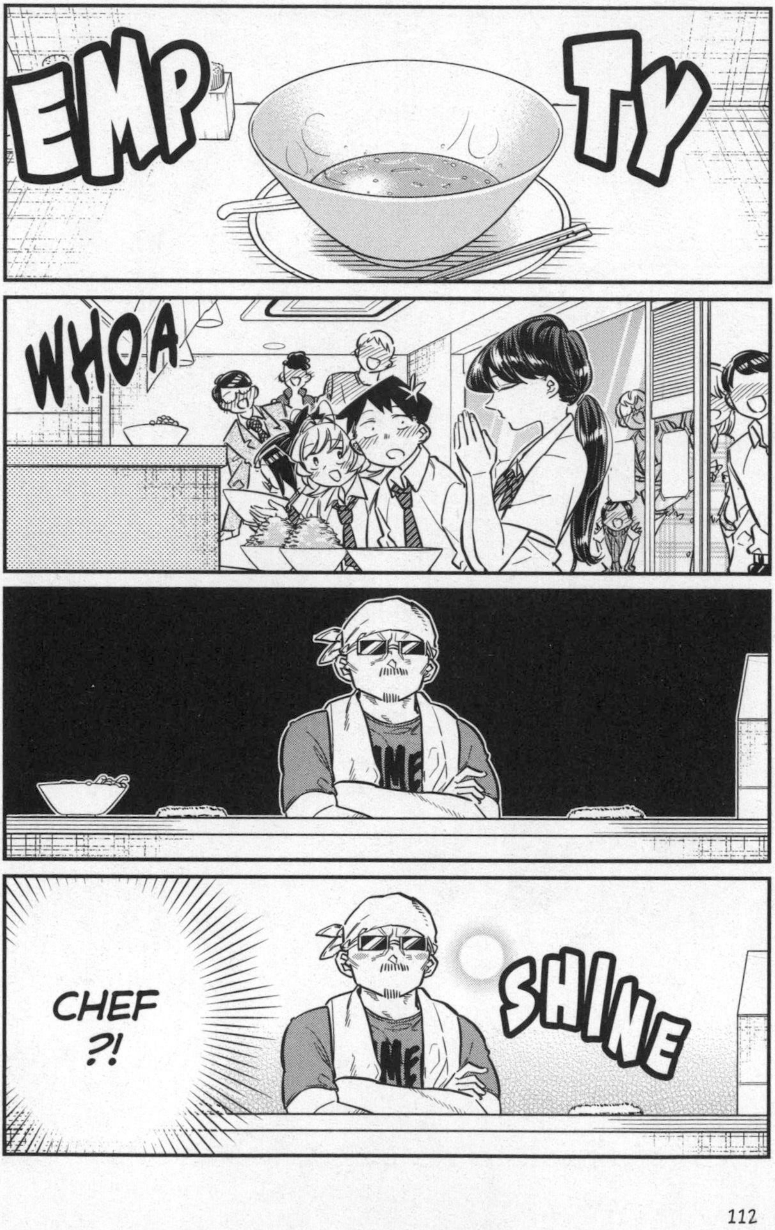
EMP
TY
WHOA
CHEF ?!
SHINE

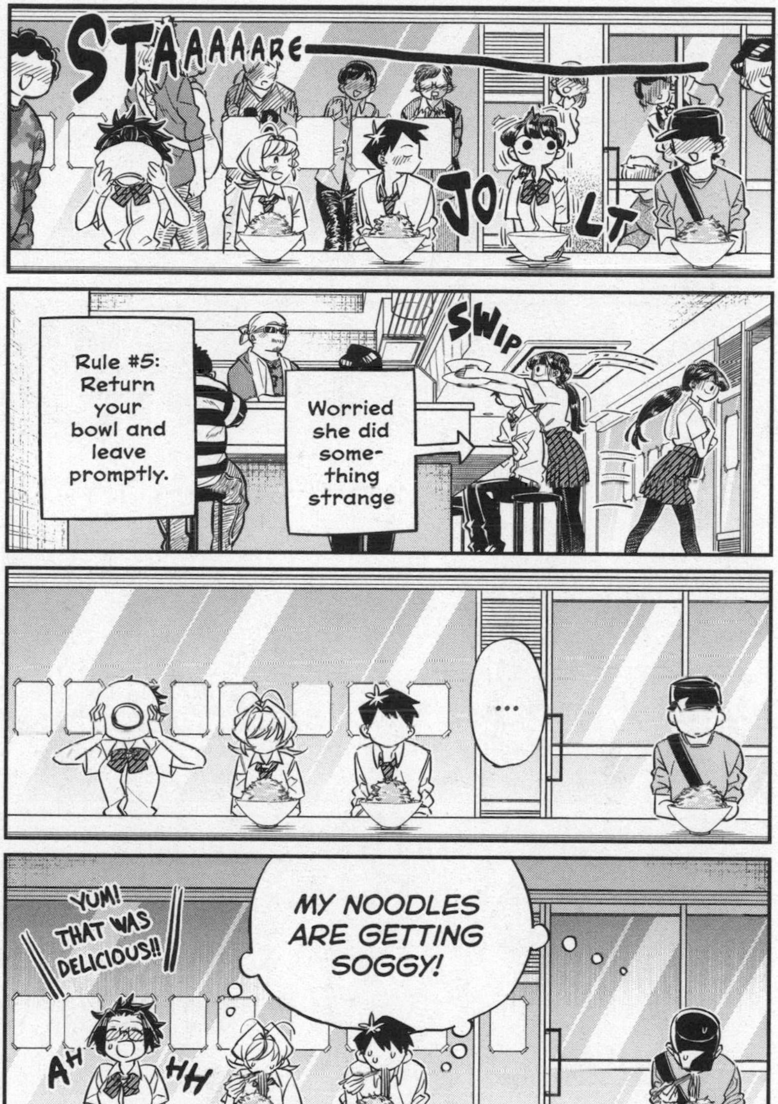
STAAAAARE
JOLT
SWIP
Worried she did something strange
Rule #5: Return your bowl and leave promptly.
...
MY NOODLES ARE GETTING SOGGY!
YUM! THAT WAS DELICIOUS!!
AHHH

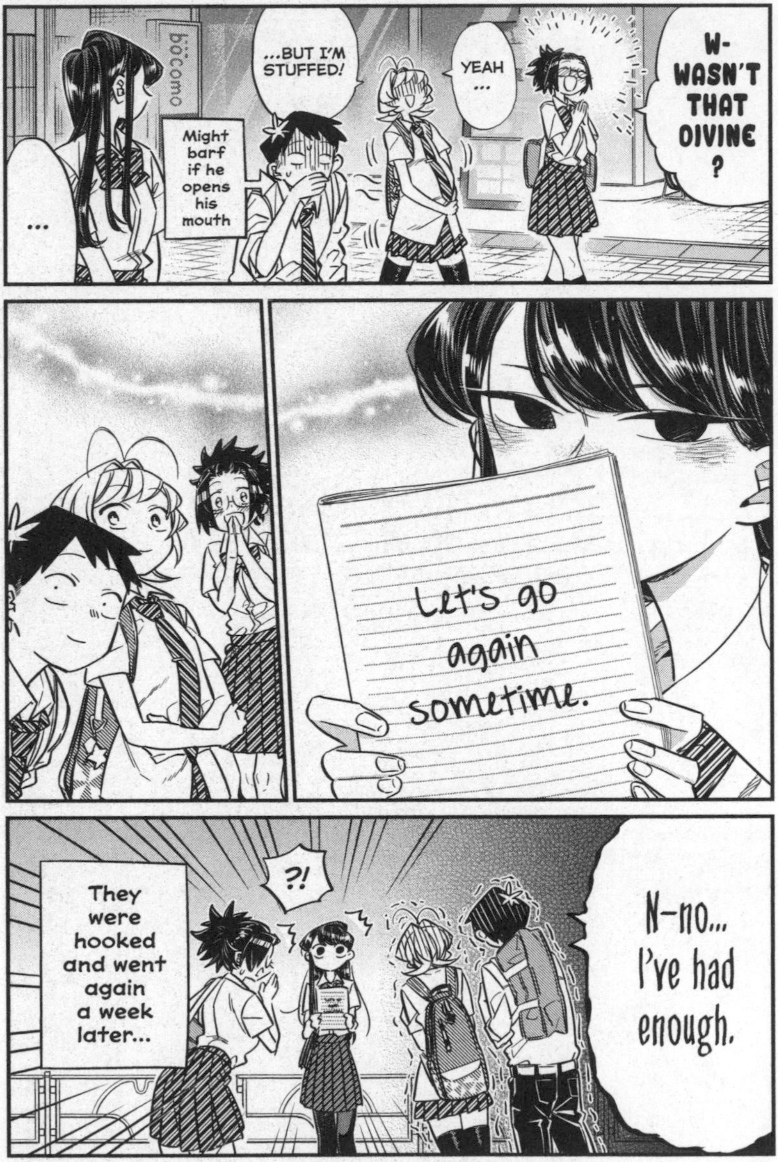
W-WASN'T THAT DIVINE?
YEAH ...
...BUT I'M STUFFED!
Might barf if he opens his mouth
...
docomo
Let's go again sometime.
N-no... I've had enough.
?!
They were hooked and went again a week later...

Communication 28 – The End

Komi Can't Communicate

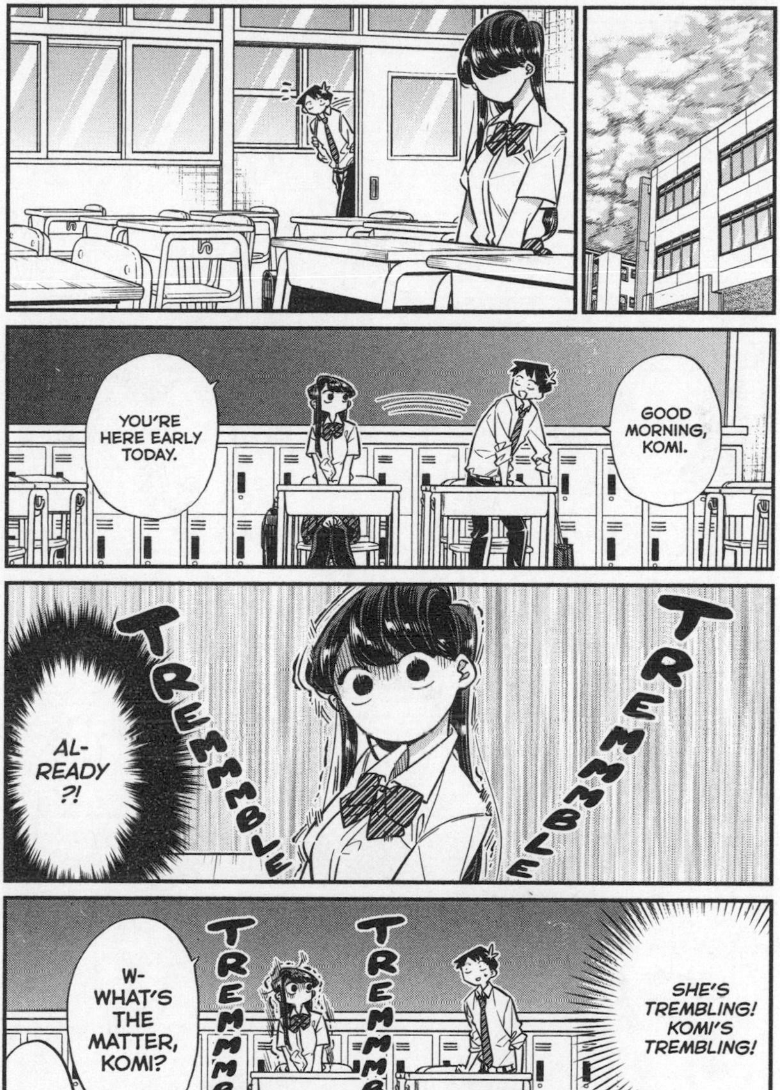
GOOD MORNING, KOMI.
YOU'RE HERE EARLY TODAY.
TREMMBLE
TREMMBLE
AL-READY ?!
SHE'S TREMBLING! KOMI'S TREMBLING!
TREMMBLE
TREMMBLE
W-WHAT'S THE MATTER, KOMI?
...

SHAKE
SHAKE
SHAKE
SHAKE
SHAKE
I CAN ACTUALLY HEAR HER HEART-BEAT!
SWIP
FWIP
W...
TH-THMP
TH-THMP
WHAT IS SHE SO NERVOUS ABOUT TELLING ME?
When a clock is hungry, it goes back four seconds.
Shoko Komi
?!

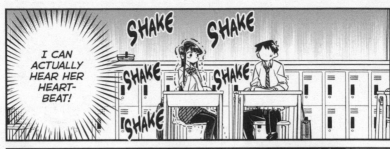

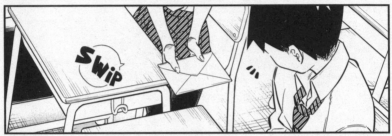

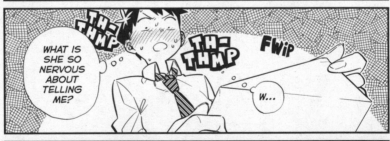

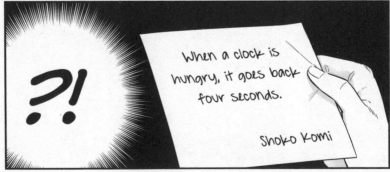

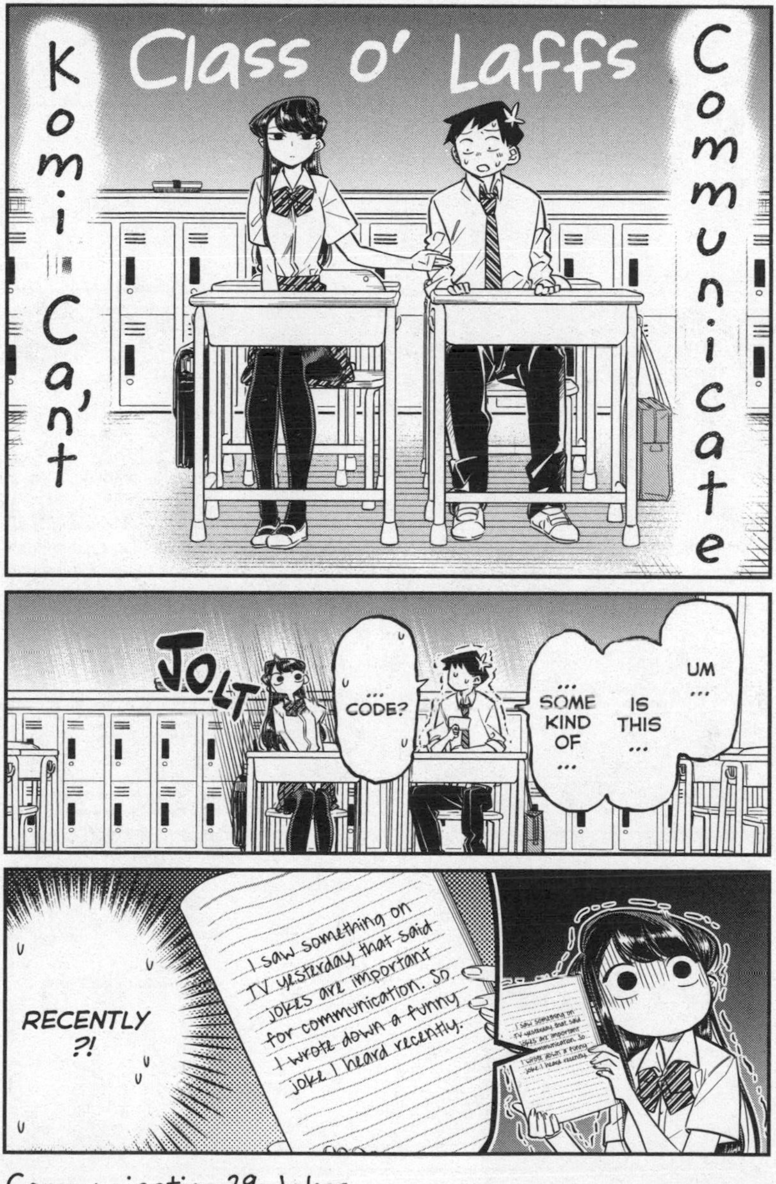
Komi Can't Communicate
Class o' Laffs
UM ...
IS THIS ...
... SOME KIND OF ...
... CODE?
JOLT
I saw something on TV yesterday that said jokes are important for communication. So I wrote down a funny joke I heard recently.
RECENTLY ?!

Communication 29: Jokes

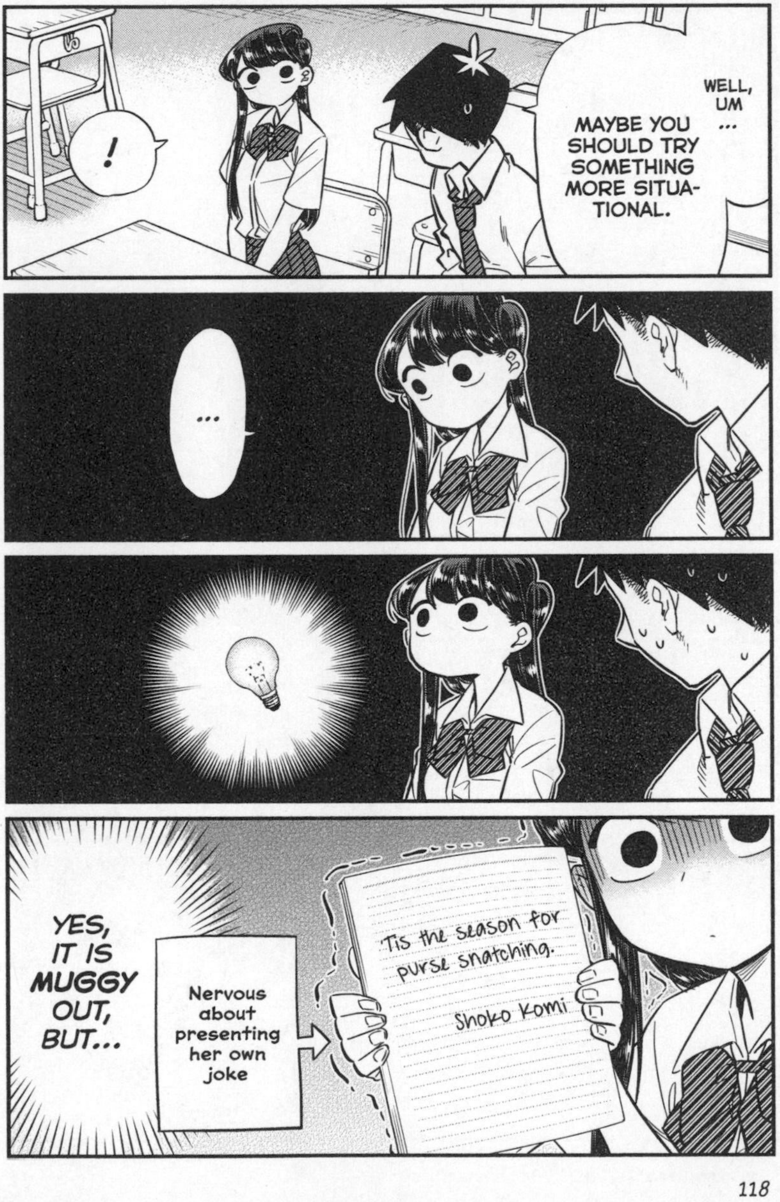
WELL, UM ...
MAYBE YOU SHOULD TRY SOMETHING MORE SITUATIONAL.
!
...
Tis the season for purse snatching.
Shoko Komi
Nervous about presenting her own joke
YES, IT IS MUGGY OUT, BUT...

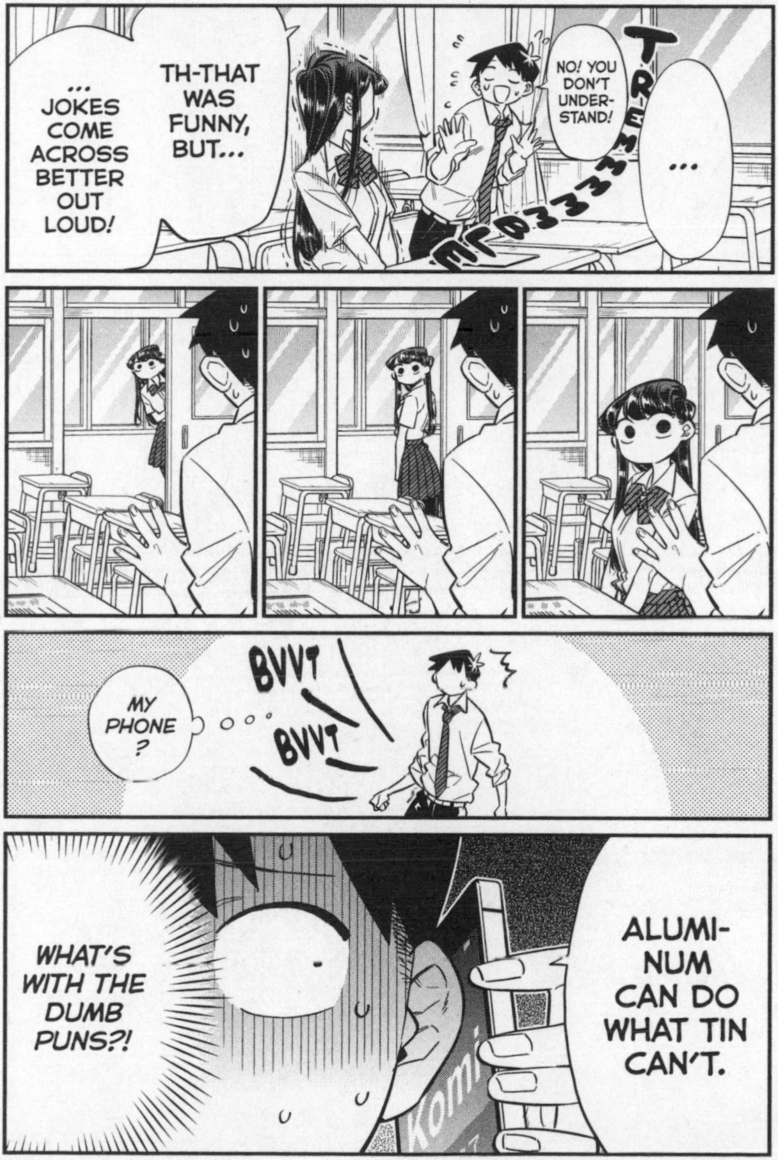
...
TREMMMMMBLE
NO! YOU DON'T UNDER-STAND!
TH-THAT WAS FUNNY, BUT...
... JOKES COME ACROSS BETTER OUT LOUD!
BVVT
BVVT
MY PHONE ?
ALUMI-NUM CAN DO WHAT TIN CAN'T.
Komi
WHAT'S WITH THE DUMB PUNS?!

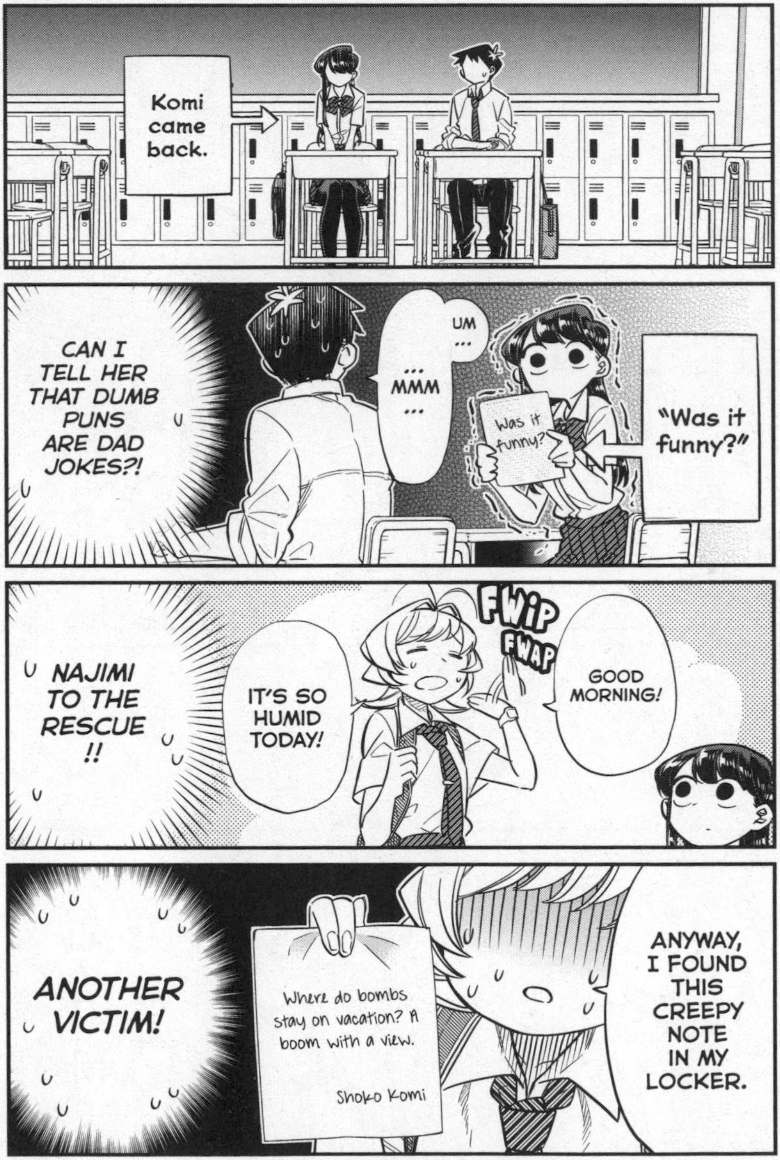
Komi came back.
"Was it funny?"
Was it funny?
UM ...
... MMM ...
CAN I TELL HER THAT DUMB PUNS ARE DAD JOKES?!
FWIP FWAP
GOOD MORNING!
IT'S SO HUMID TODAY!
NAJIMI TO THE RESCUE!!
ANYWAY, I FOUND THIS CREEPY NOTE IN MY LOCKER.
Where do bombs stay on vacation? A boom with a view.
Shoko Komi
ANOTHER VICTIM!

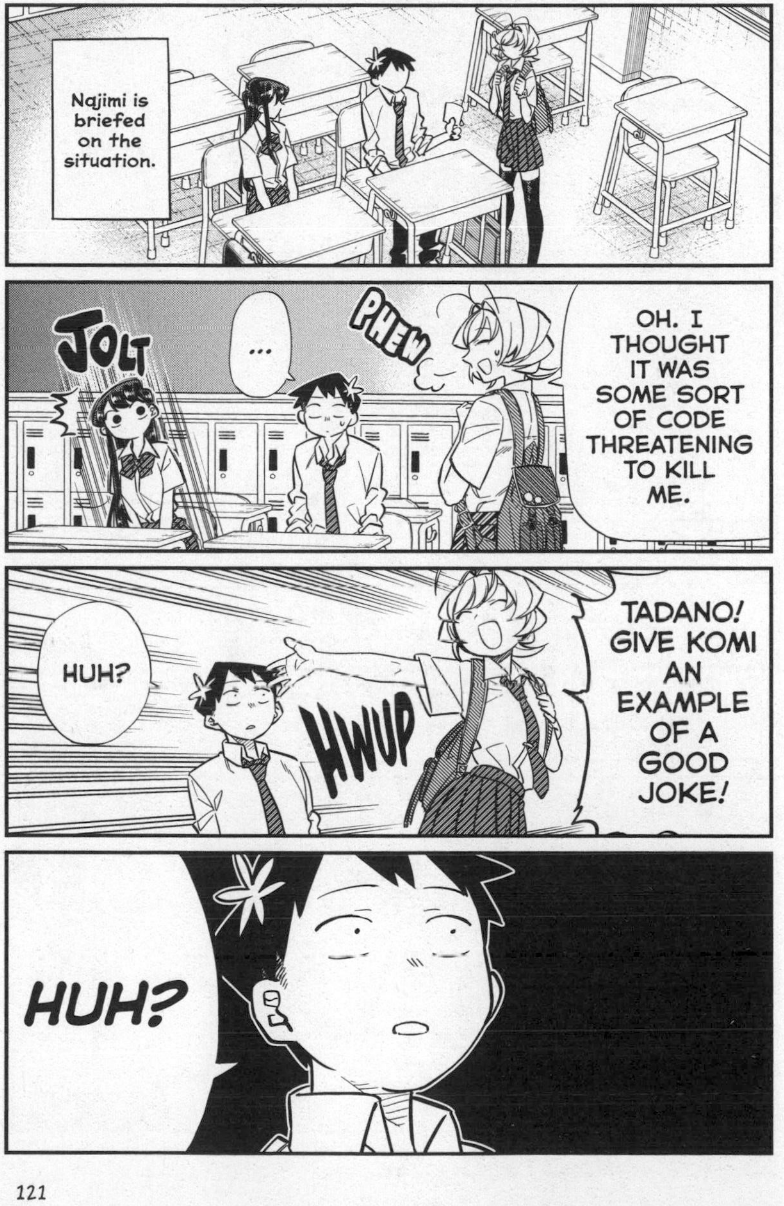

Najimi is briefed on the situation.
OH. I THOUGHT IT WAS SOME SORT OF CODE THREATENING TO KILL ME.
PHEW
...
JOLT
TADANO! GIVE KOMI AN EXAMPLE OF A GOOD JOKE!
HWUP
HUH?
HUH?

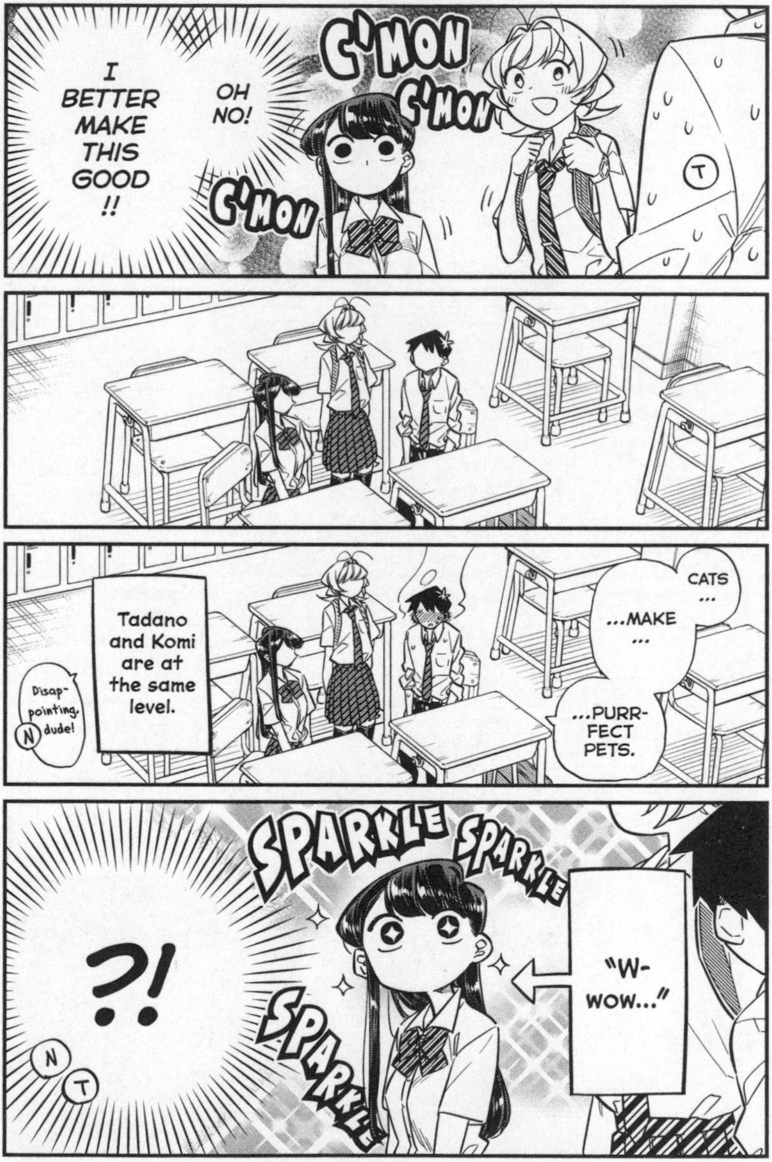
C'MON
C'MON
OH NO!
C'MON
I BETTER MAKE THIS GOOD!!
CATS...
...MAKE...
...PURR-FECT PETS.
Tadano and Komi are at the same level.
Disap-pointing, dude!
SPARKLE
SPARKLE
"W-WOW..."
SPARKLE
?!

Communication 29 – The End

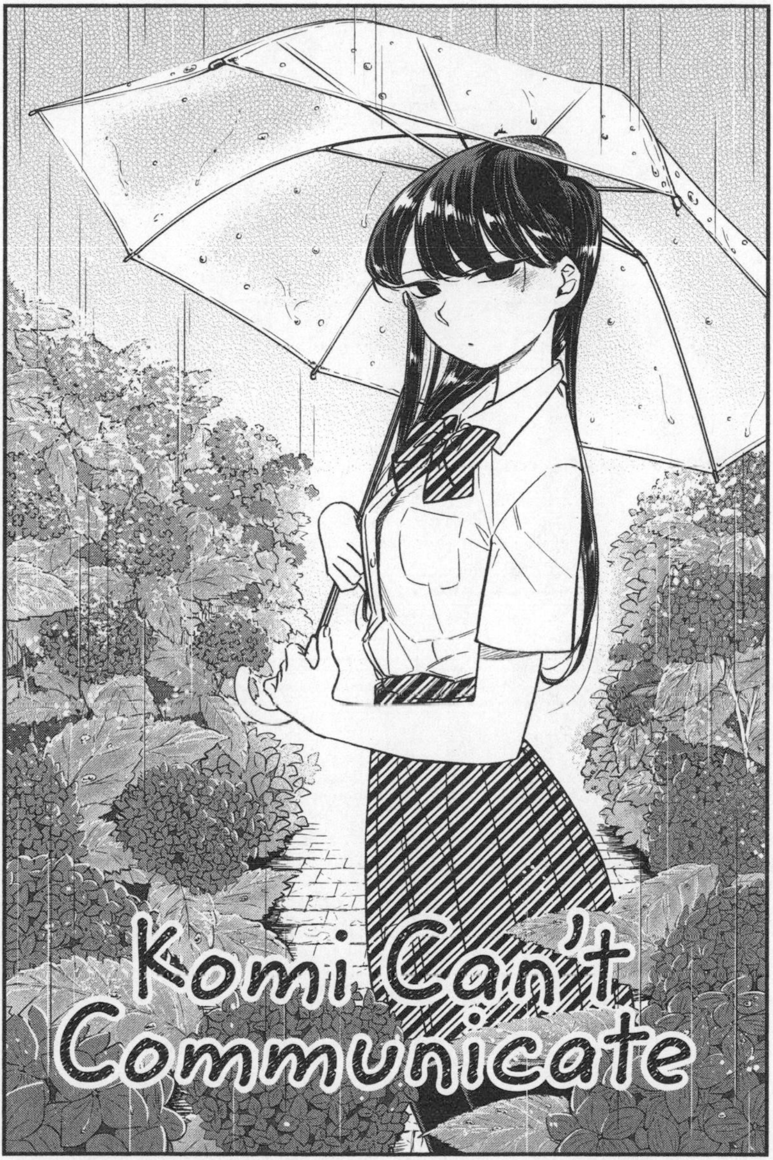
Komi Can't Communicate

Communication 30: Rain

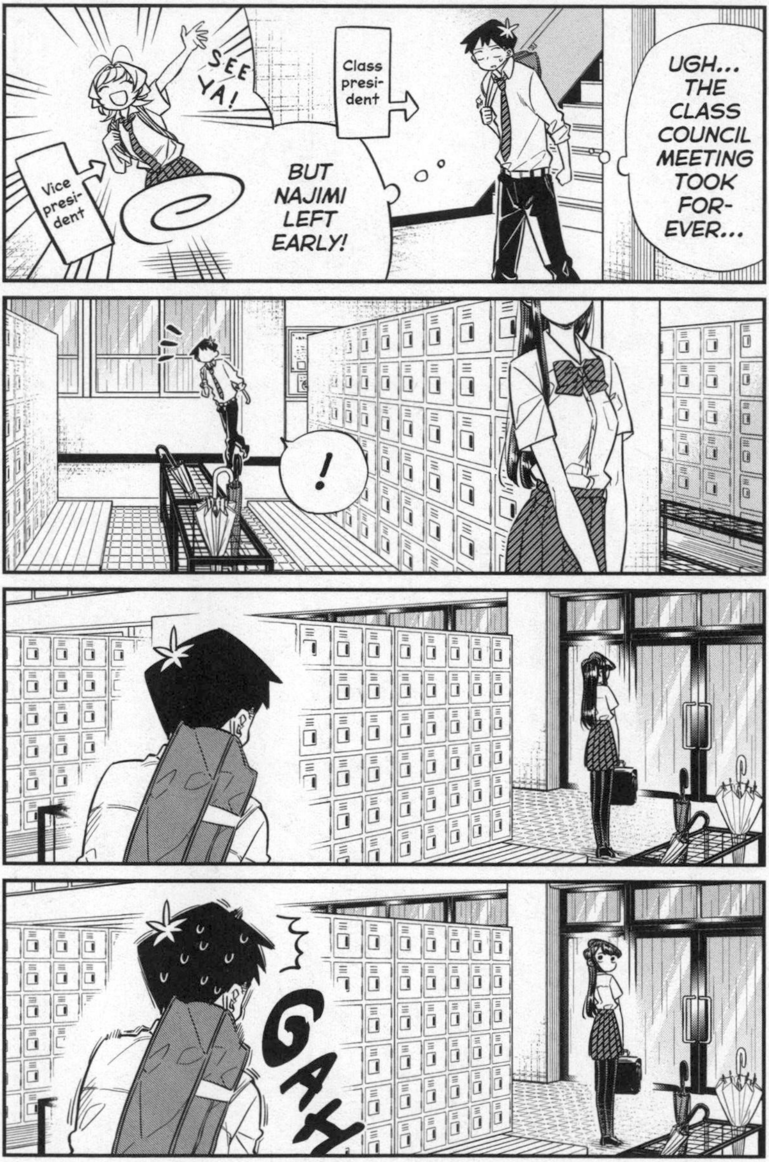
UGH... THE CLASS COUNCIL MEETING TOOK FOR-EVER...
Class presi-dent
BUT NAJIMI LEFT EARLY!
SEE YA!
Vice presi-dent
!
GAH

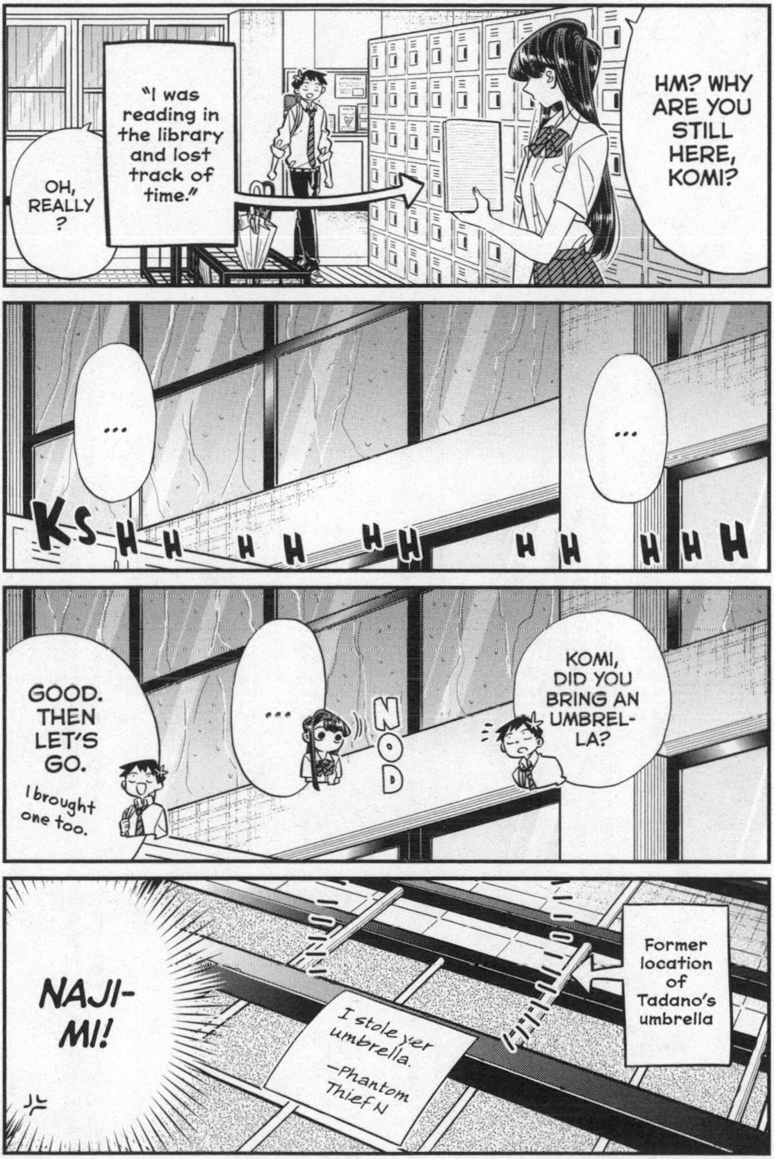
HM? WHY ARE YOU STILL HERE, KOMI?
"I was reading in the library and lost track of time."
OH, REALLY?
...
...
KSHHHHHHHHHHH
KOMI, DID YOU BRING AN UMBREL-LA?
...
NOD
GOOD. THEN LET'S GO.
I brought one too.
Former location of Tadano's umbrella
I stole yer umbrella. —Phantom Thief N
NAJI-MI!

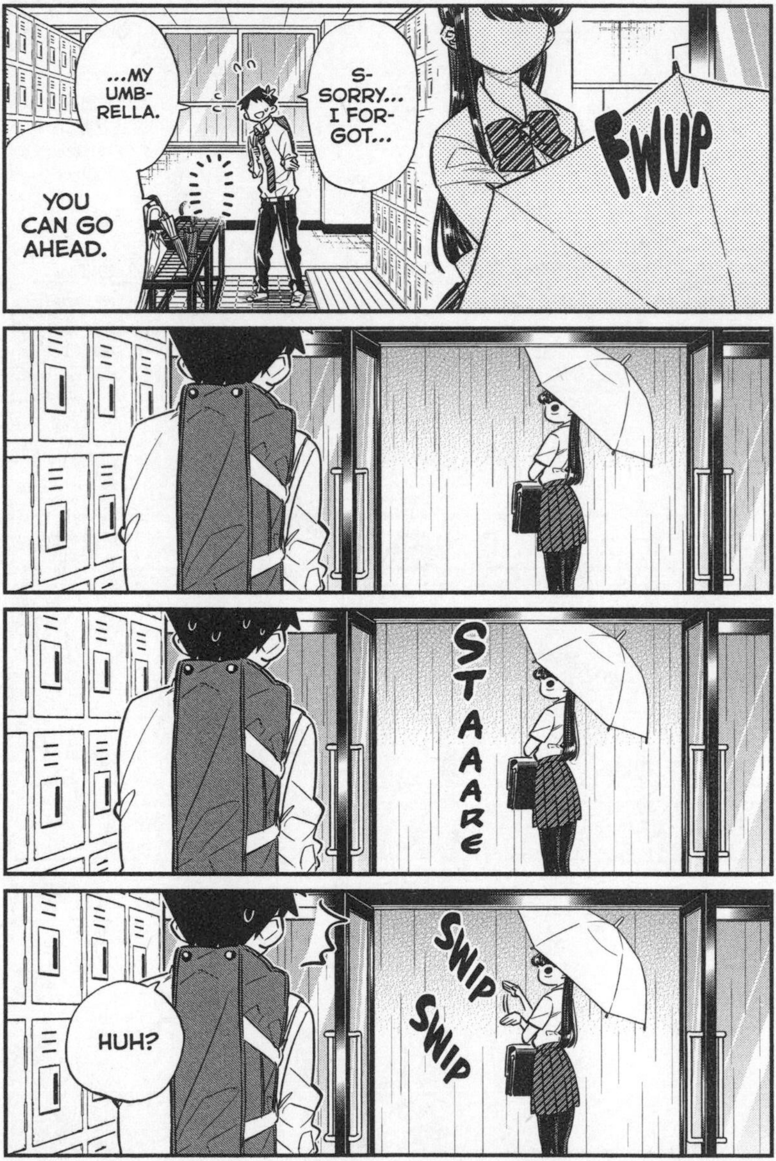
FWUP
S-SORRY... I FORGOT...
...MY UMBRELLA.
YOU CAN GO AHEAD.
STAAARE
SWIP SWIP
HUH?

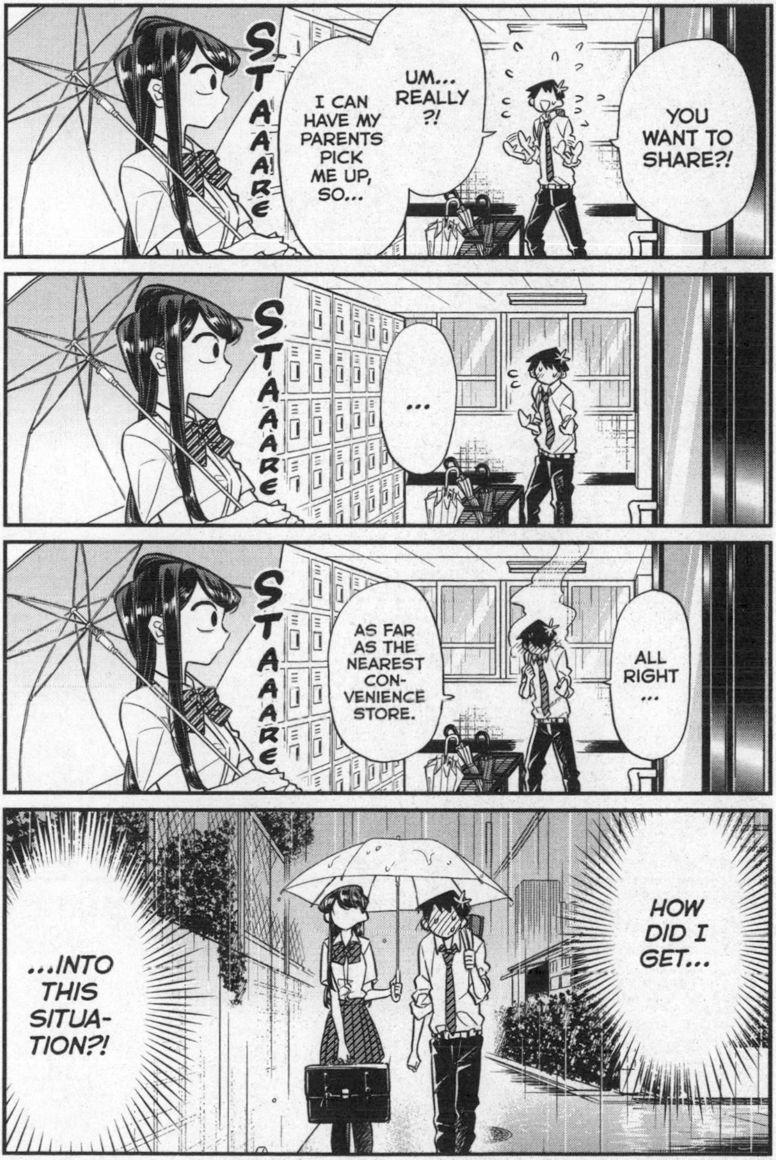
YOU WANT TO SHARE?!
UM... REALLY ?!
I CAN HAVE MY PARENTS PICK ME UP, SO...
STAAARE
...
STAAARE
ALL RIGHT ...
AS FAR AS THE NEAREST CON-VENIENCE STORE.
STAAARE
HOW DID I GET...
...INTO THIS SITUA-TION?!

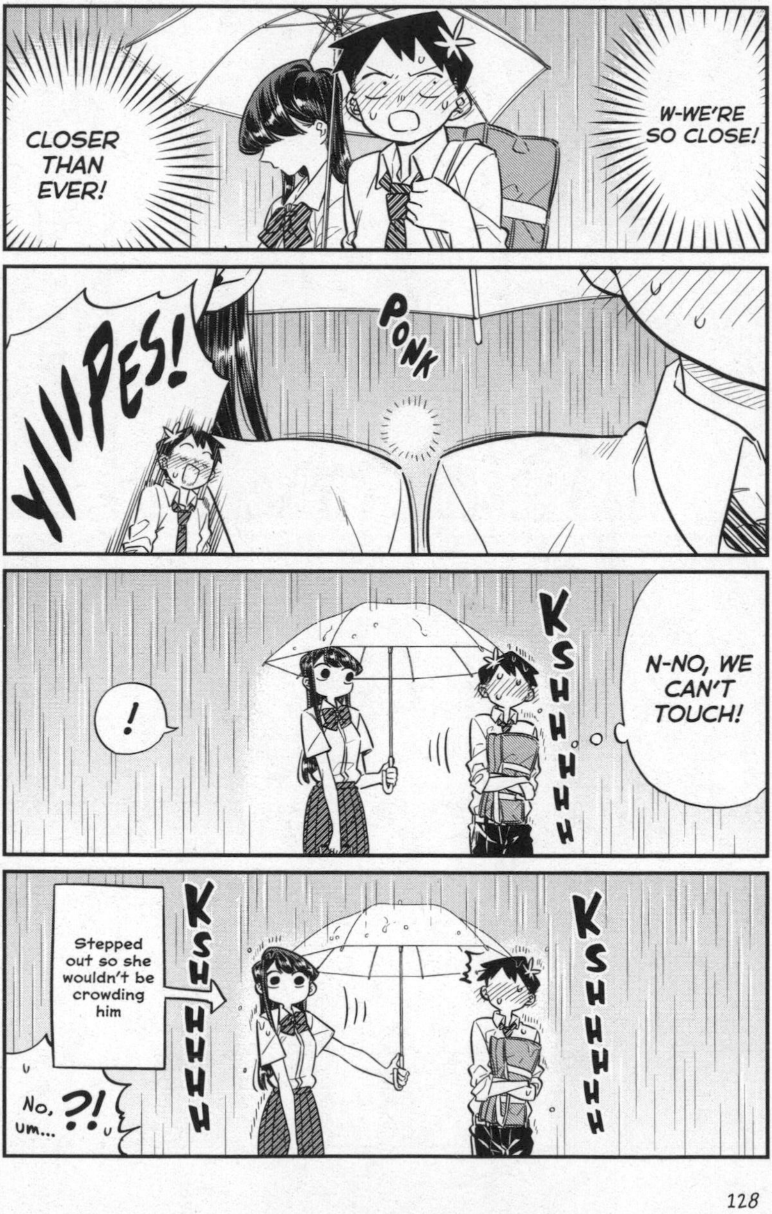
W-WE'RE SO CLOSE!
CLOSER THAN EVER!
PONK
YIIIPES!
N-NO, WE CAN'T TOUCH!
KSHHHHH
!
KSHHHHHH
Stepped out so she wouldn't be crowding him
KSHHHHHH
?!
No, um...

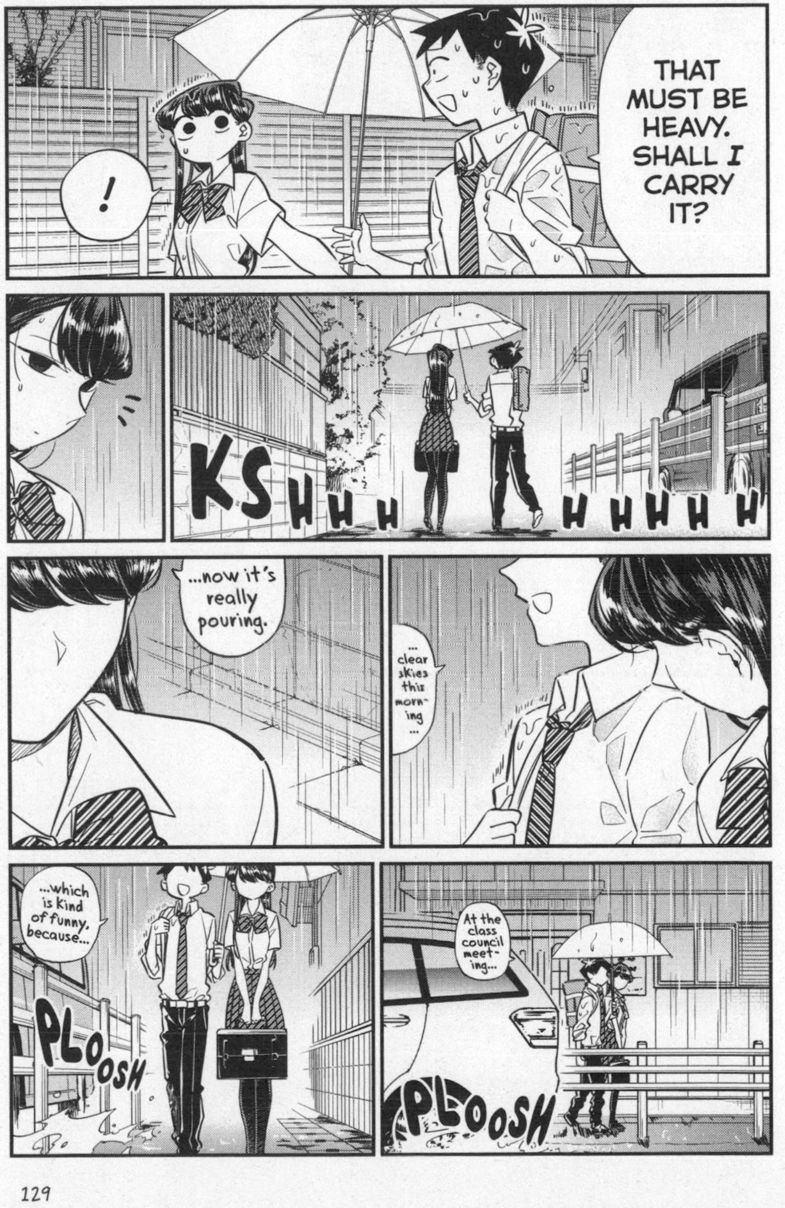
THAT MUST BE HEAVY. SHALL I CARRY IT?
!
KSHHH HHHHH
... clear skies this morn-ing ...
...now it's really pouring.
At the class council meet-ing...
PLOOSH
...which is kind of funny, because...
PLOOSH

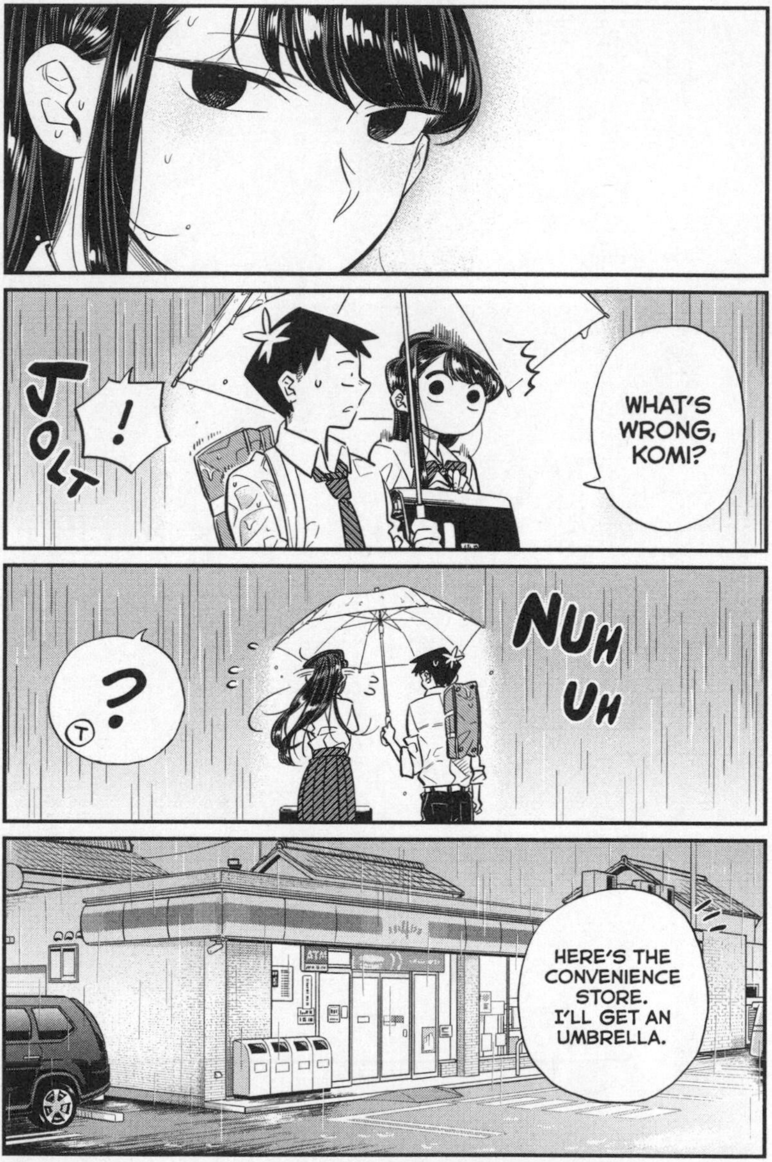
WHAT'S WRONG, KOMI?
!
JOLT
NUH UH
?
HERE'S THE CONVENIENCE STORE. I'LL GET AN UMBRELLA.

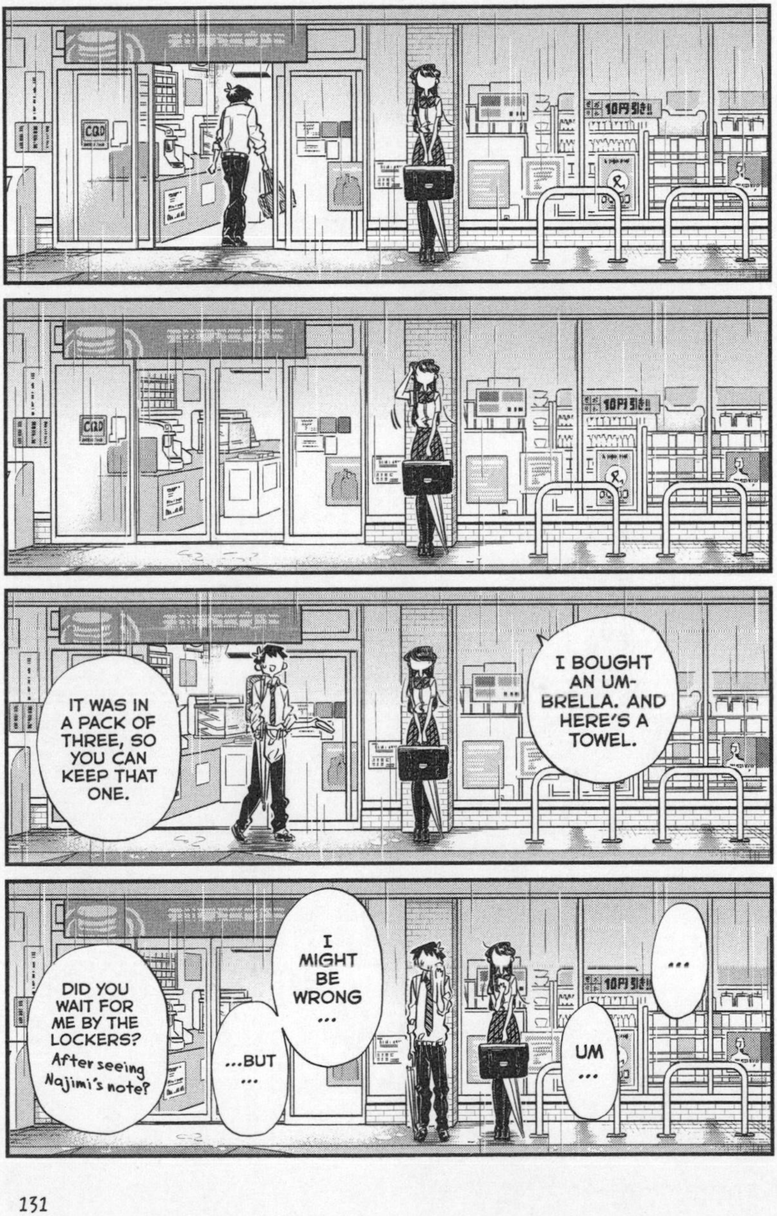
I BOUGHT AN UM-BRELLA. AND HERE'S A TOWEL.
IT WAS IN A PACK OF THREE, SO YOU CAN KEEP THAT ONE.
...
UM ...
I MIGHT BE WRONG ...
...BUT ...
DID YOU WAIT FOR ME BY THE LOCKERS?
After seeing Najimi's note?

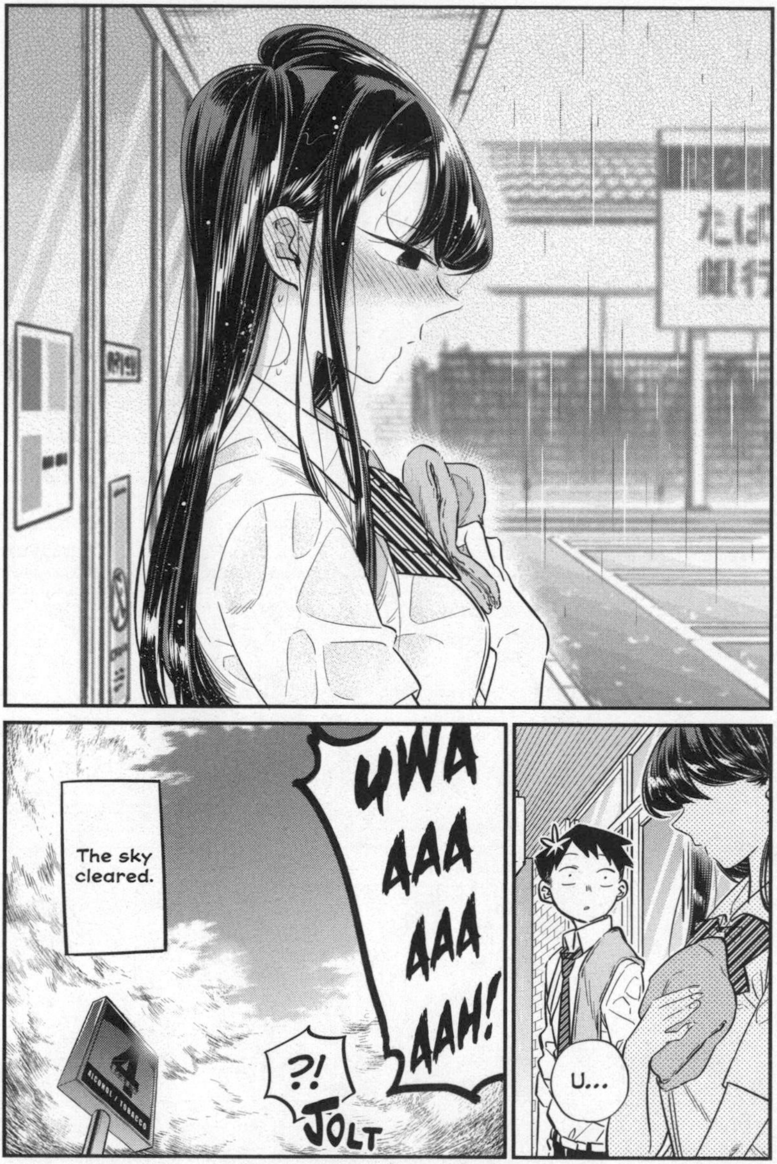
U...
UWAAAAAAAAAAAH!
The sky cleared.
?!
JOLT

Communication 30 — The End

Komi Can't Communicate

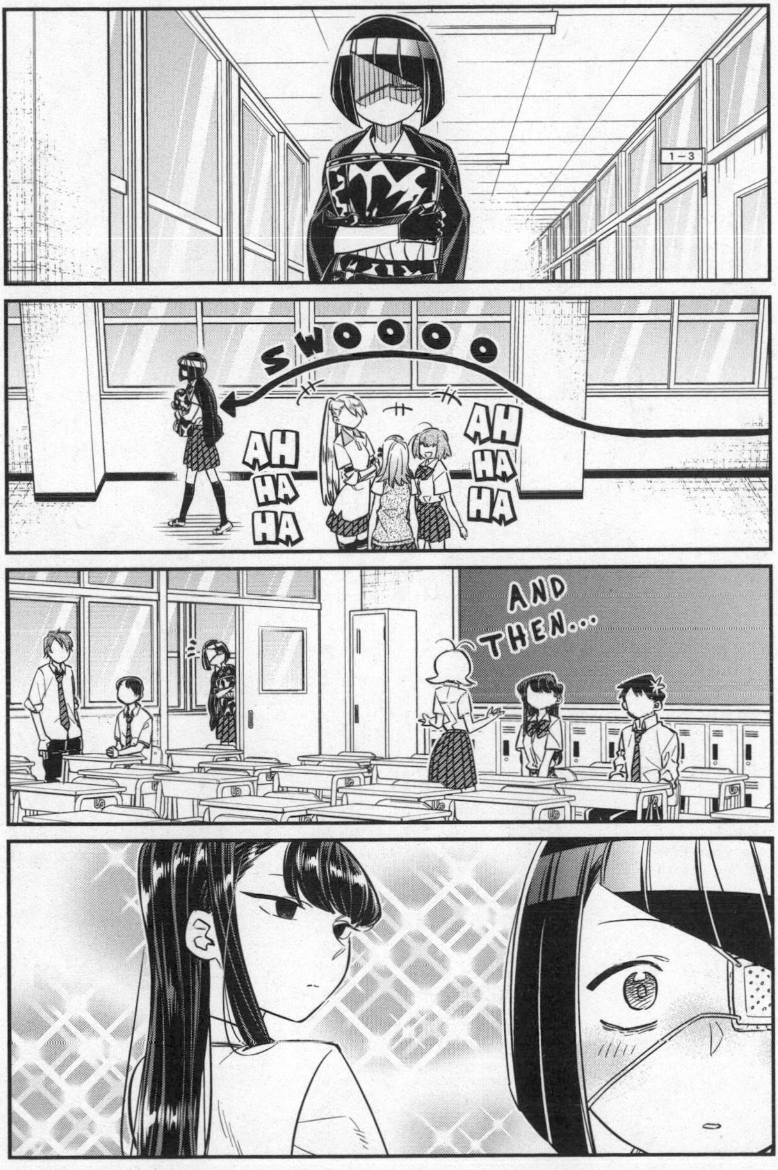

1-3
SWOOOO
AH HA HA
AH HA HA HA
AND THEN...

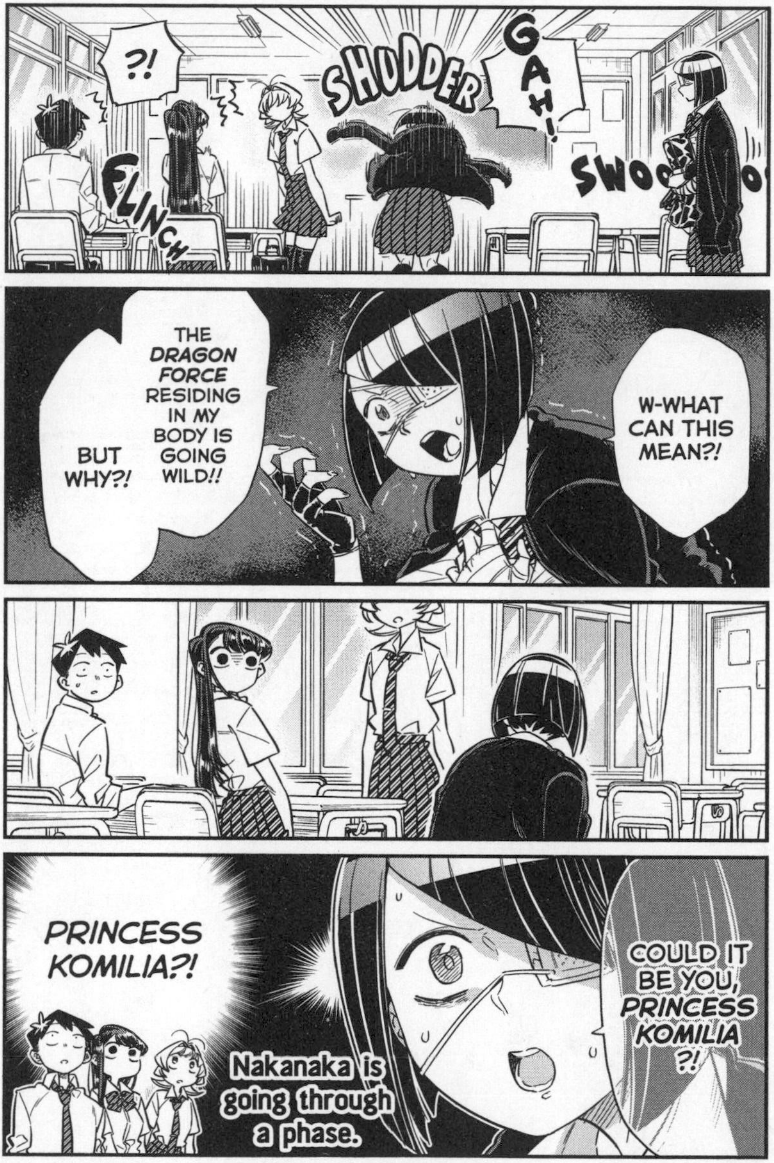
SWOO
GAH!
SHUDDER
?!
FLINCH
W-WHAT CAN THIS MEAN?!
THE DRAGON FORCE RESIDING IN MY BODY IS GOING WILD!!
BUT WHY?!
COULD IT BE YOU, PRINCESS KOMILIA?!
PRINCESS KOMILIA?!
Nakanaka is going through a phase.

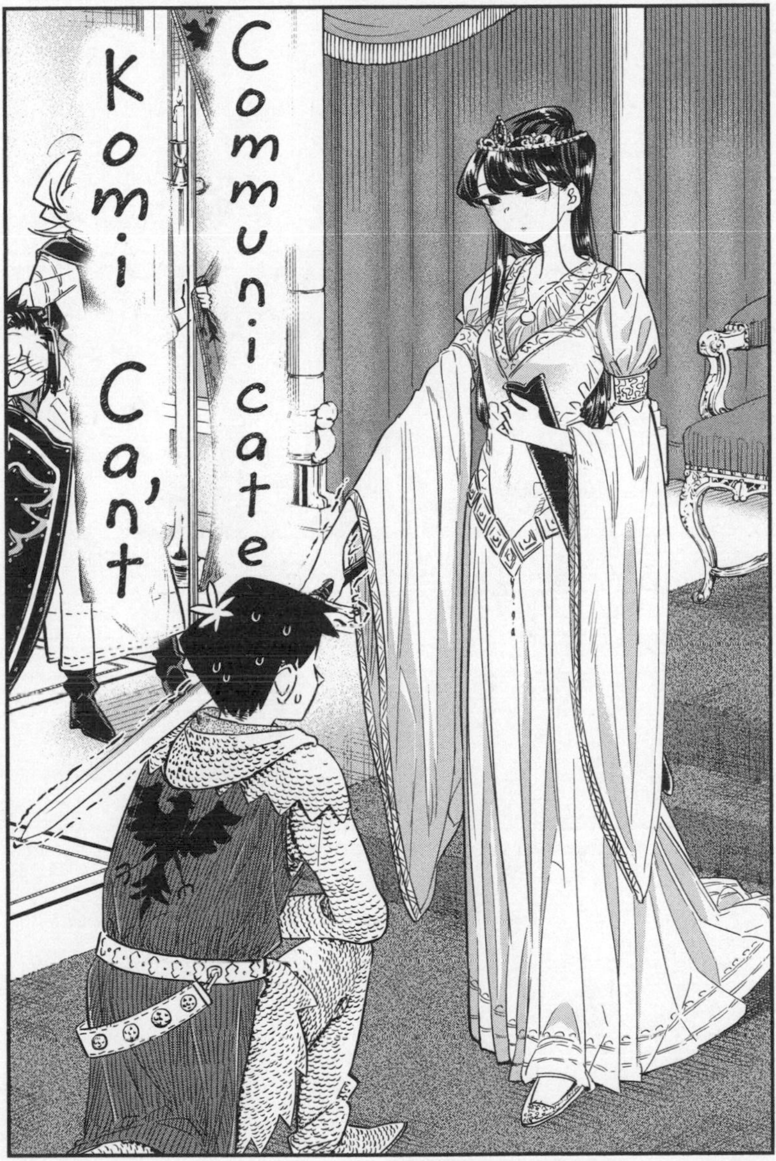
Komi Can't
Communicate

Communication 31: Blood Contract

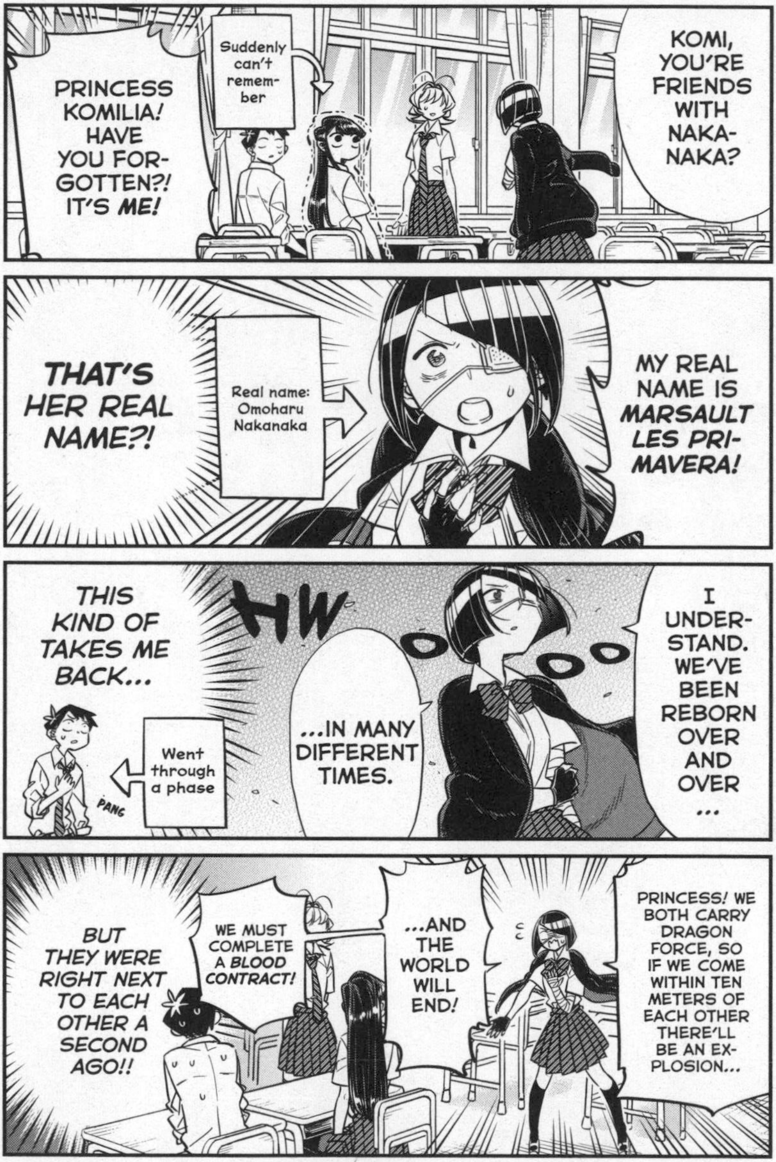
KOMI, YOU'RE FRIENDS WITH NAKA-NAKA?
Suddenly can't remem-ber
PRINCESS KOMILIA! HAVE YOU FOR-GOTTEN?! IT'S *ME!*
MY REAL NAME IS *MARSAULT LES PRI-MAVERA!*
Real name: Omoharu Nakanaka
THAT'S HER REAL NAME?!
I UNDER-STAND. WE'VE BEEN REBORN OVER AND OVER ...
...IN MANY DIFFERENT TIMES.
HW
Went through a phase
PANG
THIS KIND OF TAKES ME BACK...
PRINCESS! WE BOTH CARRY DRAGON FORCE, SO IF WE COME WITHIN TEN METERS OF EACH OTHER THERE'LL BE AN EX-PLOSION...
...AND THE WORLD WILL END!
WE MUST COMPLETE A *BLOOD CONTRACT!*
BUT THEY WERE RIGHT NEXT TO EACH OTHER A SECOND AGO!!

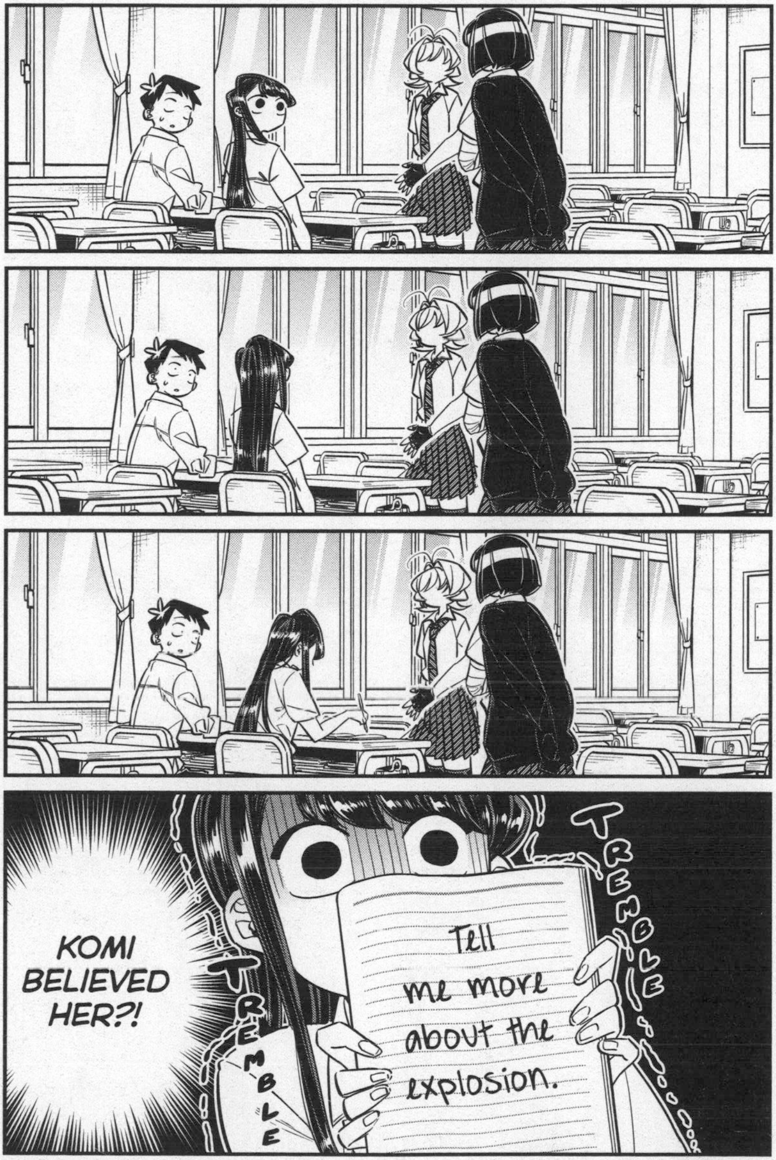
KOMI BELIEVED HER?!
TREMBLE
TREMBLE
Tell me more about the explosion.

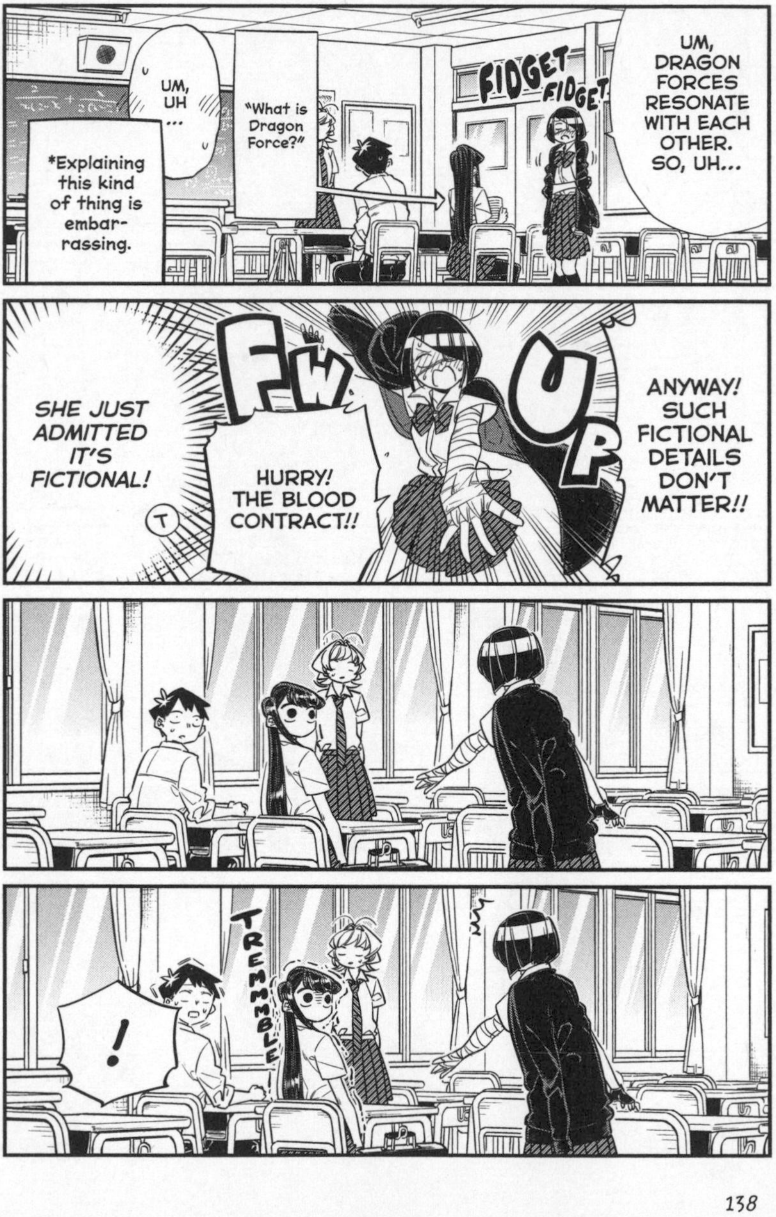
UM, DRAGON FORCES RESONATE WITH EACH OTHER. SO, UH...
FIDGET
FIDGET
"What is Dragon Force?"
UM, UH ...
*Explaining this kind of thing is embarrassing.
ANYWAY! SUCH FICTIONAL DETAILS DON'T MATTER!!
FWUP
HURRY! THE BLOOD CONTRACT!!
SHE JUST ADMITTED IT'S FICTIONAL!
T
TREMMMBLE
!

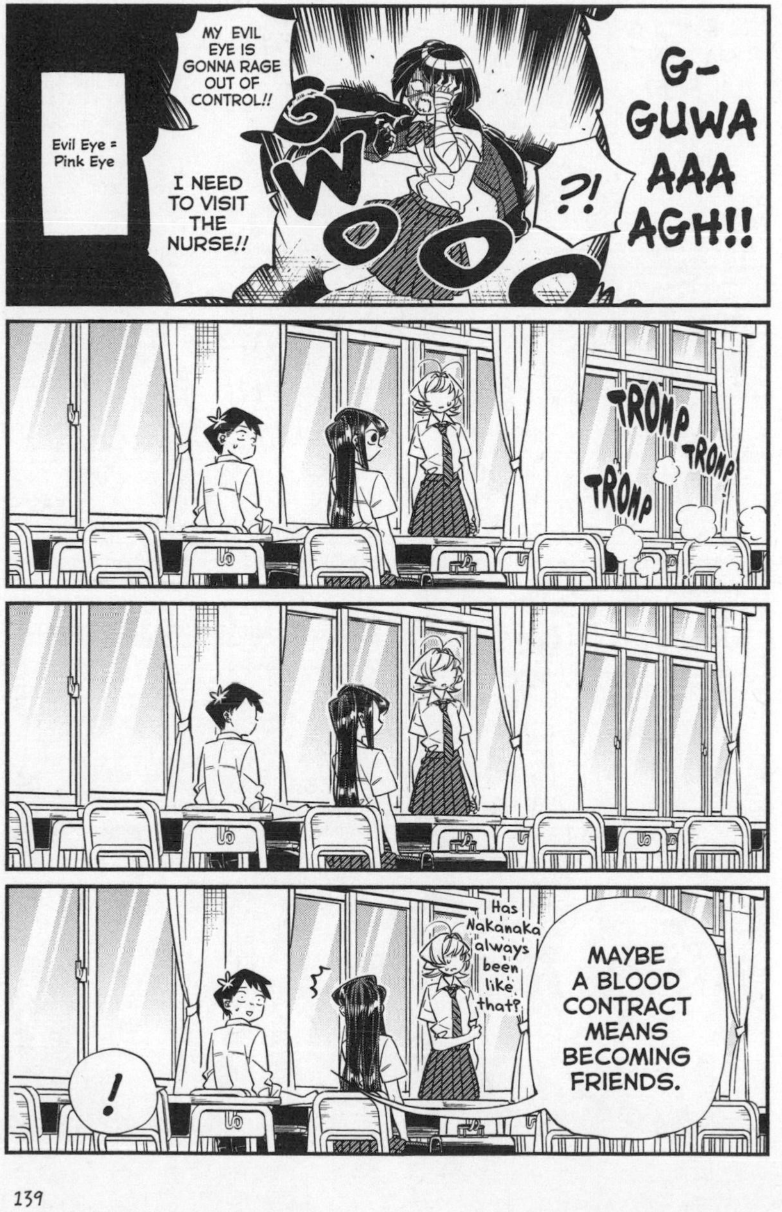
G-GUWAAAAGH!!
?!
WOOOO
MY EVIL EYE IS GONNA RAGE OUT OF CONTROL!!
I NEED TO VISIT THE NURSE!!
Evil Eye = Pink Eye
TROMP
TROMP
TROMP
MAYBE A BLOOD CONTRACT MEANS BECOMING FRIENDS.
Has Nakanaka always been like that?
!

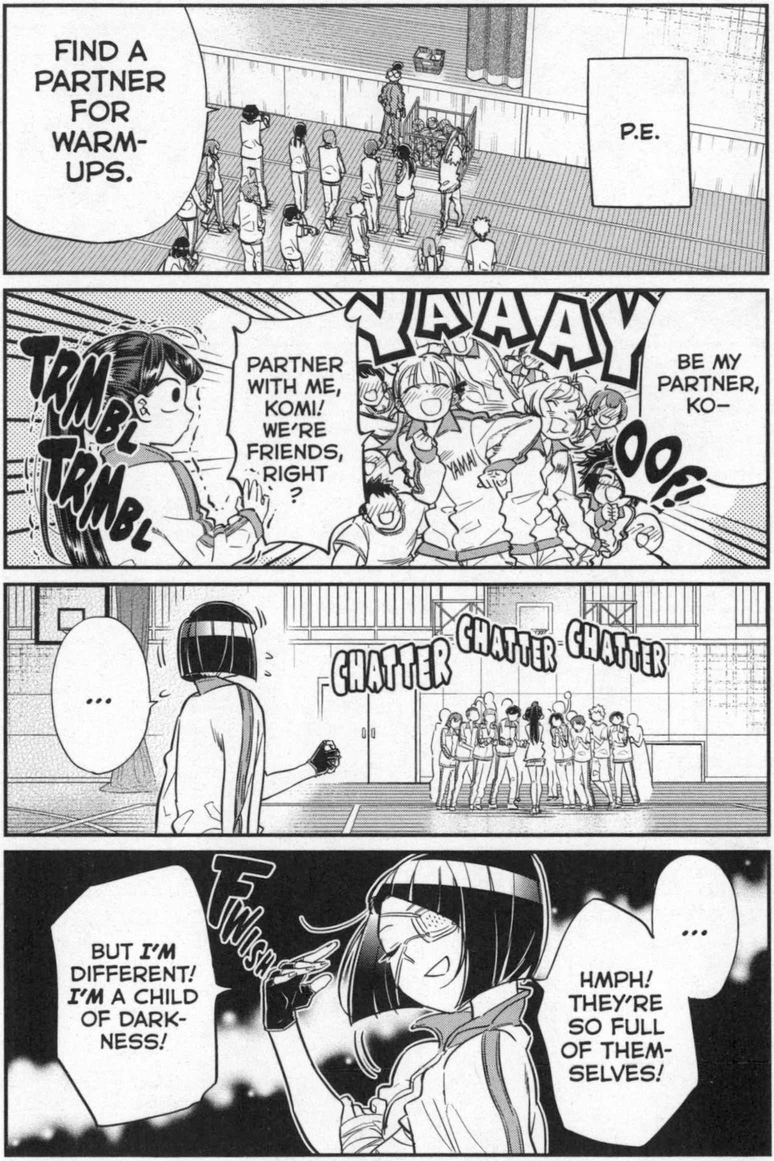
P.E.
FIND A PARTNER FOR WARM-UPS.
BE MY PARTNER, KO—
OOF!
YAAAY
PARTNER WITH ME, KOMI! WE'RE FRIENDS, RIGHT?
TRMBL TRMBL
CHATTER CHATTER CHATTER
...
...
HMPH! THEY'RE SO FULL OF THEM-SELVES!
FWISH
BUT *I'M* DIFFERENT! *I'M* A CHILD OF DARK-NESS!

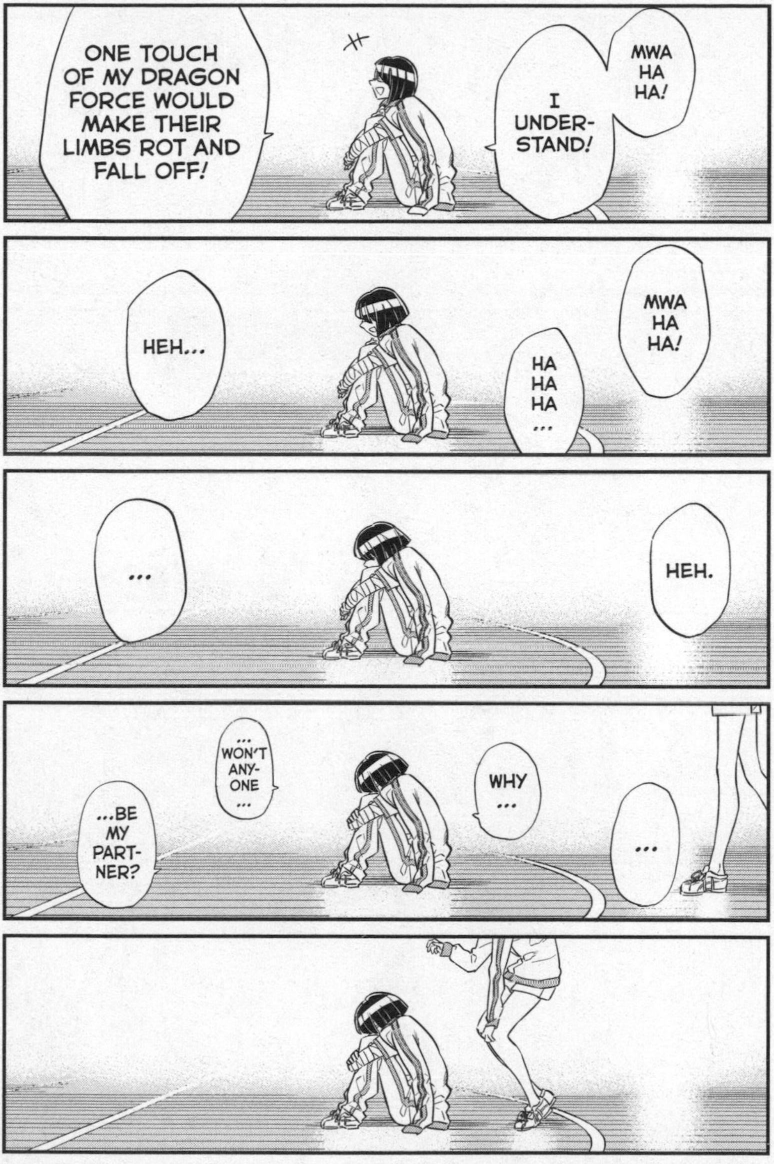
MWA HA HA!
I UNDER-STAND!
ONE TOUCH OF MY DRAGON FORCE WOULD MAKE THEIR LIMBS ROT AND FALL OFF!
MWA HA HA!
HA HA HA ...
HEH...
HEH.
...
...
WHY ...
... WON'T ANY-ONE ...
...BE MY PART-NER?

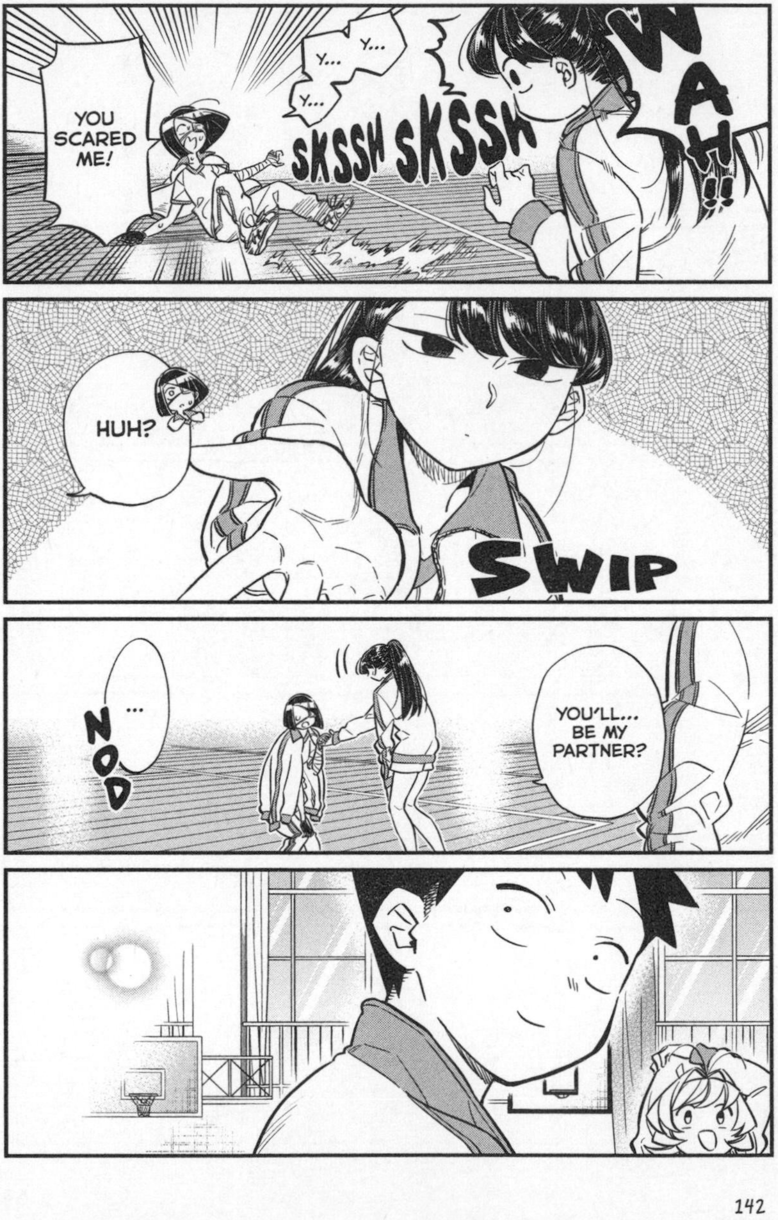
WAH!!
Y...
Y...
Y...
SKSSH SKSSH
YOU SCARED ME!
SWIP
HUH?
YOU'LL... BE MY PARTNER?
...
NOD

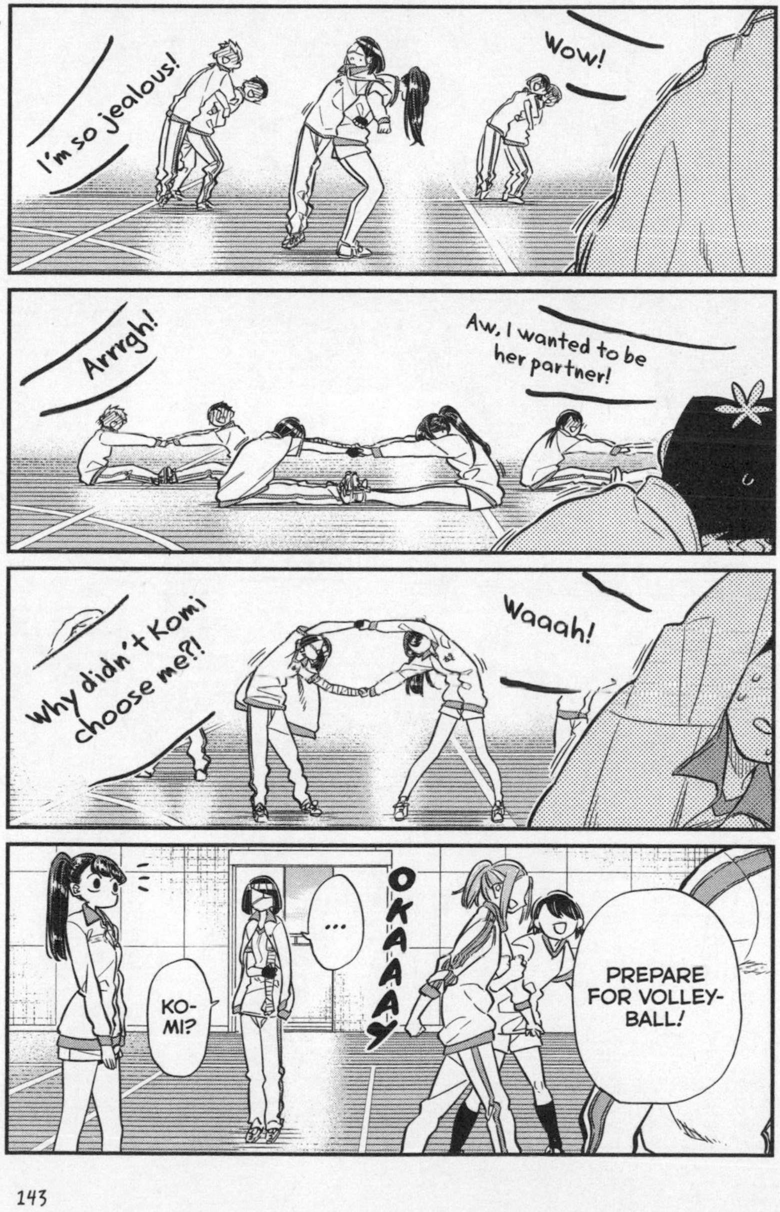
Wow!
I'm so jealous!
Aw, I wanted to be her partner!
Arrrgh!
Waaah!
Why didn't Komi choose me?!
PREPARE FOR VOLLEY-BALL!
OKAAAAY
...
KO-MI?

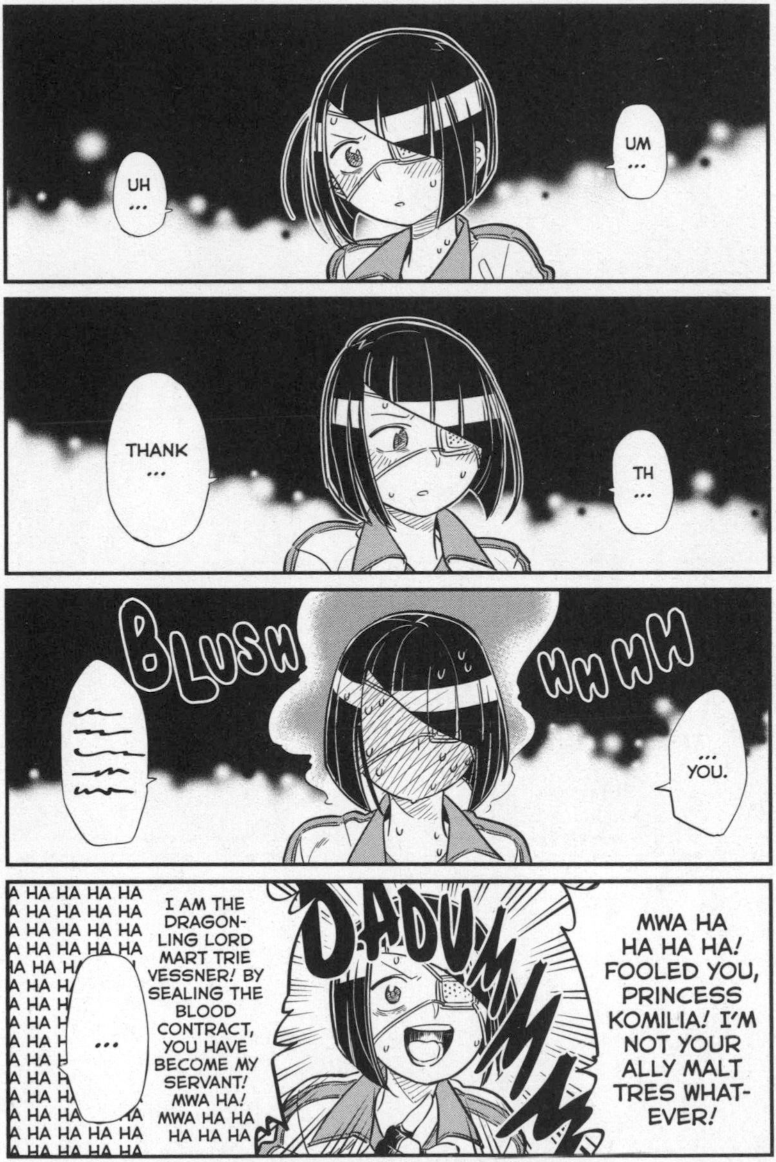
UM ...
UH ...
TH ...
THANK ...
BLUSHHHHH
... YOU.
MWA HA HA HA HA! FOOLED YOU, PRINCESS KOMILIA! I'M NOT YOUR ALLY MALT TRES WHATEVER!
DADUMMM
I AM THE DRAGONLING LORD MART TRIE VESSNER! BY SEALING THE BLOOD CONTRACT, YOU HAVE BECOME MY SERVANT! MWA HA! MWA HA HA HA HA HA
...
HA HA HA HA HA HA HA HA HA HA

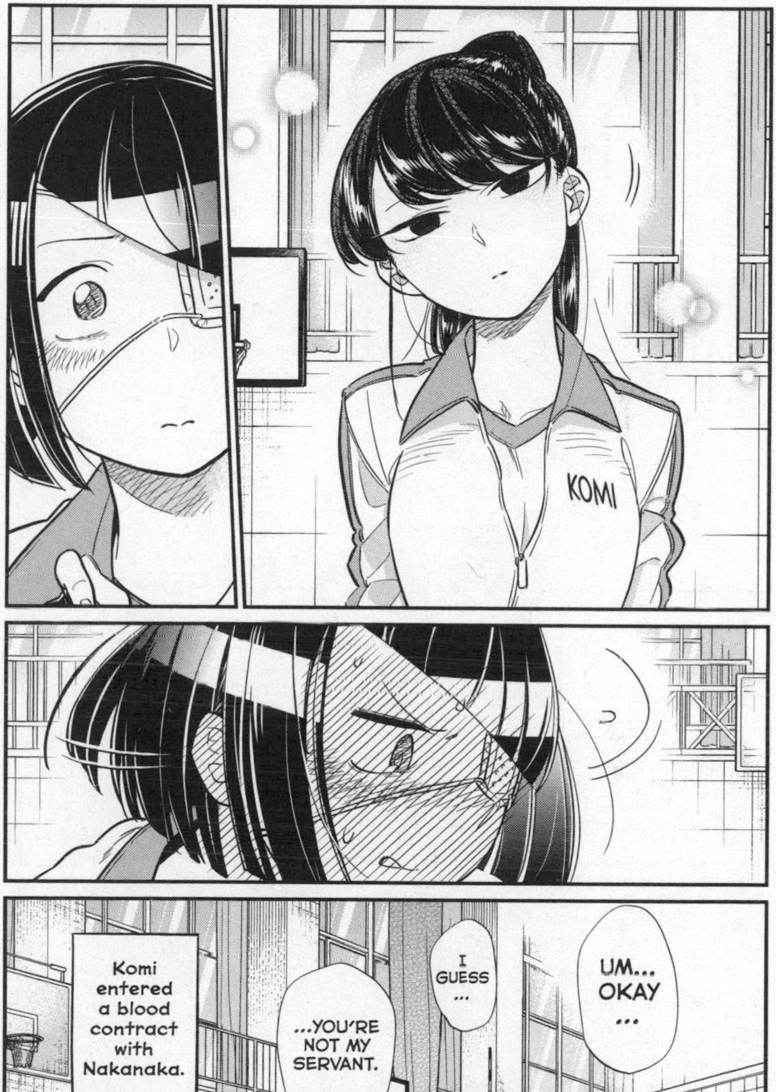
KOMI
UM... OKAY ...
I GUESS ...
...YOU'RE NOT MY SERVANT.
Komi entered a blood contract with Nakanaka.

Communication 31 — The End

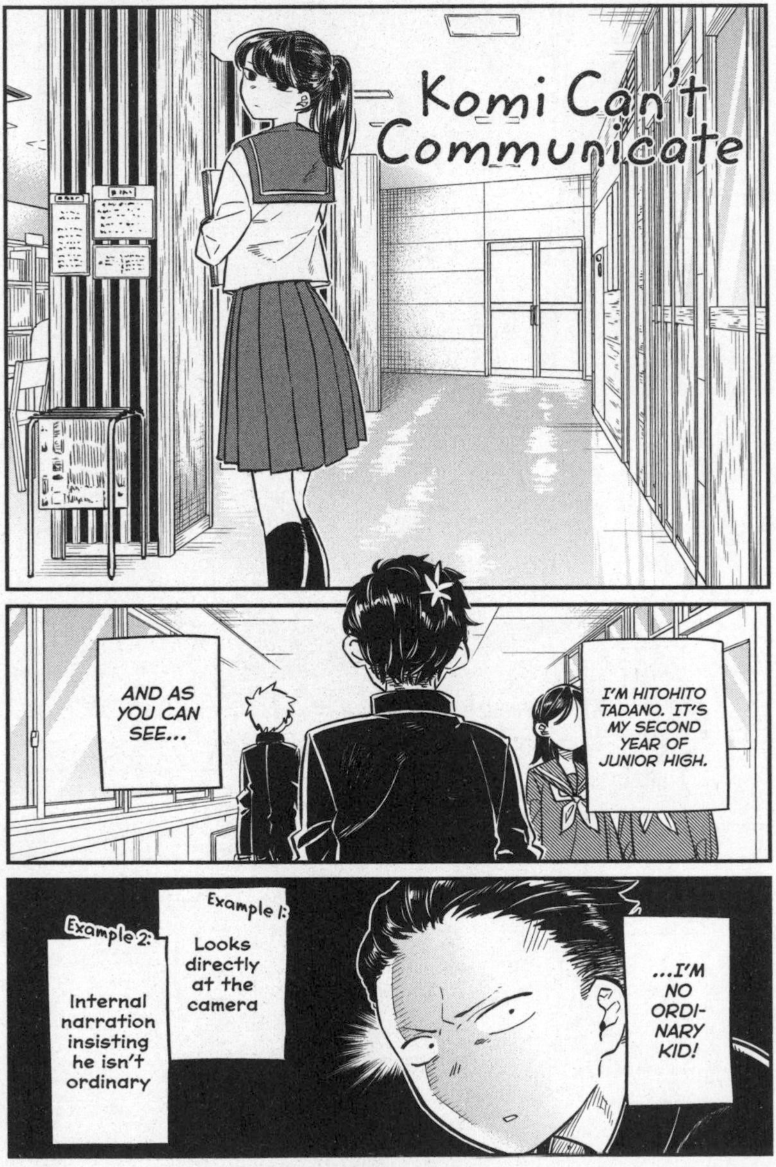
Komi Can't Communicate
I'M HITOHITO TADANO. IT'S MY SECOND YEAR OF JUNIOR HIGH.
AND AS YOU CAN SEE...
...I'M NO ORDINARY KID!
Example 1:
Looks directly at the camera
Example 2:
Internal narration insisting he isn't ordinary

Communication 32: Tadano in Junior High

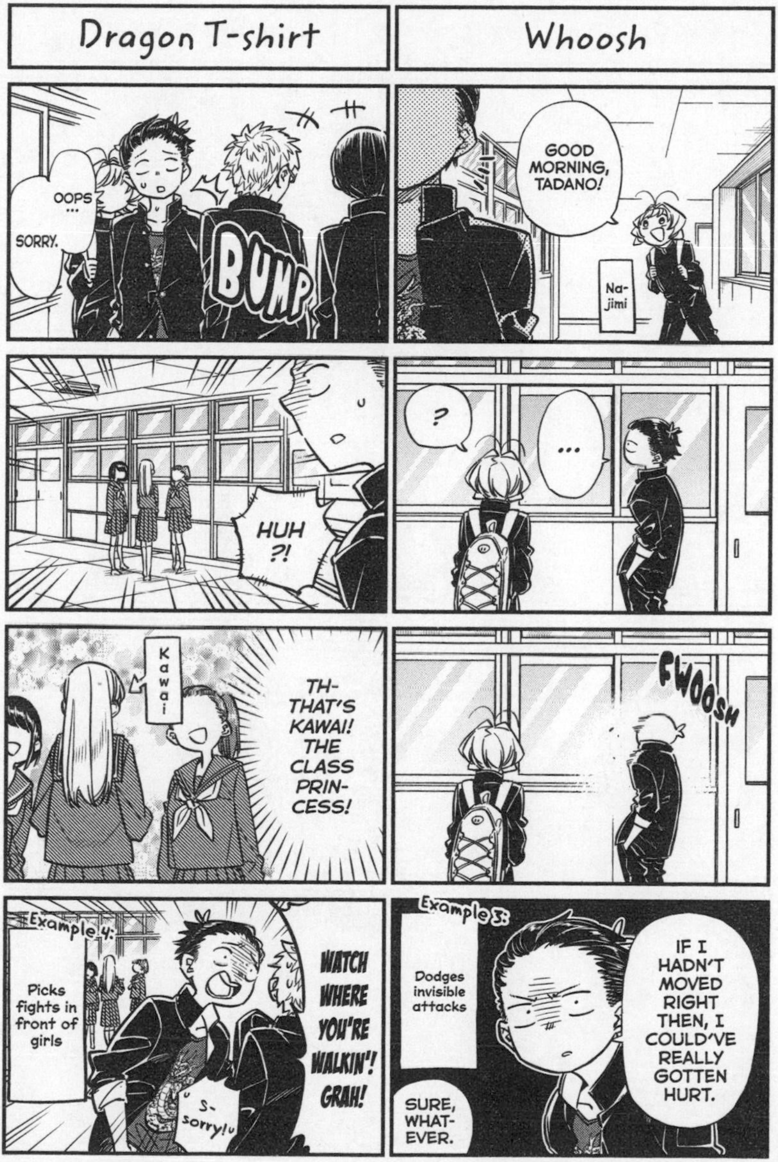
Whoosh
GOOD MORNING, TADANO!
Na-jimi
...
?
FWOOSH
Example 3:
IF I HADN'T MOVED RIGHT THEN, I COULD'VE REALLY GOTTEN HURT.
Dodges invisible attacks
SURE, WHAT-EVER.
Dragon T-shirt
BUMP
OOPS... SORRY.
HUH?!
TH-THAT'S KAWAI! THE CLASS PRIN-CESS!
Kawai
Example 4:
WATCH WHERE YOU'RE WALKIN'! GRAH!
Picks fights in front of girls
S-sorry!

"You-Know-What"

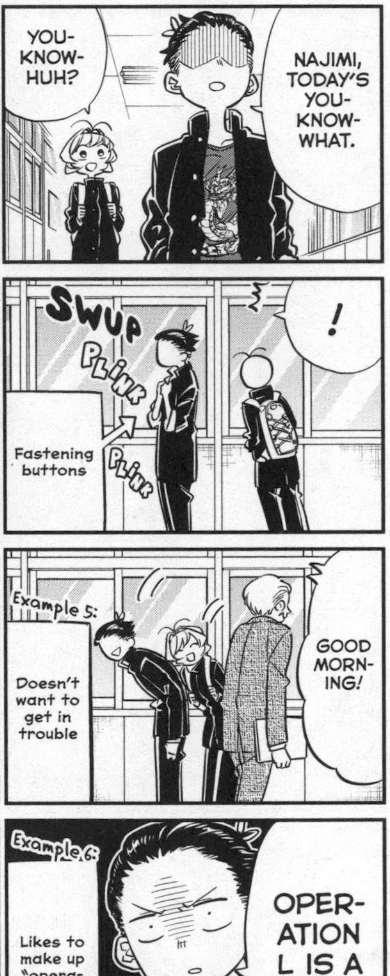
NAJIMI, TODAY'S YOU-KNOW-WHAT.
YOU-KNOW-HUH?
!
SWUP
PLINK
Fastening buttons
PLINK
GOOD MORNING!
Example 5:
Doesn't want to get in trouble
OPERATION L IS A GO!
Example 6:
Likes to make up "operations"
PLINK

The L in "Operation L" Means Love

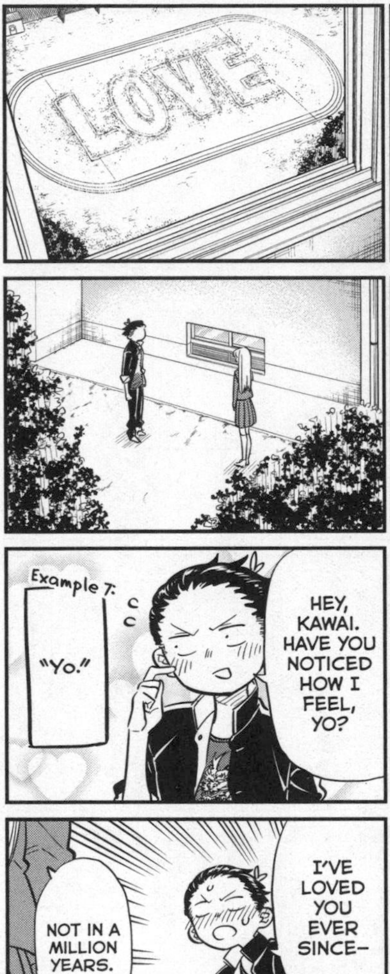
LOVE
HEY, KAWAI. HAVE YOU NOTICED HOW I FEEL, YO?
Example 7:
"Yo."
I'VE LOVED YOU EVER SINCE—
NOT IN A MILLION YEARS.

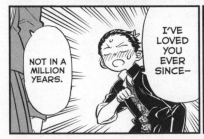

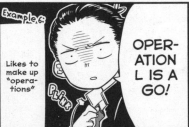

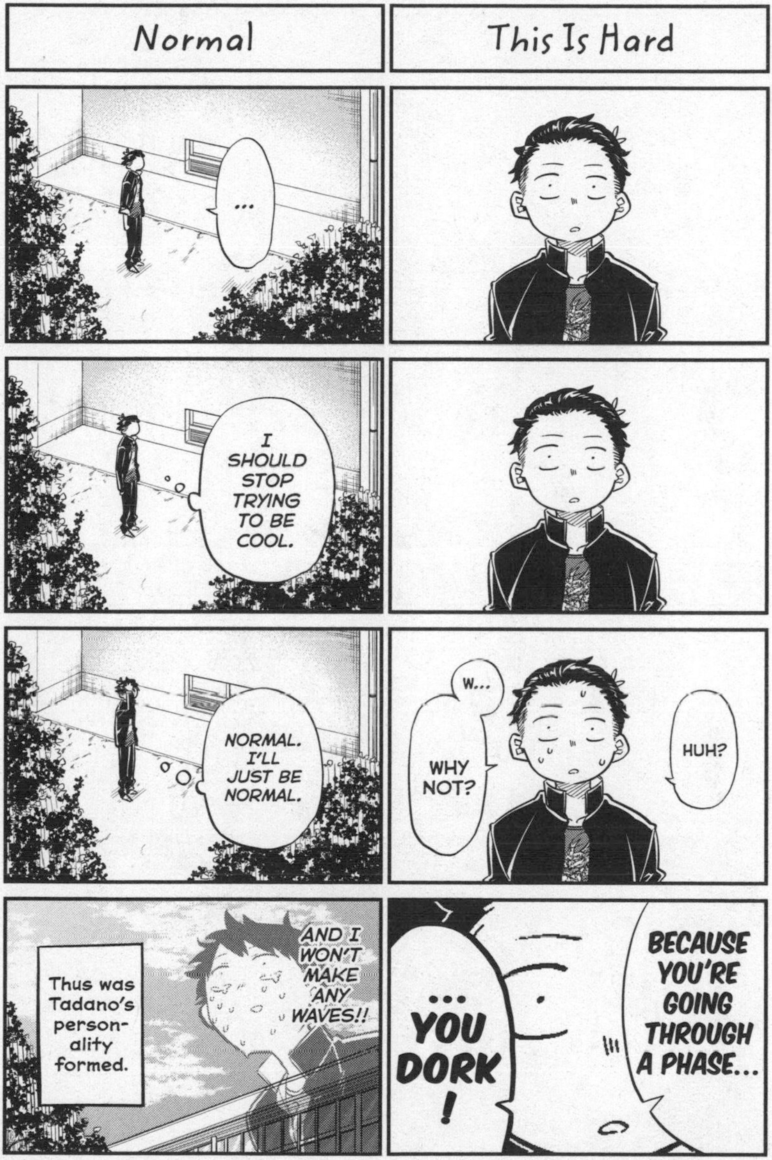
This Is Hard
HUH?
W...
WHY NOT?
BECAUSE YOU'RE GOING THROUGH A PHASE...
...YOU DORK!
Normal
...
I SHOULD STOP TRYING TO BE COOL.
NORMAL. I'LL JUST BE NORMAL.
AND I WON'T MAKE ANY WAVES!!
Thus was Tadano's personality formed.

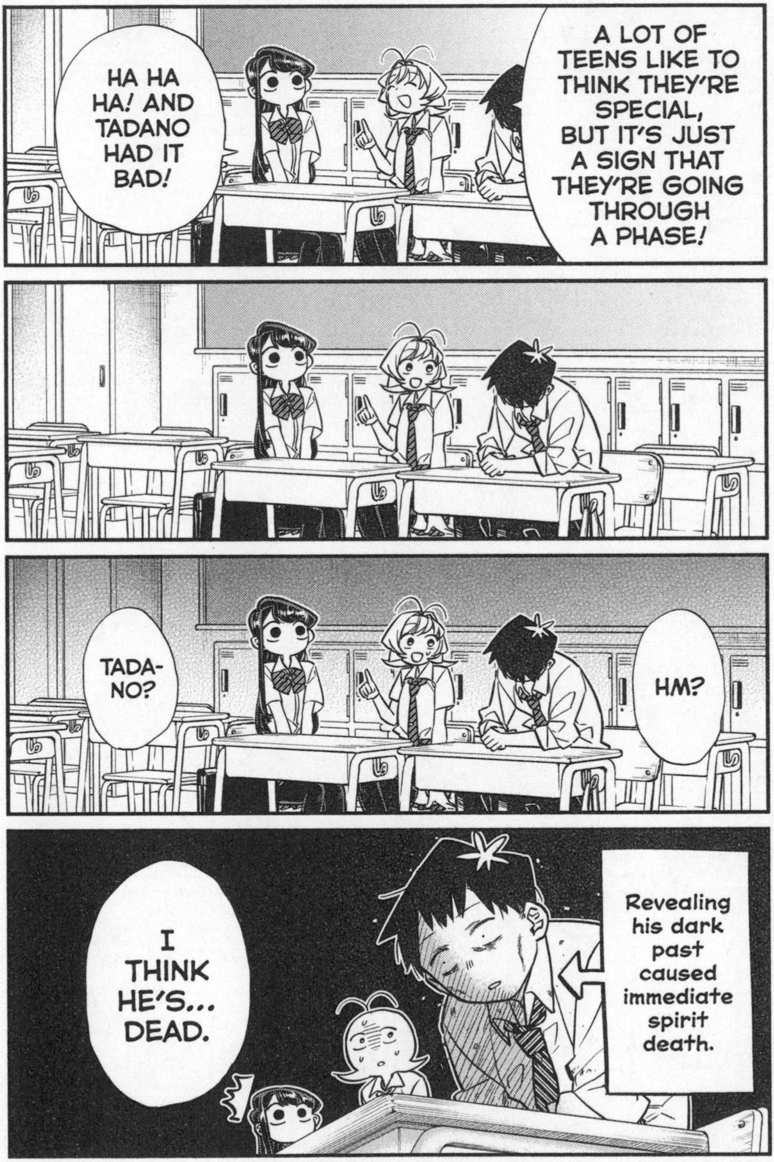
A LOT OF TEENS LIKE TO THINK THEY'RE SPECIAL, BUT IT'S JUST A SIGN THAT THEY'RE GOING THROUGH A PHASE!
HA HA HA! AND TADANO HAD IT BAD!
HM?
TADA-NO?
Revealing his dark past caused immediate spirit death.
I THINK HE'S... DEAD.

Communication 32 – The End

Komi Can't Communicate

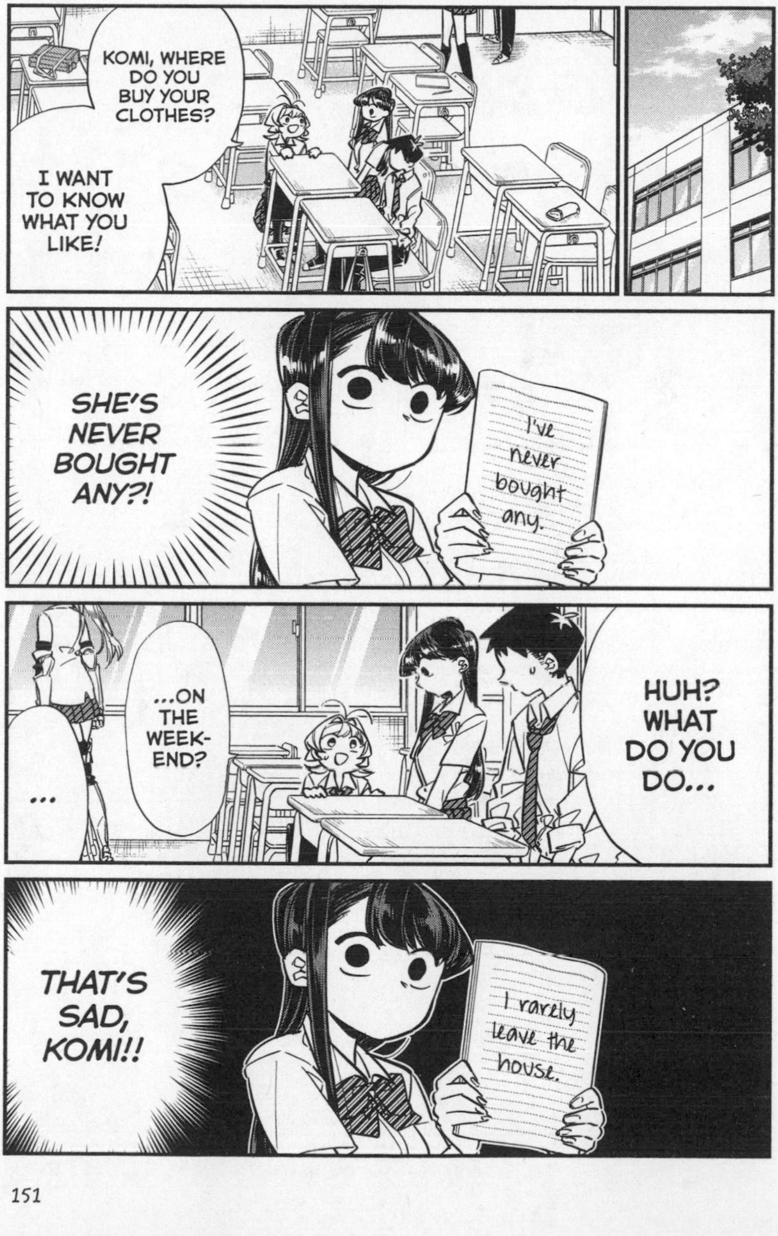
KOMI, WHERE DO YOU BUY YOUR CLOTHES?
I WANT TO KNOW WHAT YOU LIKE!
I've never bought any.
SHE'S NEVER BOUGHT ANY?!
HUH? WHAT DO YOU DO...
...ON THE WEEKEND?
...
I rarely leave the house.
THAT'S SAD, KOMI!!

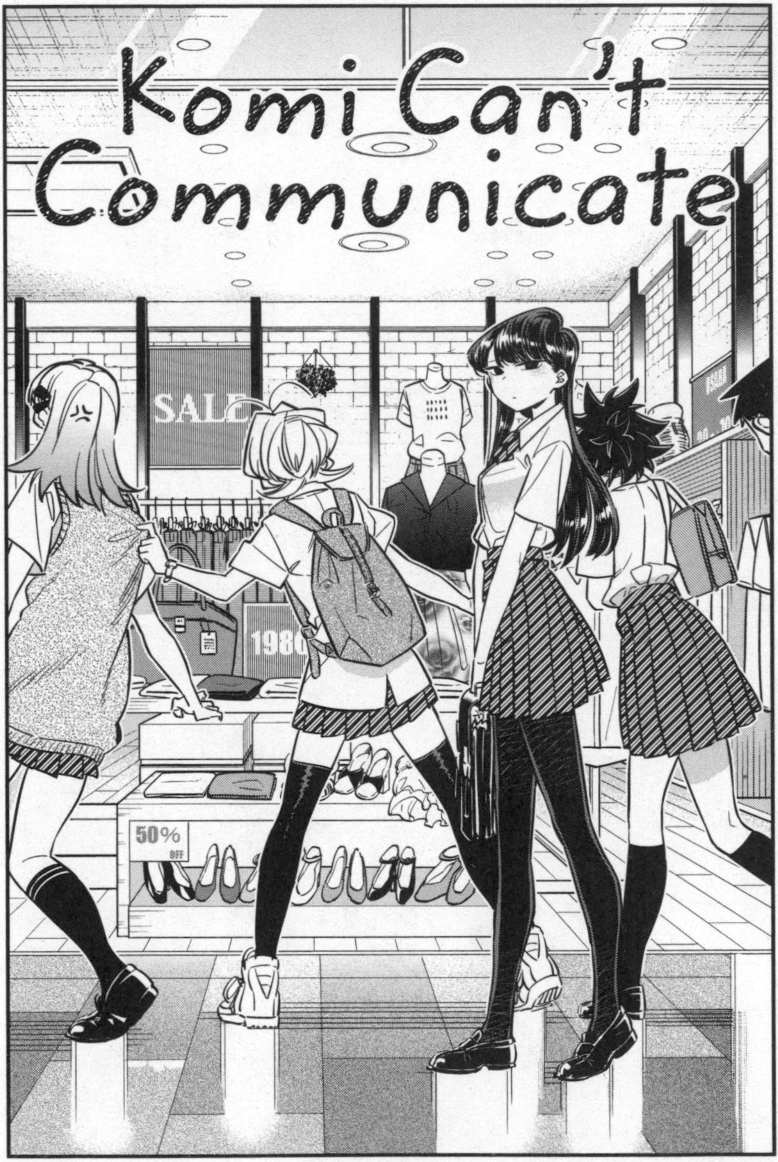
Komi Can't Communicate
SALE
1980
50% OFF

Communication 33: Shopping

Then let's go clothes shopping together!!
TO THE LOCAL STATION MALL!!
!!
"Um..."
Um, I appreciate the thought, but
"...I appreciate the thought, but..."
TRMBL TRMBL TRMBL TRMBL
I'm scared.
SHE'S SCARED?!

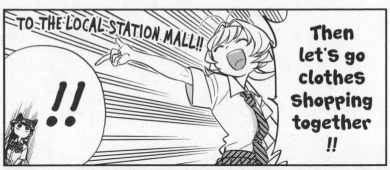

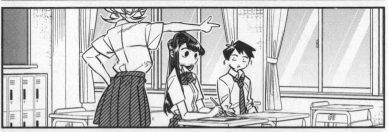

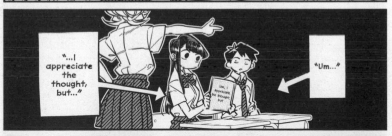

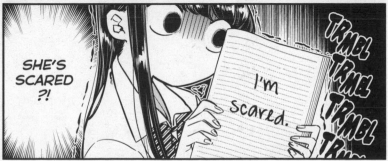

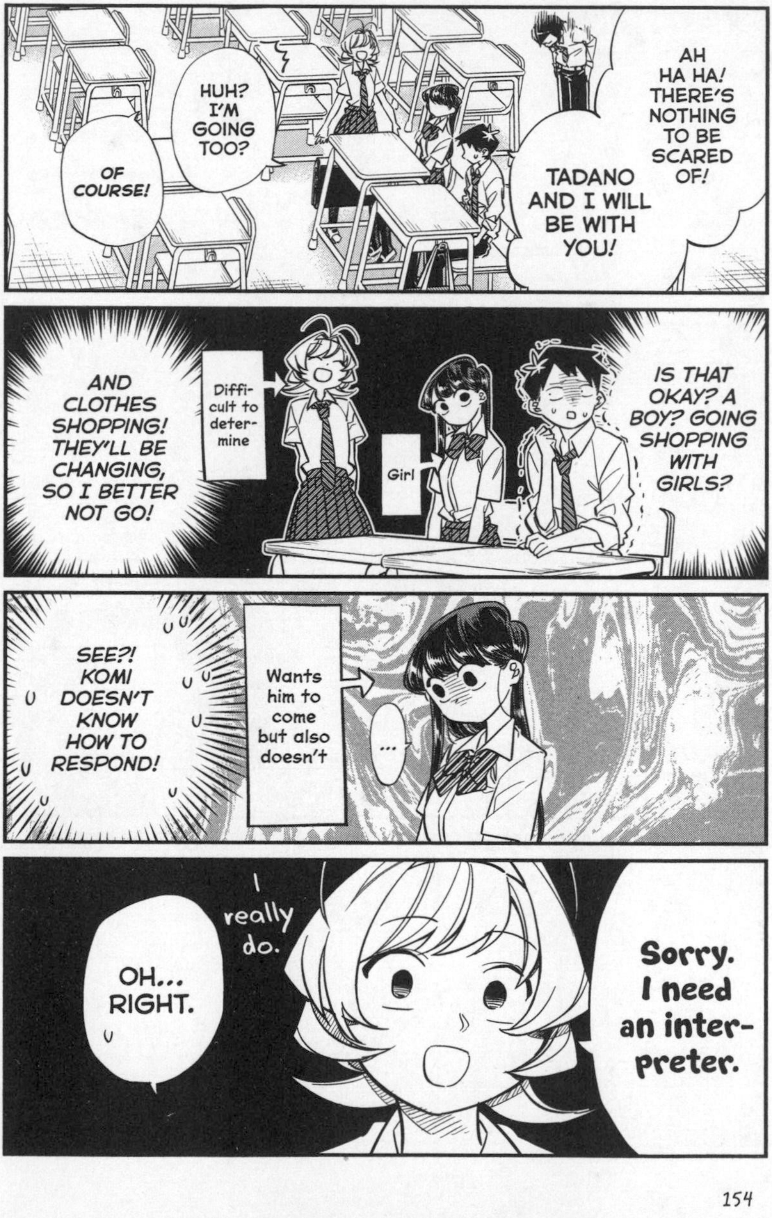
AH HA HA! THERE'S NOTHING TO BE SCARED OF!
TADANO AND I WILL BE WITH YOU!
HUH? I'M GOING TOO?
OF COURSE!
IS THAT OKAY? A BOY? GOING SHOPPING WITH GIRLS?
Girl
Diffi-cult to deter-mine
AND CLOTHES SHOPPING! THEY'LL BE CHANGING, SO I BETTER NOT GO!
...
Wants him to come but also doesn't
SEE?! KOMI DOESN'T KNOW HOW TO RESPOND!
Sorry. I need an inter-preter.
I really do.
OH... RIGHT.

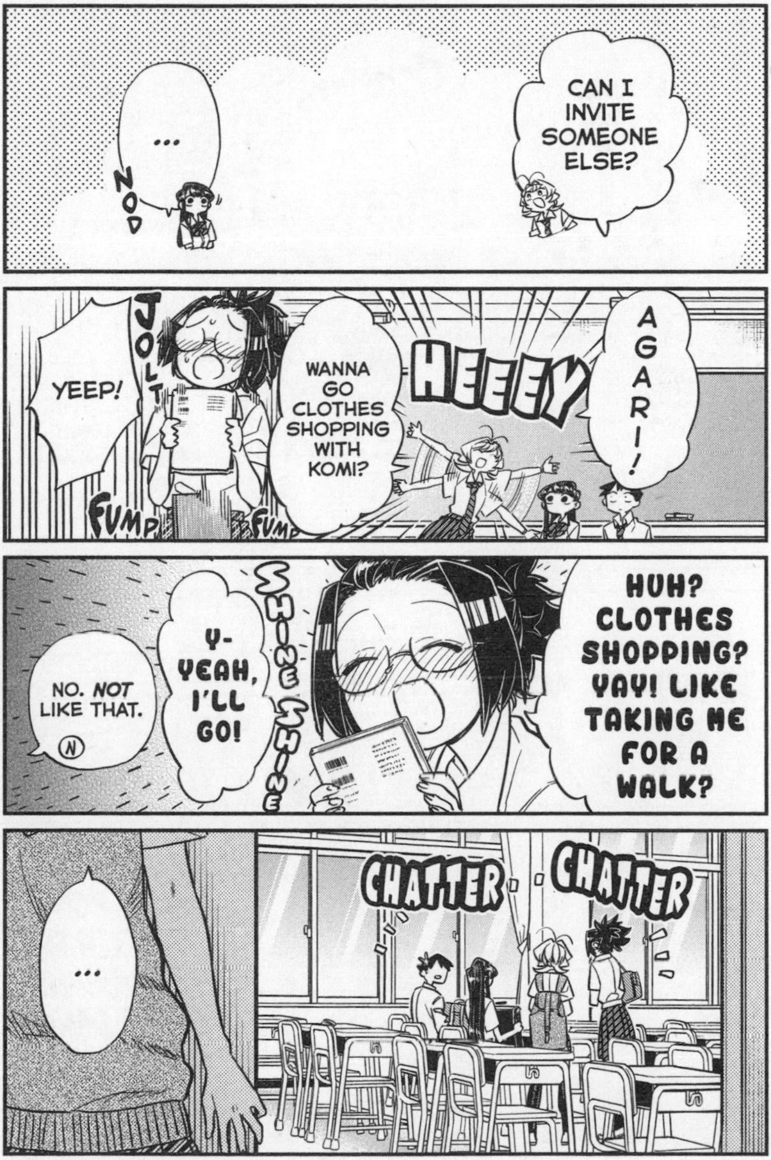
CAN I INVITE SOMEONE ELSE?
...
NOD
AGARI!
HEEEY
WANNA GO CLOTHES SHOPPING WITH KOMI?
JOLT
YEEP!
FUMP
FUMP
HUH? CLOTHES SHOPPING? YAY! LIKE TAKING ME FOR A WALK?
SHINE SHINE
Y-YEAH, I'LL GO!
NO. *NOT* LIKE THAT.
CHATTER
CHATTER
...

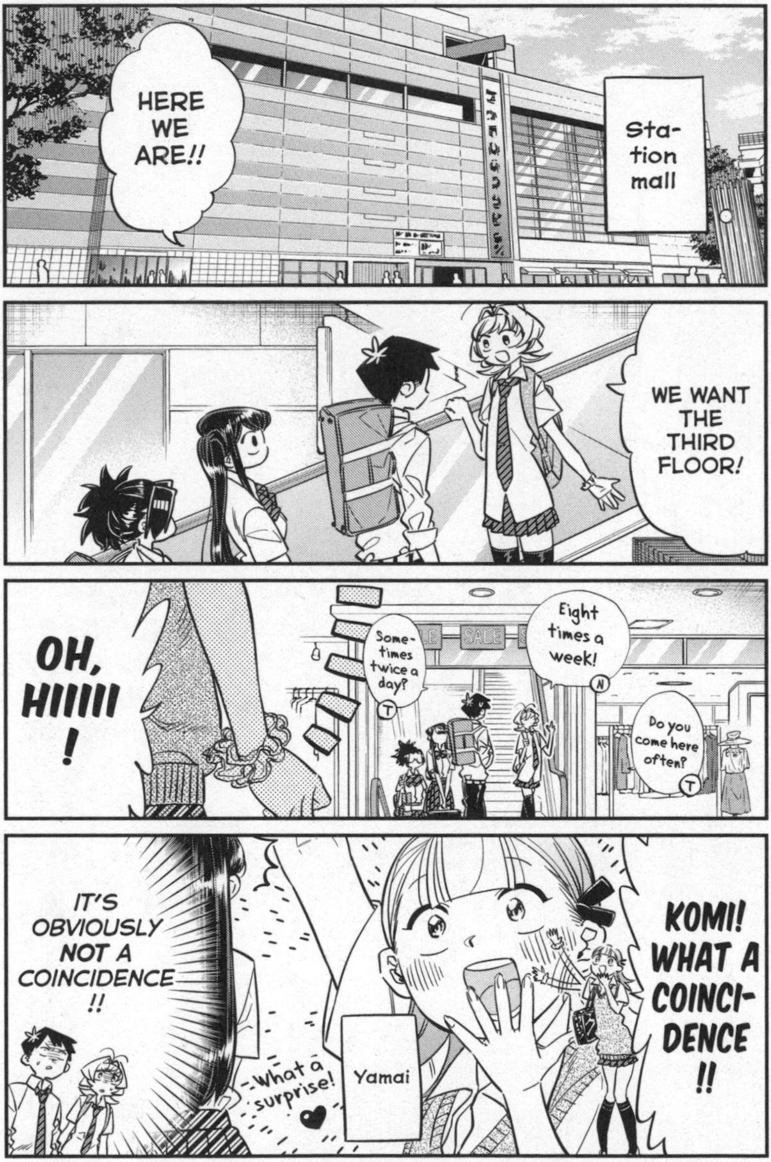
Station mall
HERE WE ARE!!
WE WANT THE THIRD FLOOR!
Do you come here often?
Eight times a week!
Sometimes twice a day?
OH, HIIIII!
KOMI! WHAT A COINCIDENCE!!
Yamai
What a surprise!
IT'S OBVIOUSLY NOT A COINCIDENCE!!

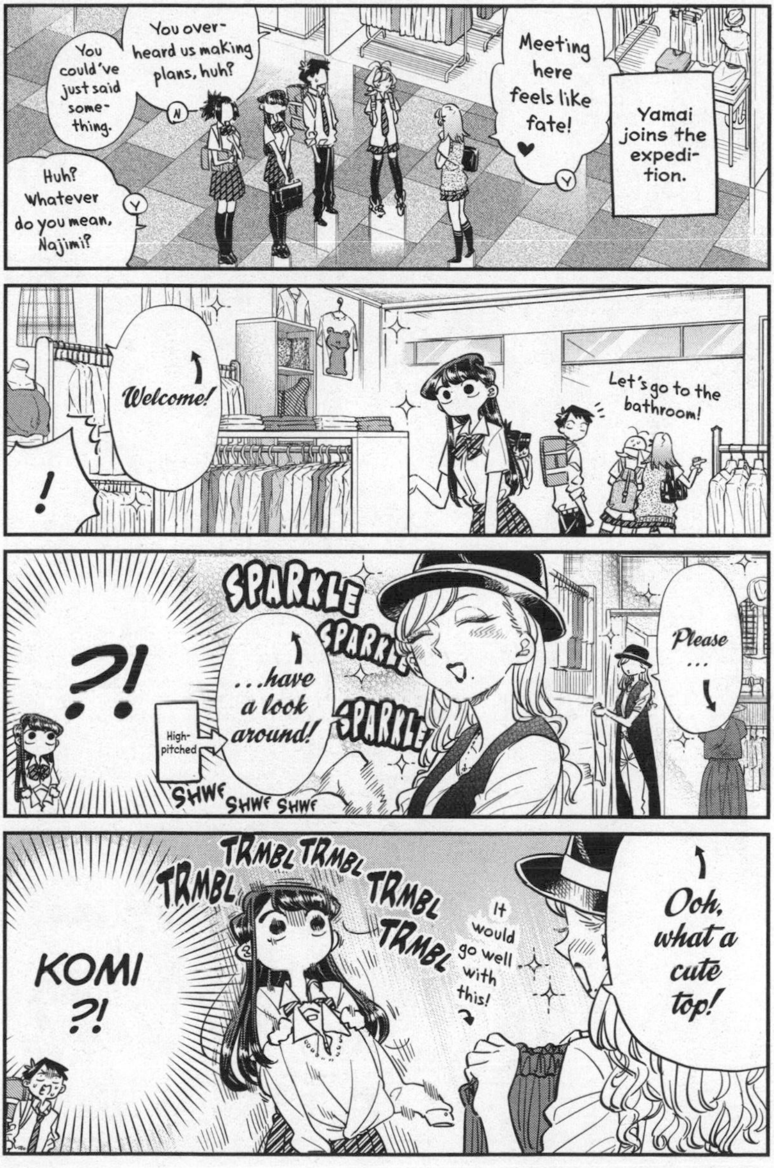
Yamai joins the expedition.
Meeting here feels like fate! ♥
You over-heard us making plans, huh?
You could've just said some-thing.
Huh? Whatever do you mean, Najimi?
Let's go to the bathroom!
Welcome!
!
Please ...
SPARKLE
SPARKLE
...have a look around!
High-pitched
SPARKLE
SHWF SHWF SHWF
?!
Ooh, what a cute top!
It would go well with this!
TRMBL TRMBL TRMBL TRMBL TRMBL
KOMI ?!

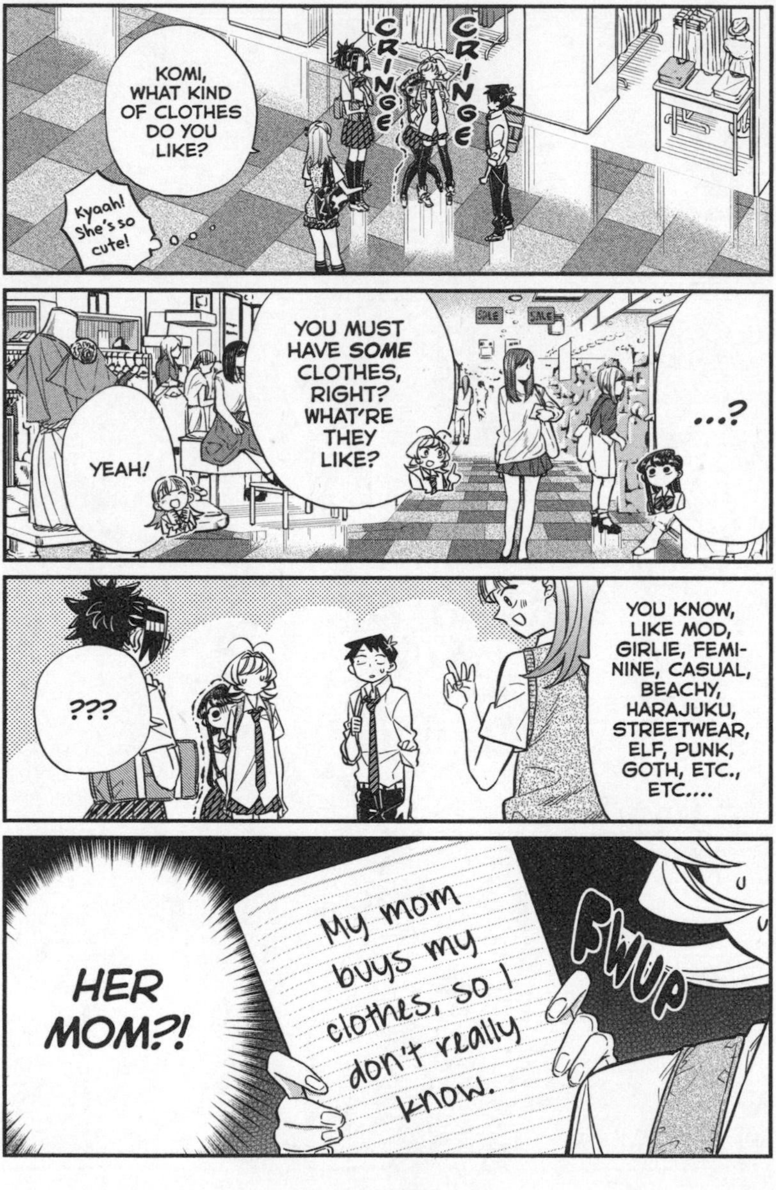
CRINGE
CRINGE
KOMI, WHAT KIND OF CLOTHES DO YOU LIKE?
Kyaah! She's so cute!
...?
YOU MUST HAVE SOME CLOTHES, RIGHT? WHAT'RE THEY LIKE?
YEAH!
YOU KNOW, LIKE MOD, GIRLIE, FEMI-NINE, CASUAL, BEACHY, HARAJUKU, STREETWEAR, ELF, PUNK, GOTH, ETC., ETC....
???
FWUP
My mom buys my clothes, so I don't really know.
HER MOM?!

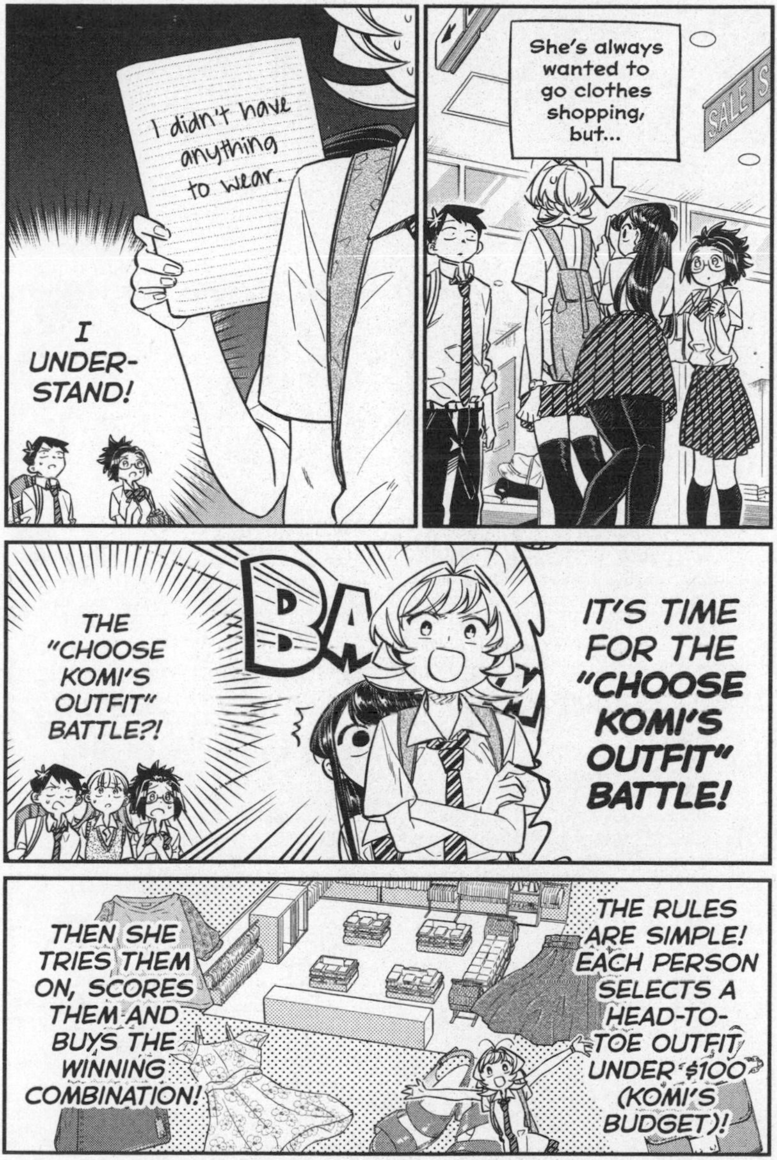
She's always wanted to go clothes shopping, but...
SALE
I didn't have anything to wear.
I UNDER-STAND!
IT'S TIME FOR THE "CHOOSE KOMI'S OUTFIT" BATTLE!
THE "CHOOSE KOMI'S OUTFIT" BATTLE?!
THE RULES ARE SIMPLE! EACH PERSON SELECTS A HEAD-TO-TOE OUTFIT UNDER $100 (KOMI'S BUDGET)!
THEN SHE TRIES THEM ON, SCORES THEM AND BUYS THE WINNING COMBINATION!

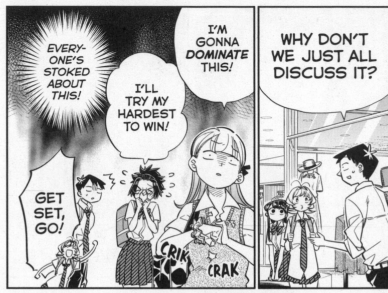

WHY DON'T WE JUST ALL DISCUSS IT?
I'M GONNA DOMINATE THIS!
I'LL TRY MY HARDEST TO WIN!
EVERY-ONE'S STOKED ABOUT THIS!
GET SET, GO!
CRIK
CRAK
What a lovely manne-quin!
It looks so real!
People think she's a manne-quin.
But why a school uniform?

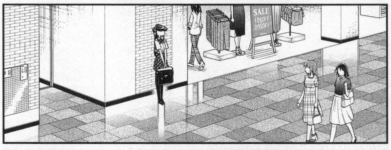

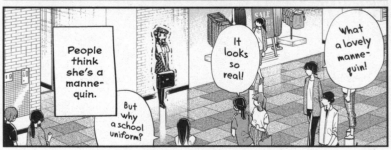

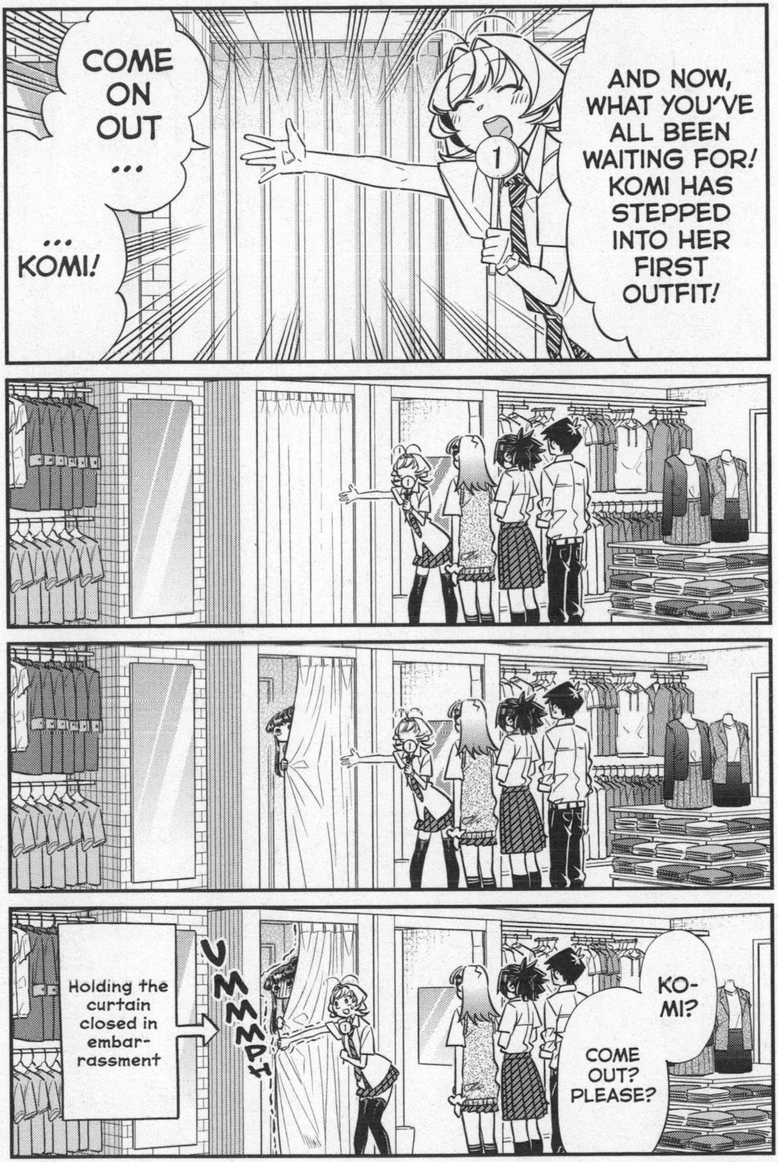
AND NOW, WHAT YOU'VE ALL BEEN WAITING FOR! KOMI HAS STEPPED INTO HER FIRST OUTFIT!
COME ON OUT ...
... KOMI!
KO-MI?
COME OUT? PLEASE?
UMMMPH
Holding the curtain closed in embar-rassment

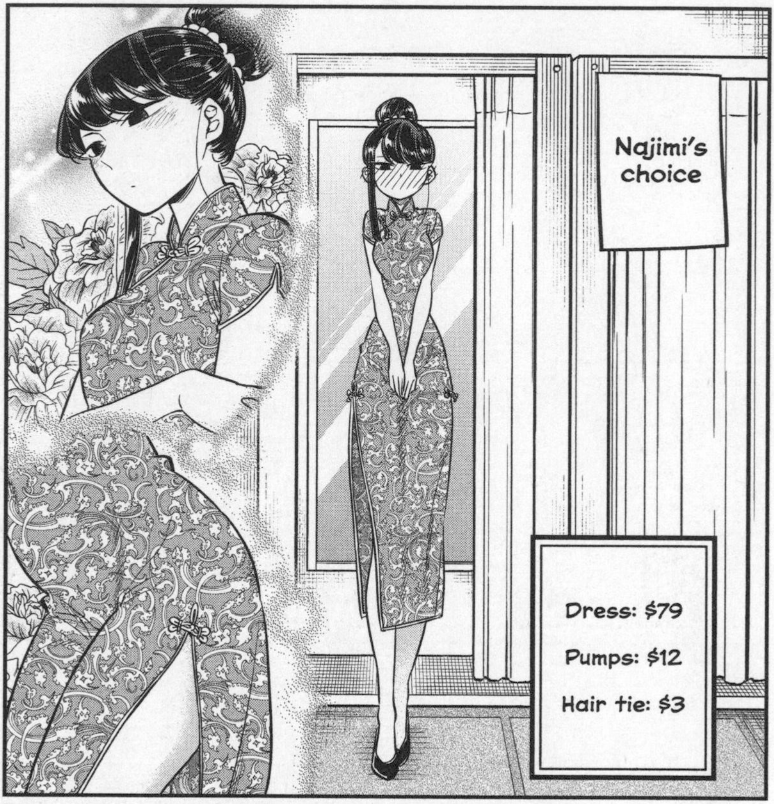
Najimi's choice
Dress: $79
Pumps: $12
Hair tie: $3

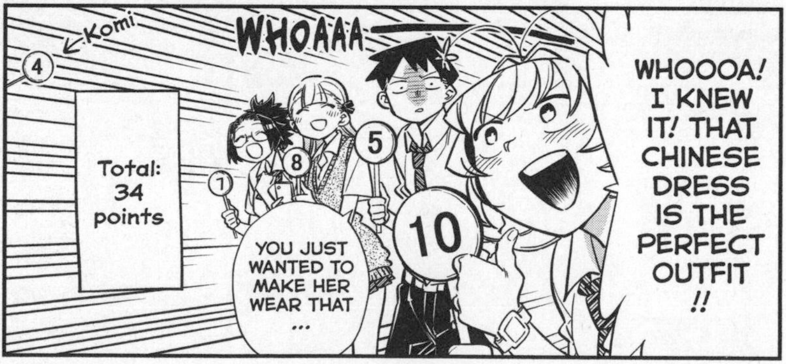
WHOOOA! I KNEW IT! THAT CHINESE DRESS IS THE PERFECT OUTFIT!!
WHOAAA
10
YOU JUST WANTED TO MAKE HER WEAR THAT...
5
8
7
Total: 34 points
4
← Komi

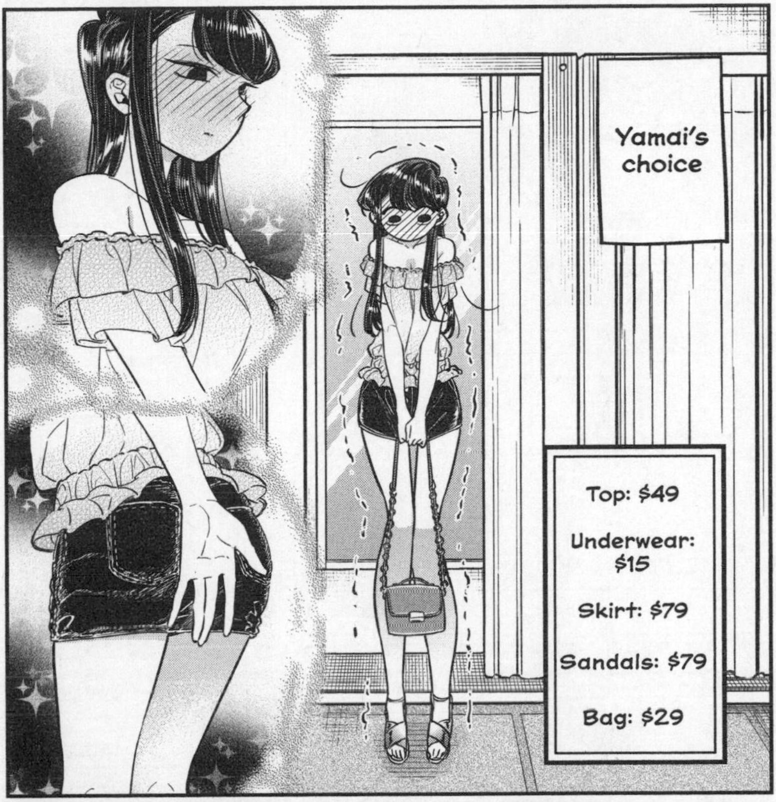
Yamai's choice
Top: $49
Underwear: $15
Skirt: $79
Sandals: $79
Bag: $29

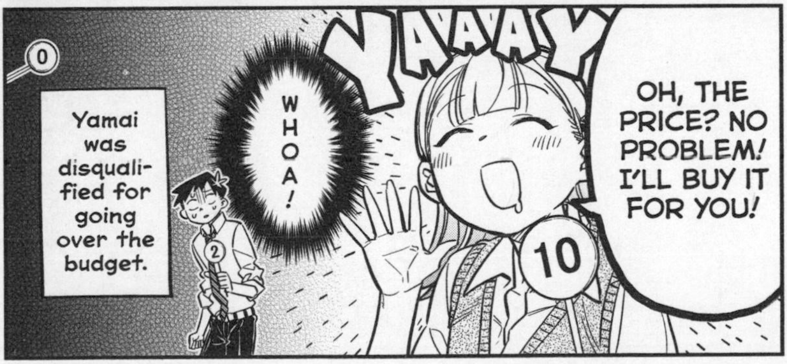
YAAAY
OH, THE PRICE? NO PROBLEM! I'LL BUY IT FOR YOU!
10
WHOA!
0
Yamai was disquali-fied for going over the budget.
2

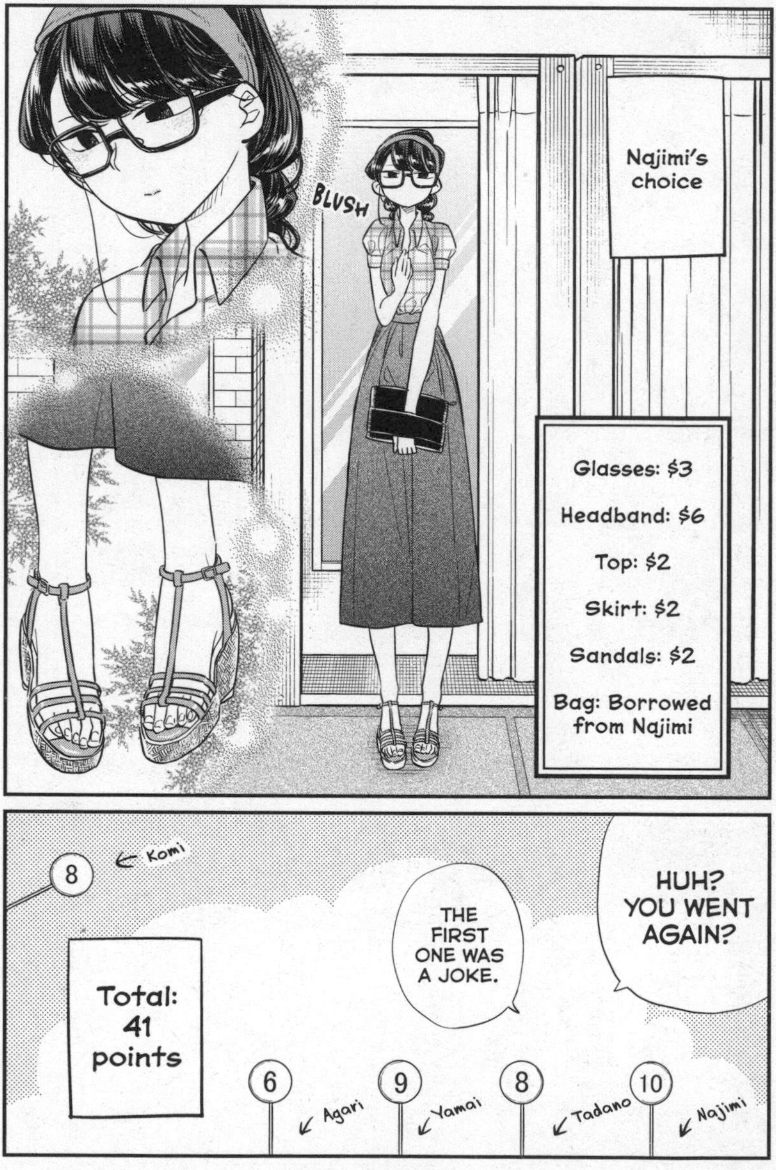

Najimi's choice
BLUSH
Glasses: $3
Headband: $6
Top: $2
Skirt: $2
Sandals: $2
Bag: Borrowed from Najimi
HUH? YOU WENT AGAIN?
THE FIRST ONE WAS A JOKE.
8 ← Komi
10 ← Najimi
8 ← Tadano
9 ← Yamai
6 ← Agari
Total: 41 points

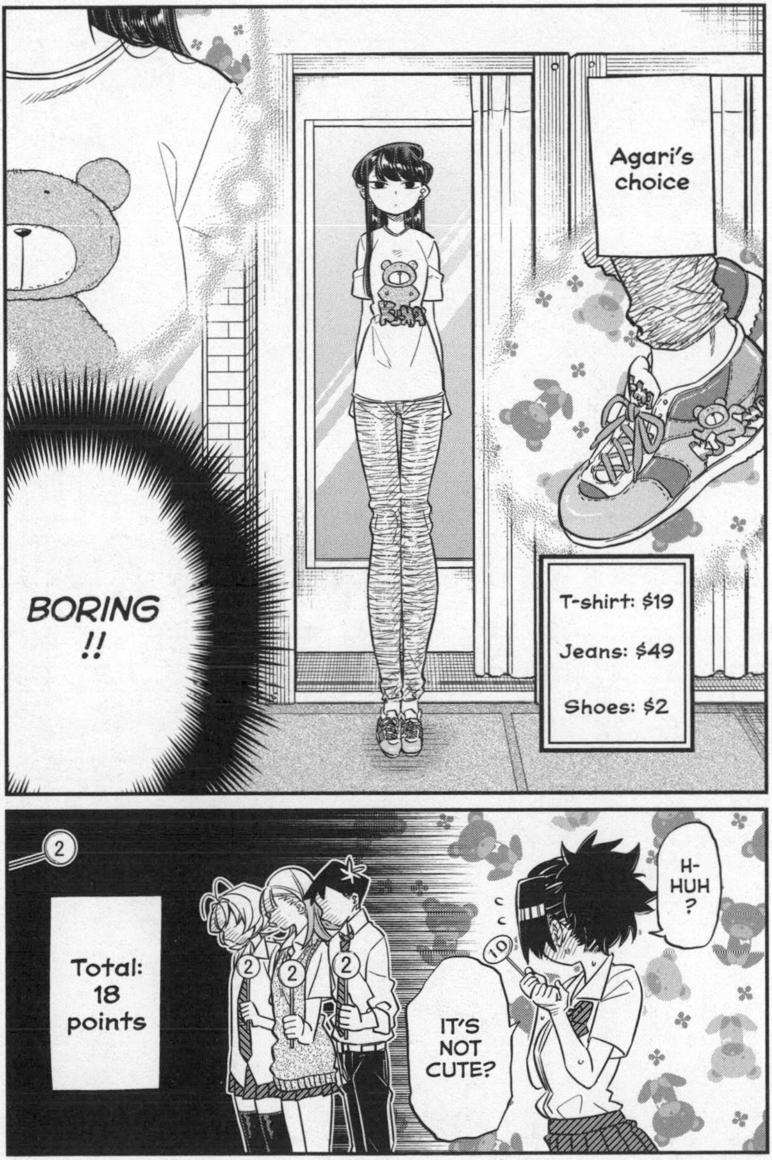
Agari's choice
T-shirt: $19
Jeans: $49
Shoes: $2
BORING !!
H-HUH ?
IT'S NOT CUTE?
Total: 18 points

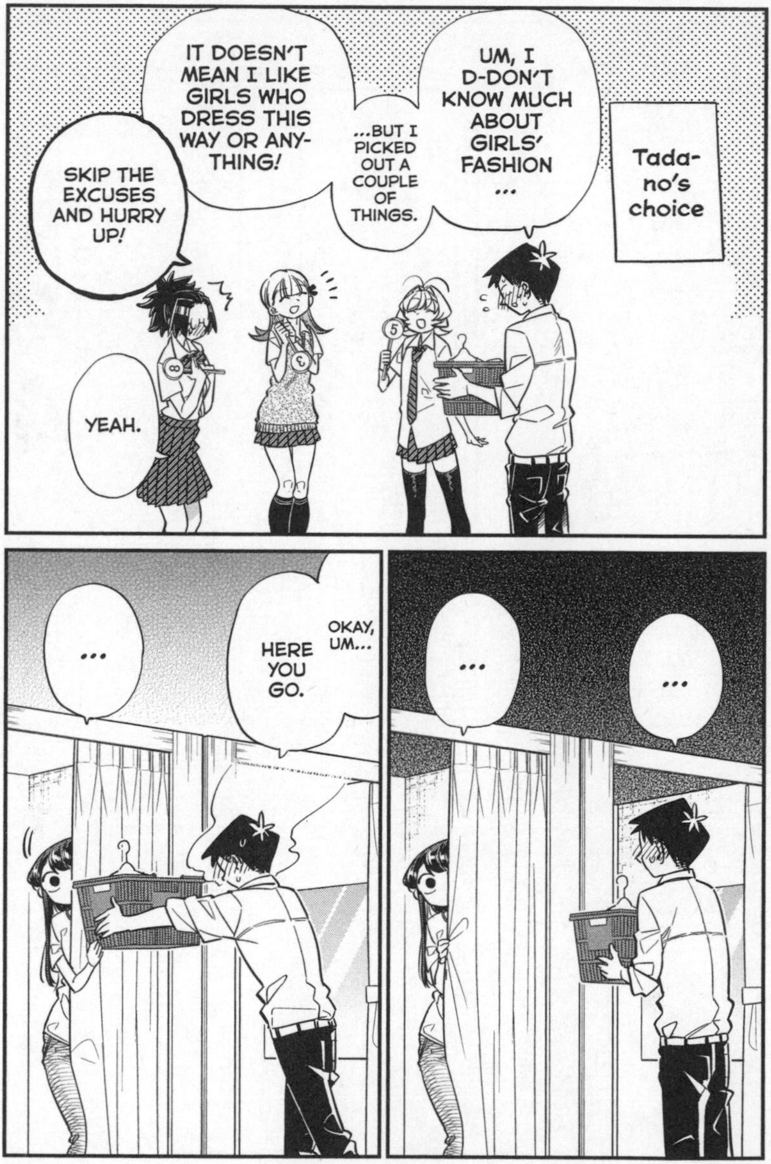
Tada-no's choice
UM, I D-DON'T KNOW MUCH ABOUT GIRLS' FASHION...
...BUT I PICKED OUT A COUPLE OF THINGS.
IT DOESN'T MEAN I LIKE GIRLS WHO DRESS THIS WAY OR ANY-THING!
SKIP THE EXCUSES AND HURRY UP!
YEAH.
...
...
OKAY, UM...
HERE YOU GO.
...

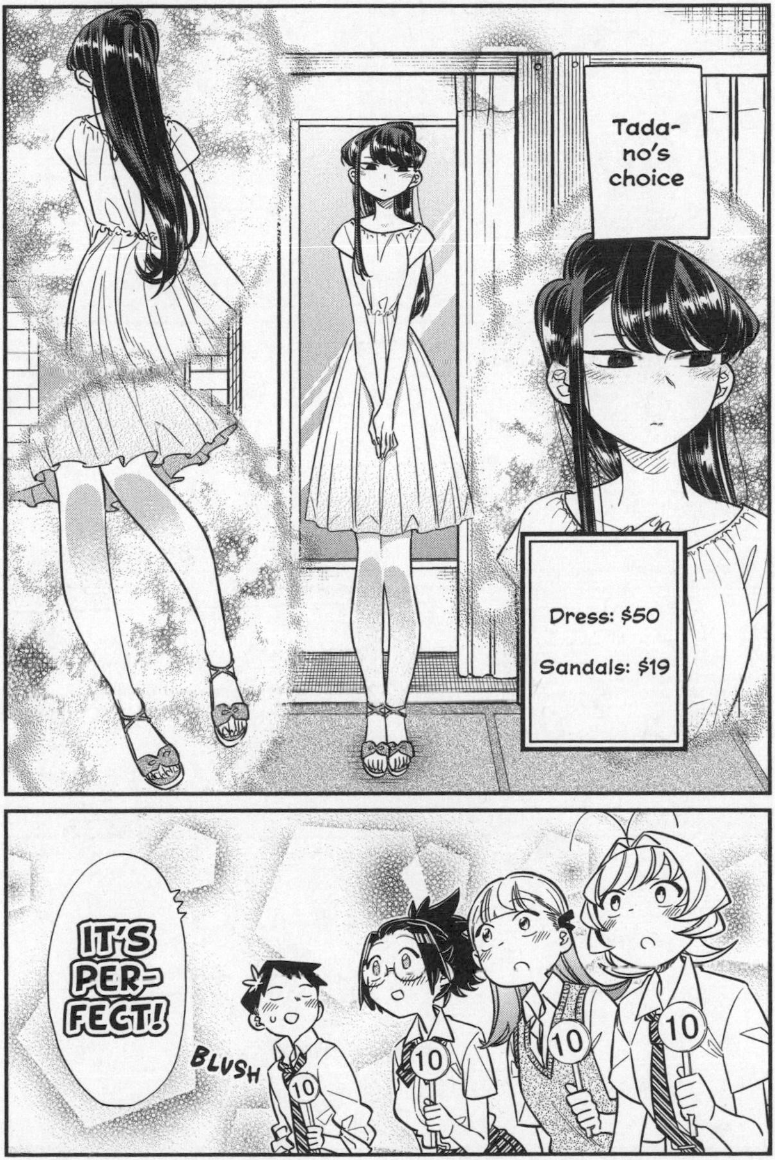

Tada-
no's
choice
Dress: $50
Sandals: $19
10
10
10
10
BLUSH
IT'S PER-FECT!

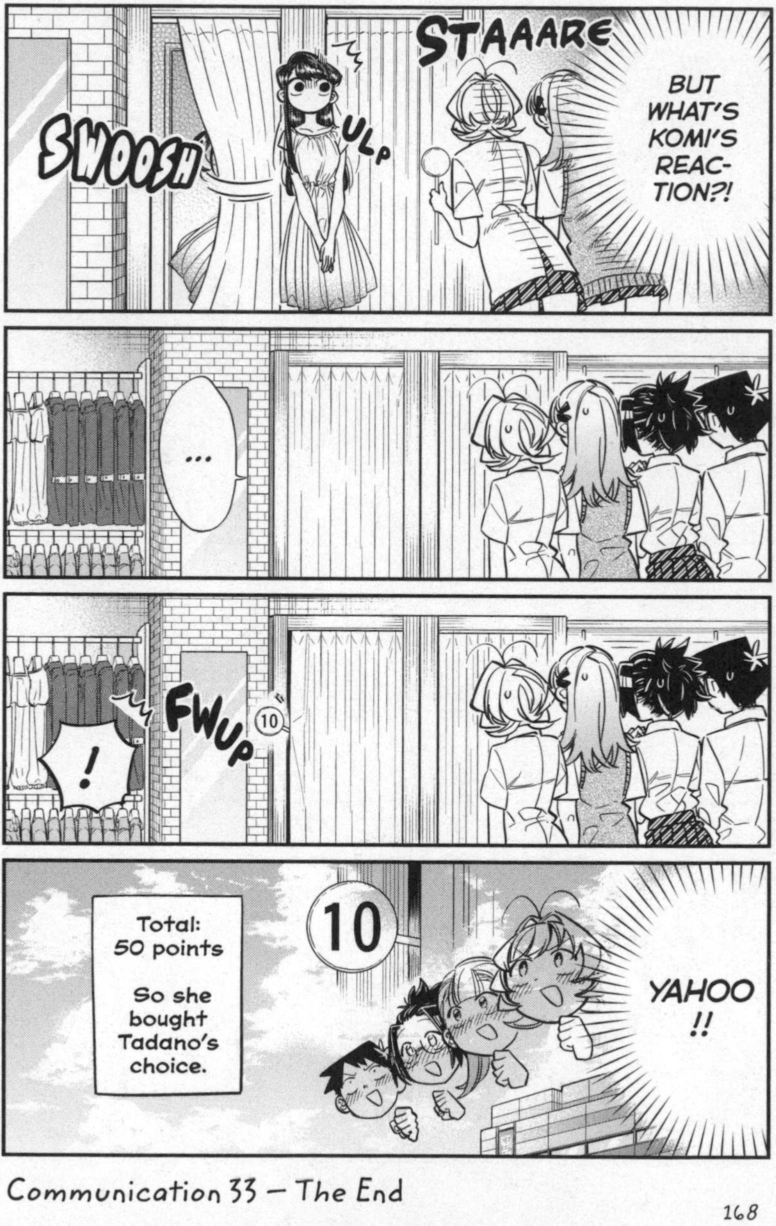

BUT WHAT'S KOMI'S REAC-TION?!
STAAARE
ULP
SWOOSH
...
FWUP
10
!
YAHOO !!
10
Total: 50 points
So she bought Tadano's choice.

Communication 33 – The End

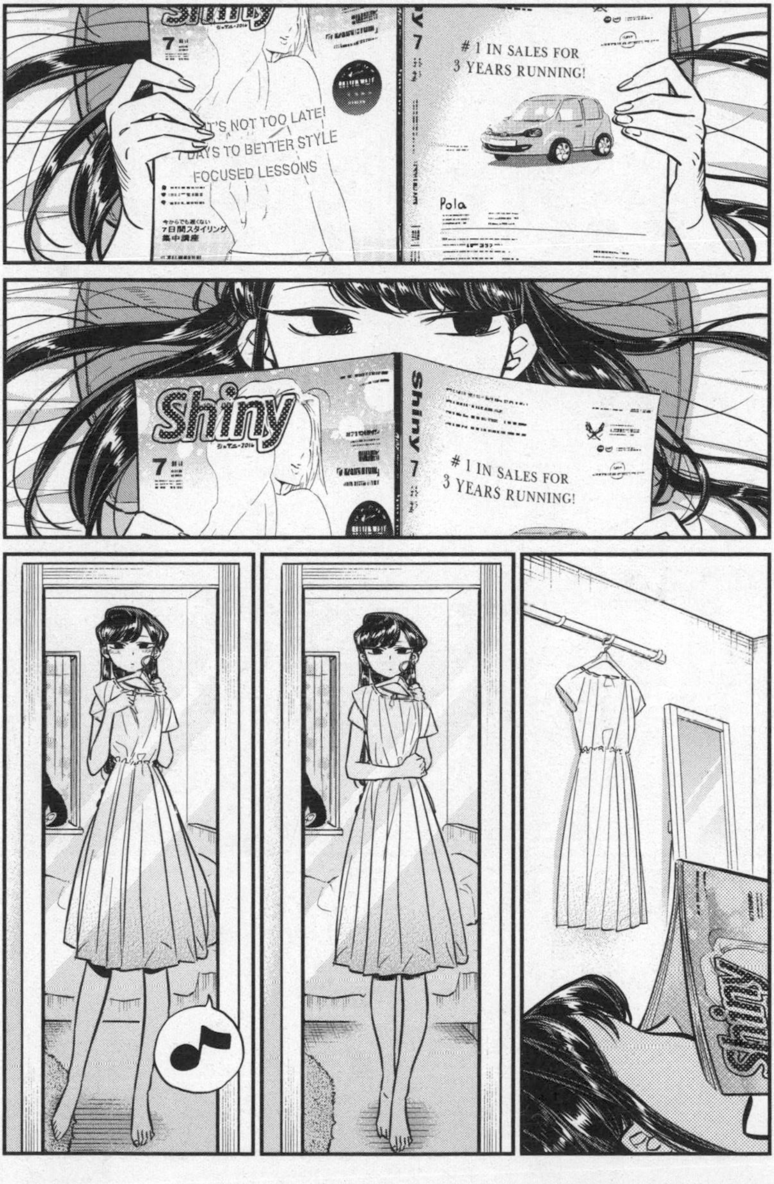

1 IN SALES FOR
3 YEARS RUNNING!
Pola
Shiny
T'S NOT TOO LATE!
7 DAYS TO BETTER STYLE
FOCUSED LESSONS
今からでも遅くない
7日間スタイリング
集中講座
Shiny
Shiny
1 IN SALES FOR
3 YEARS RUNNING!

POKE
POKE
HMPH
Made up her mind

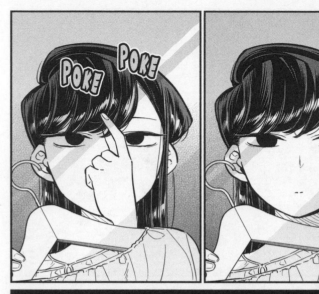

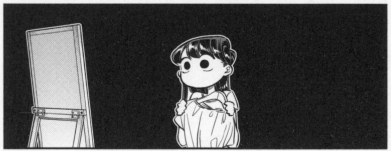

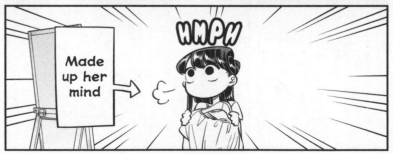

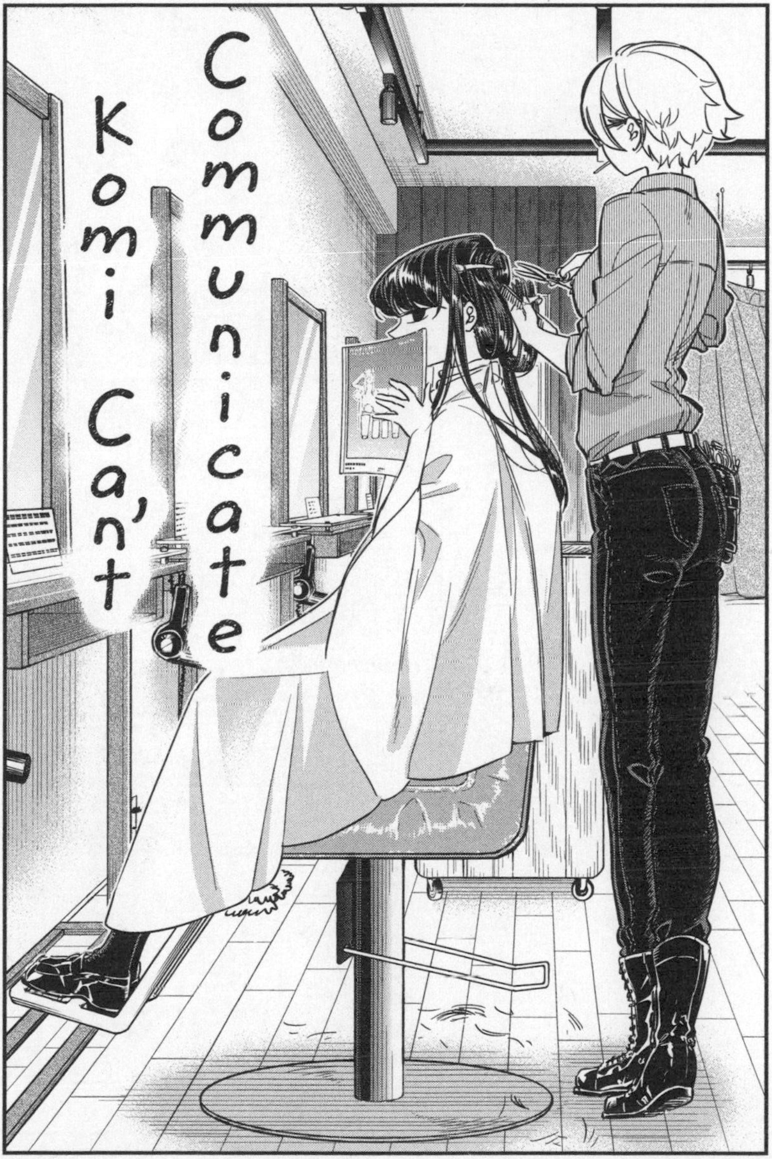
Komi Can't
Communicate

Communication 34: Beauty Salon

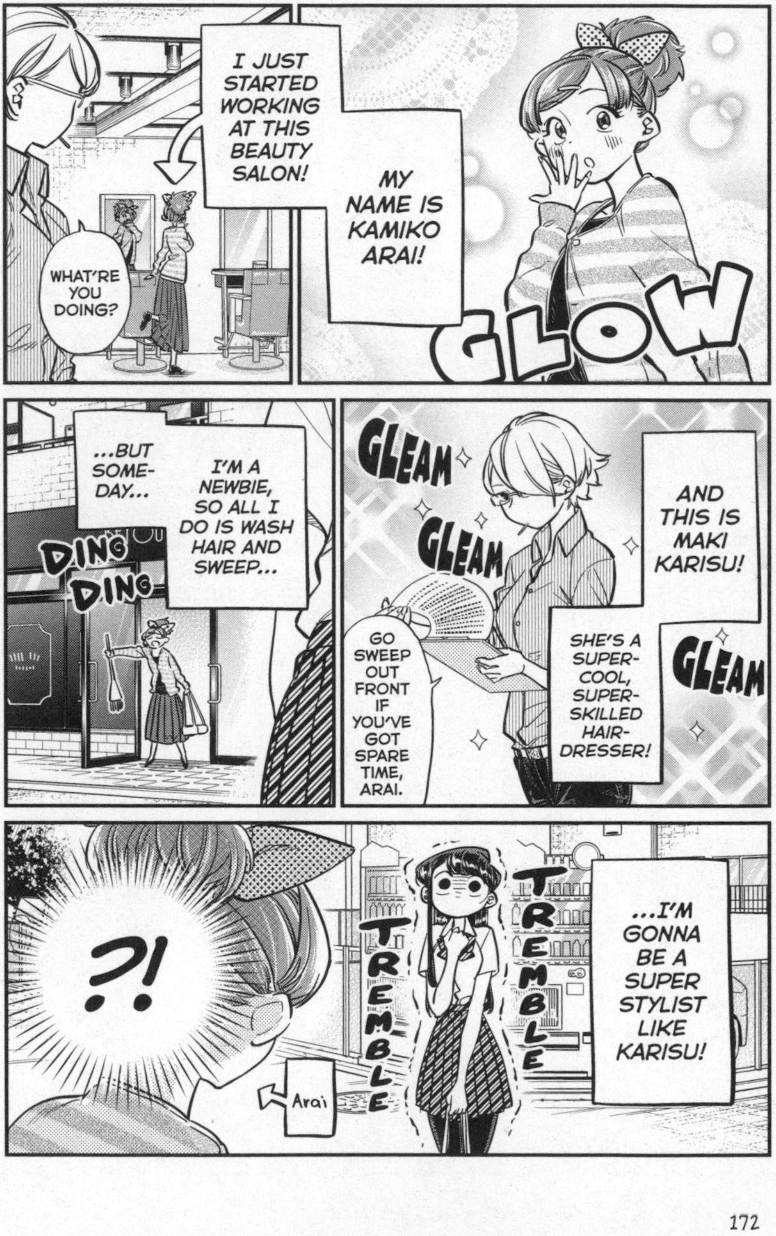
MY NAME IS KAMIKO ARAI!
I JUST STARTED WORKING AT THIS BEAUTY SALON!
GLOW
WHAT'RE YOU DOING?
AND THIS IS MAKI KARISU!
SHE'S A SUPER-COOL, SUPER-SKILLED HAIR-DRESSER!
GLEAM
GLEAM
GLEAM
GO SWEEP OUT FRONT IF YOU'VE GOT SPARE TIME, ARAI.
I'M A NEWBIE, SO ALL I DO IS WASH HAIR AND SWEEP...
...BUT SOME-DAY...
DING DING
...I'M GONNA BE A SUPER STYLIST LIKE KARISU!
TREMBLE
TREMBLE
?!
Arai

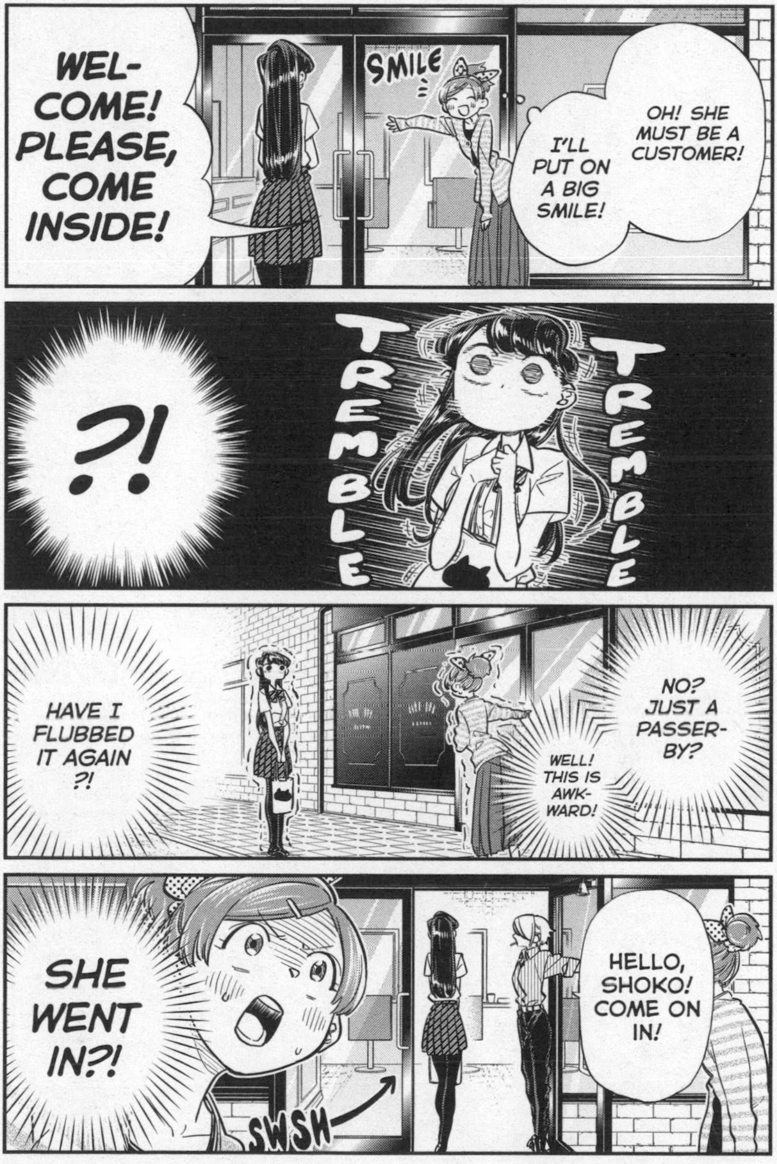
OH! SHE MUST BE A CUSTOMER!
I'LL PUT ON A BIG SMILE!
SMILE
WEL-COME! PLEASE, COME INSIDE!
TREMBLE
TREMBLE
?!
NO? JUST A PASSER-BY?
WELL! THIS IS AWK-WARD!
HAVE I FLUBBED IT AGAIN ?!
HELLO, SHOKO! COME ON IN!
SWSH
SHE WENT IN?!

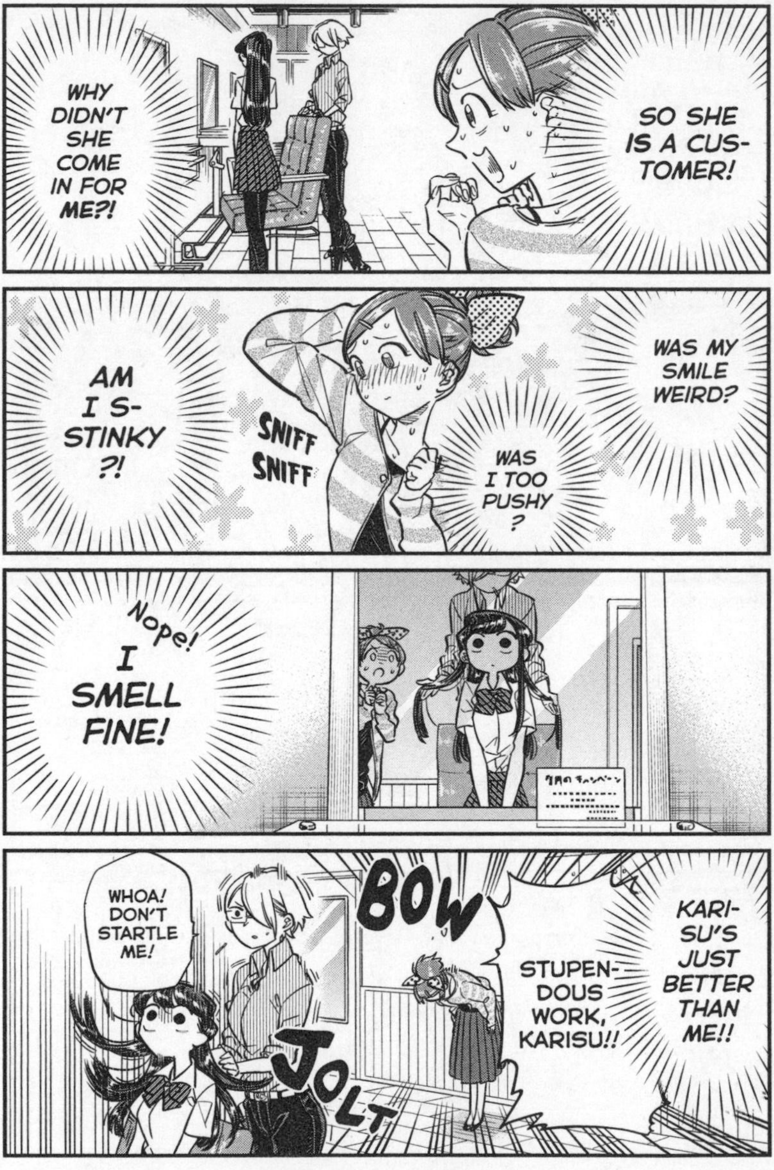
SO SHE IS A CUS-TOMER!
WHY DIDN'T SHE COME IN FOR ME?!
WAS MY SMILE WEIRD?
WAS I TOO PUSHY?
SNIFF SNIFF
AM I S-STINKY?!
Nope! I SMELL FINE!
KARI-SU'S JUST BETTER THAN ME!!
STUPEN-DOUS WORK, KARISU!!
BOW
JOLT
WHOA! DON'T STARTLE ME!

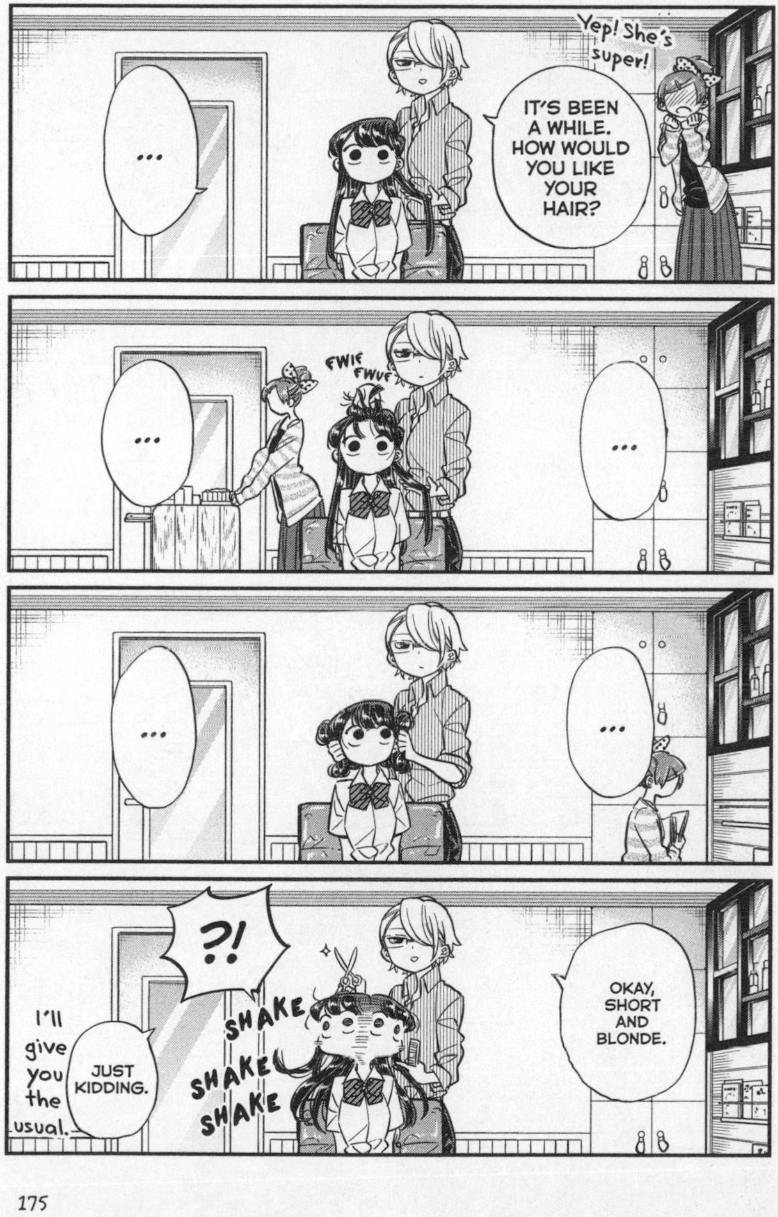
Yep! She's super!
IT'S BEEN A WHILE. HOW WOULD YOU LIKE YOUR HAIR?
...
...
FWIF FWUF
...
...
...
OKAY, SHORT AND BLONDE.
?!
SHAKE SHAKE SHAKE
JUST KIDDING.
I'll give you the usual.

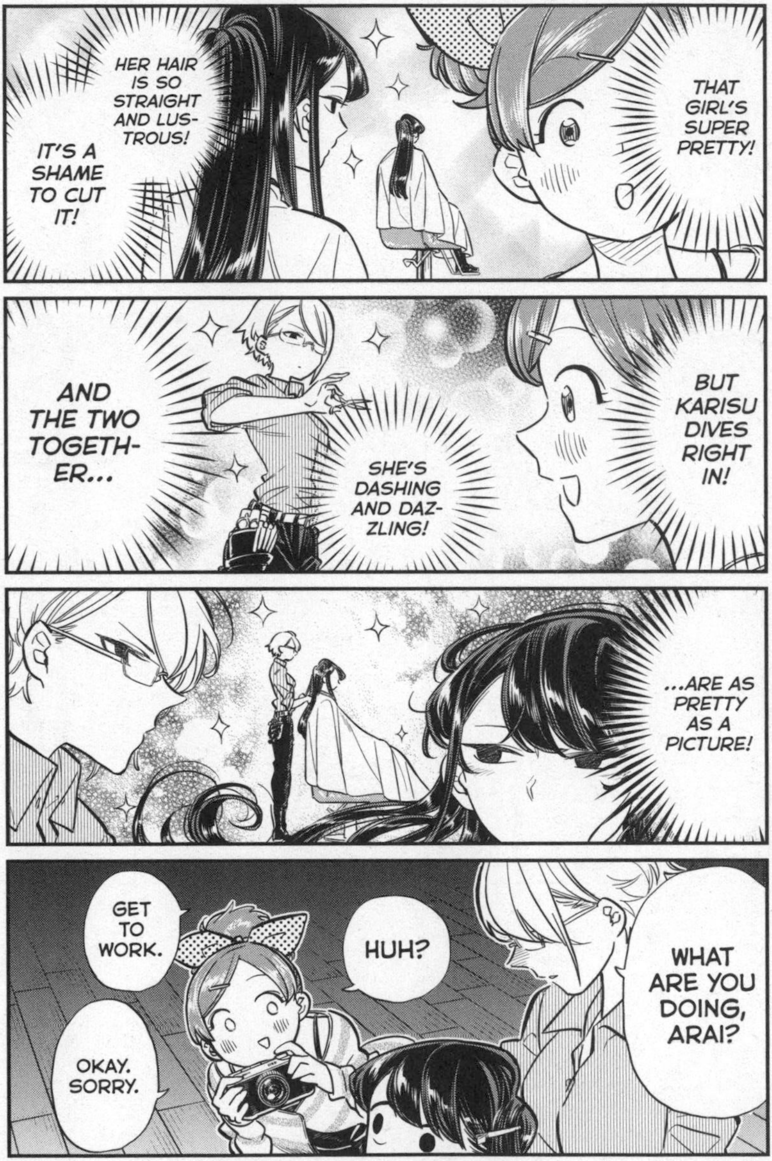
THAT GIRL'S SUPER PRETTY!
HER HAIR IS SO STRAIGHT AND LUS-TROUS!
IT'S A SHAME TO CUT IT!
BUT KARISU DIVES RIGHT IN!
SHE'S DASHING AND DAZ-ZLING!
AND THE TWO TOGETH-ER...
...ARE AS PRETTY AS A PICTURE!
WHAT ARE YOU DOING, ARAI?
HUH?
GET TO WORK.
OKAY. SORRY.

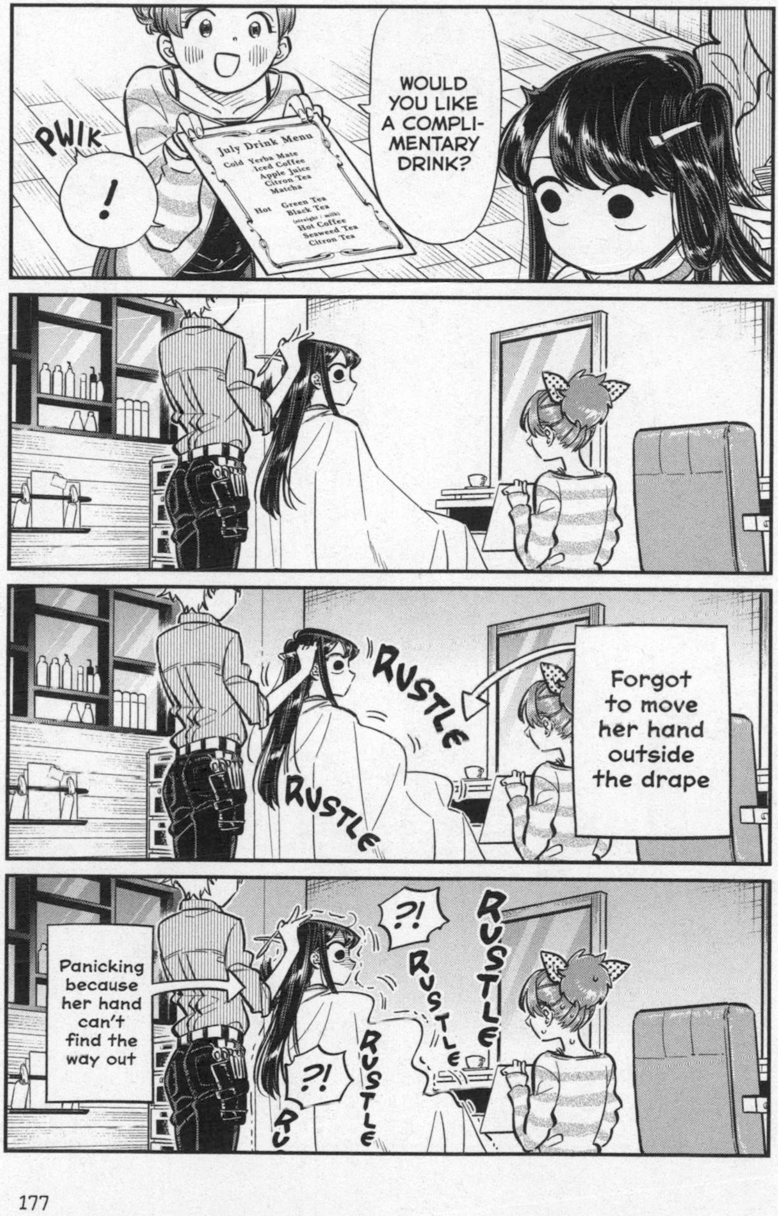
WOULD YOU LIKE A COMPLIMENTARY DRINK?
July Drink Menu
Cold Yerba Mate
Iced Coffee
Apple Juice
Citron Tea
Matcha
Hot Green Tea
Black Tea
(straight / milk)
Hot Coffee
Seaweed Tea
Citron Tea
PWIK
!
Forgot to move her hand outside the drape
RUSTLE
RUSTLE
RUSTLE
?!
RUSTLE
RUSTLE
?!
RU
Panicking because her hand can't find the way out

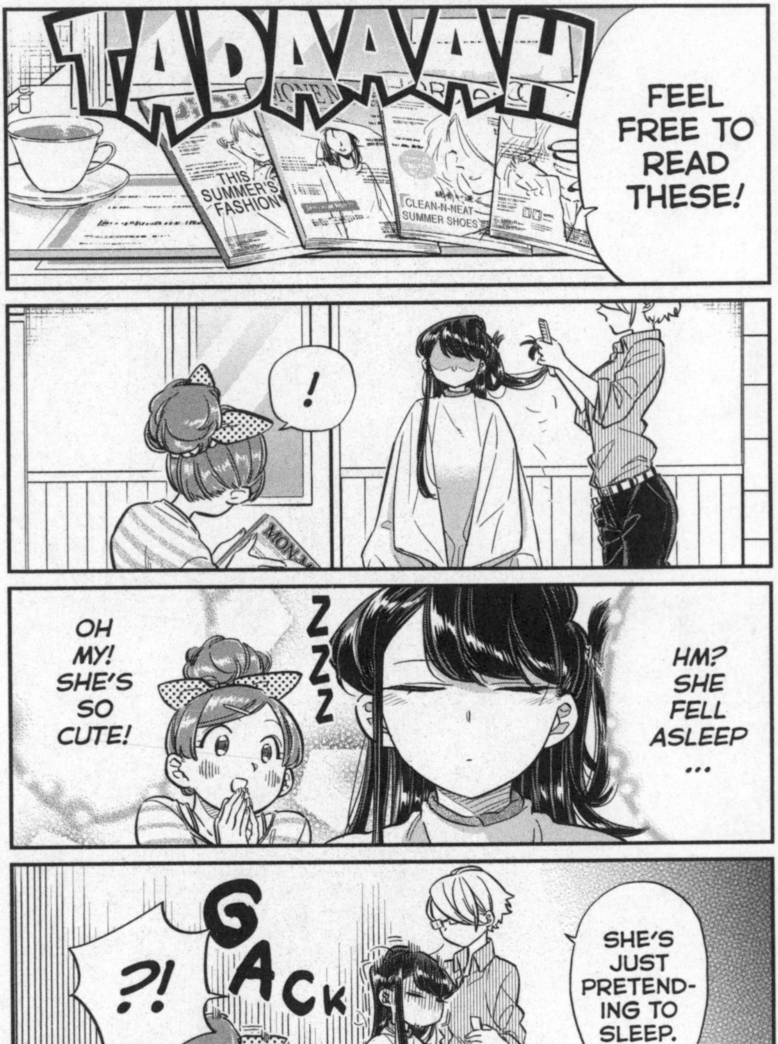
FEEL FREE TO READ THESE!
TADAAAH
CLEAN-N-NEAT SUMMER SHOES
THIS SUMMER'S FASHION
!
HM? SHE FELL ASLEEP ...
ZZZ
OH MY! SHE'S SO CUTE!
SHE'S JUST PRETEND-ING TO SLEEP.
So I won't talk to her.
GACK
?!

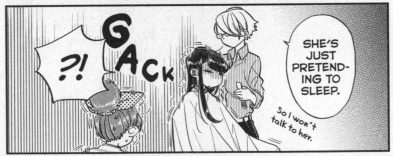

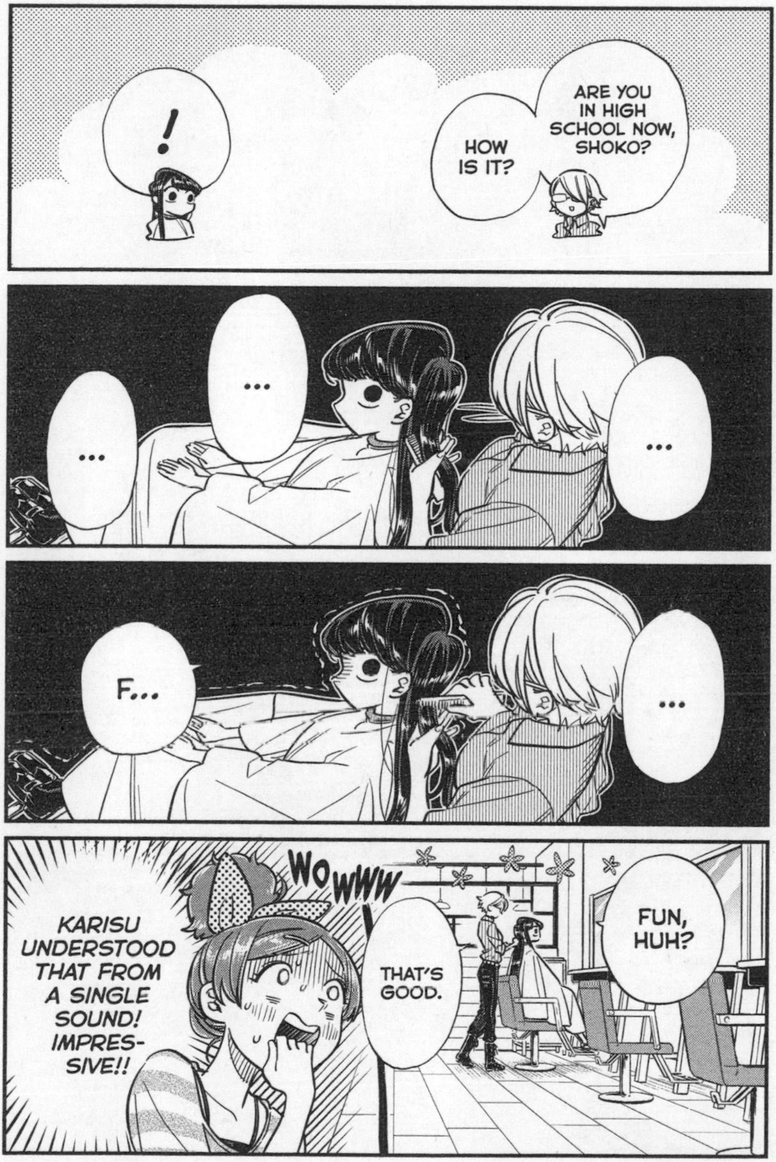
ARE YOU IN HIGH SCHOOL NOW, SHOKO?
HOW IS IT?
!
...
...
...
...
F...
FUN, HUH?
WOWWW
THAT'S GOOD.
KARISU UNDERSTOOD THAT FROM A SINGLE SOUND! IMPRES-SIVE!!

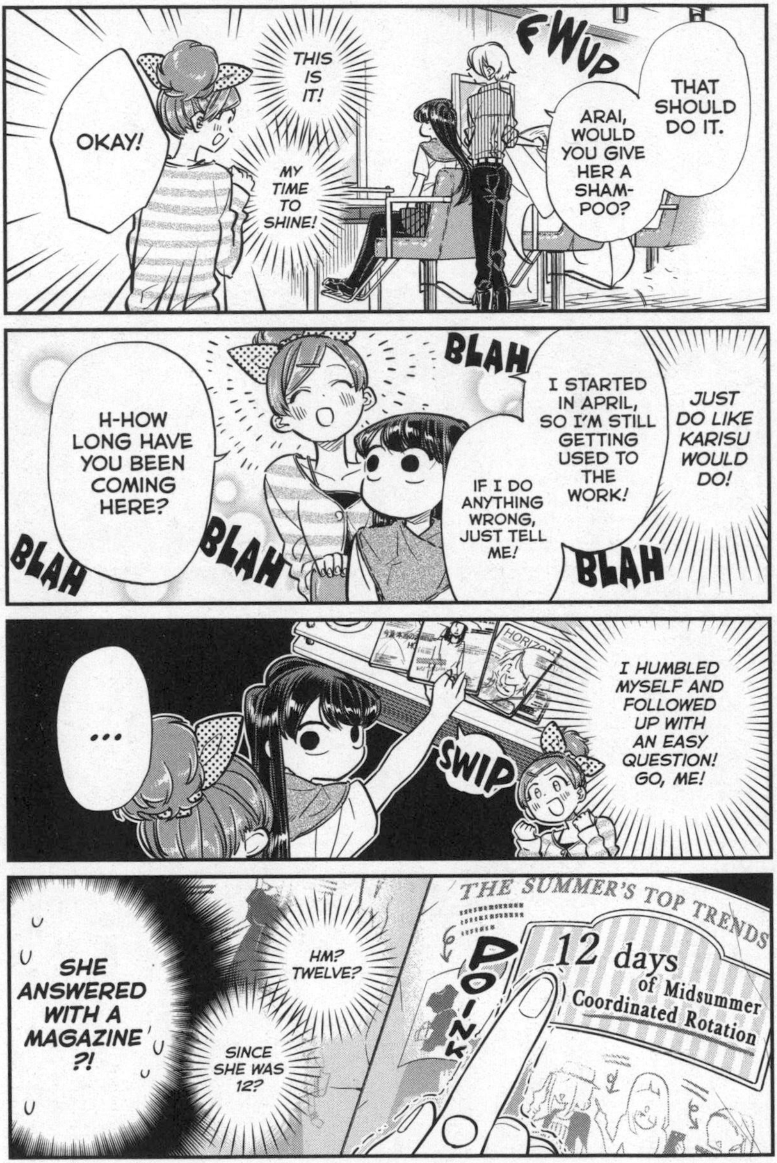
THAT SHOULD DO IT.
ARAI, WOULD YOU GIVE HER A SHAMPOO?
FWUP
THIS IS IT!
MY TIME TO SHINE!
OKAY!
JUST DO LIKE KARISU WOULD DO!
BLAH
I STARTED IN APRIL, SO I'M STILL GETTING USED TO THE WORK!
IF I DO ANYTHING WRONG, JUST TELL ME!
BLAH
BLAH
H-HOW LONG HAVE YOU BEEN COMING HERE?
BLAH
I HUMBLED MYSELF AND FOLLOWED UP WITH AN EASY QUESTION! GO, ME!
SWIP
...
THE SUMMER'S TOP TRENDS
12 days of Midsummer Coordinated Rotation
POINK
HM? TWELVE?
SINCE SHE WAS 12?
SHE ANSWERED WITH A MAGAZINE?!

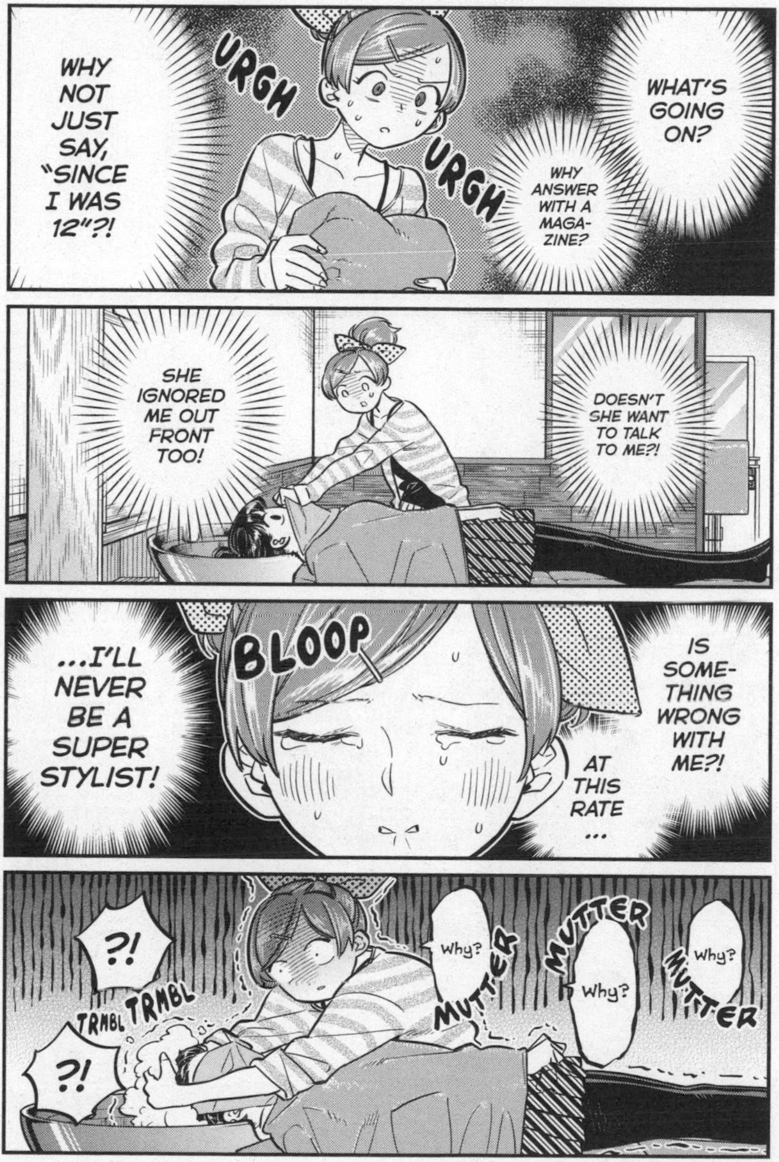
WHAT'S GOING ON?
WHY ANSWER WITH A MAGAZINE?
URGH
URGH
WHY NOT JUST SAY, "SINCE I WAS 12"?!
DOESN'T SHE WANT TO TALK TO ME?!
SHE IGNORED ME OUT FRONT TOO!
IS SOMETHING WRONG WITH ME?!
AT THIS RATE...
BLOOP
...I'LL NEVER BE A SUPER STYLIST!
Why?
MUTTER
Why?
MUTTER
Why?
MUTTER
?!
TRMBL
TRMBL
?!

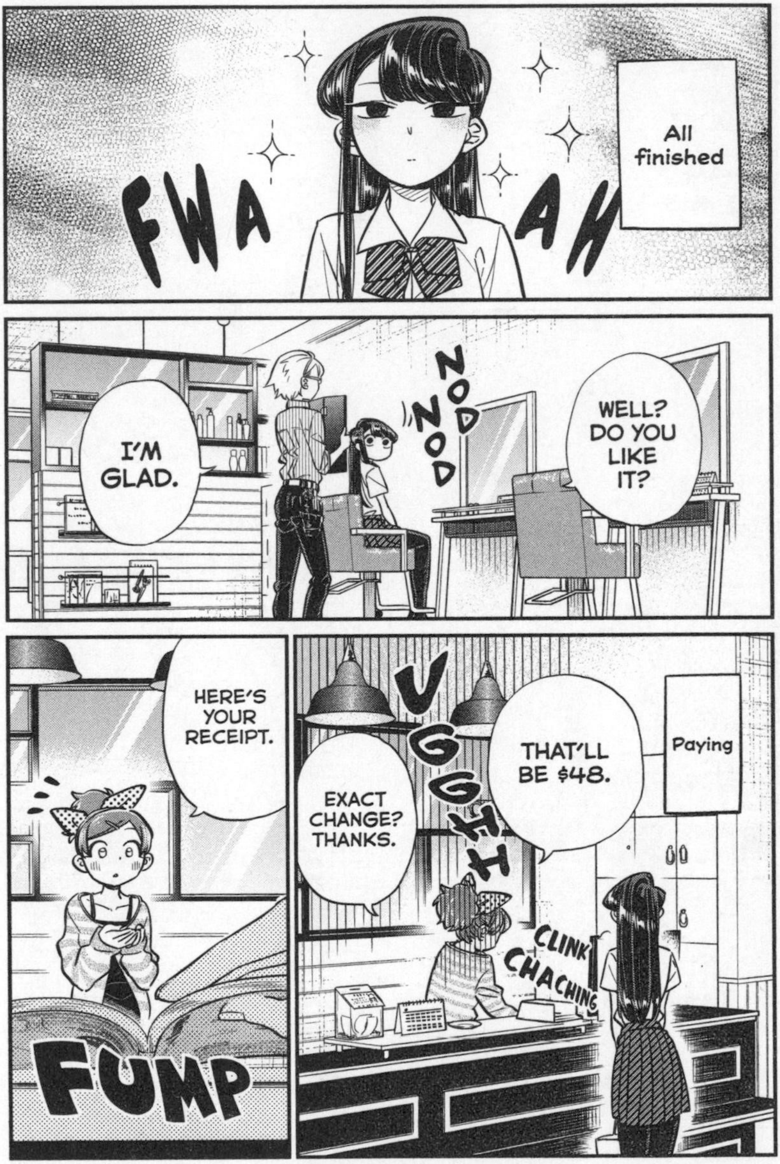
All finished
FWA AH
WELL? DO YOU LIKE IT?
NOD NOD
I'M GLAD.
Paying
THAT'LL BE $48.
UGGH
EXACT CHANGE? THANKS.
CLINK CHACHING
HERE'S YOUR RECEIPT.
FUMP

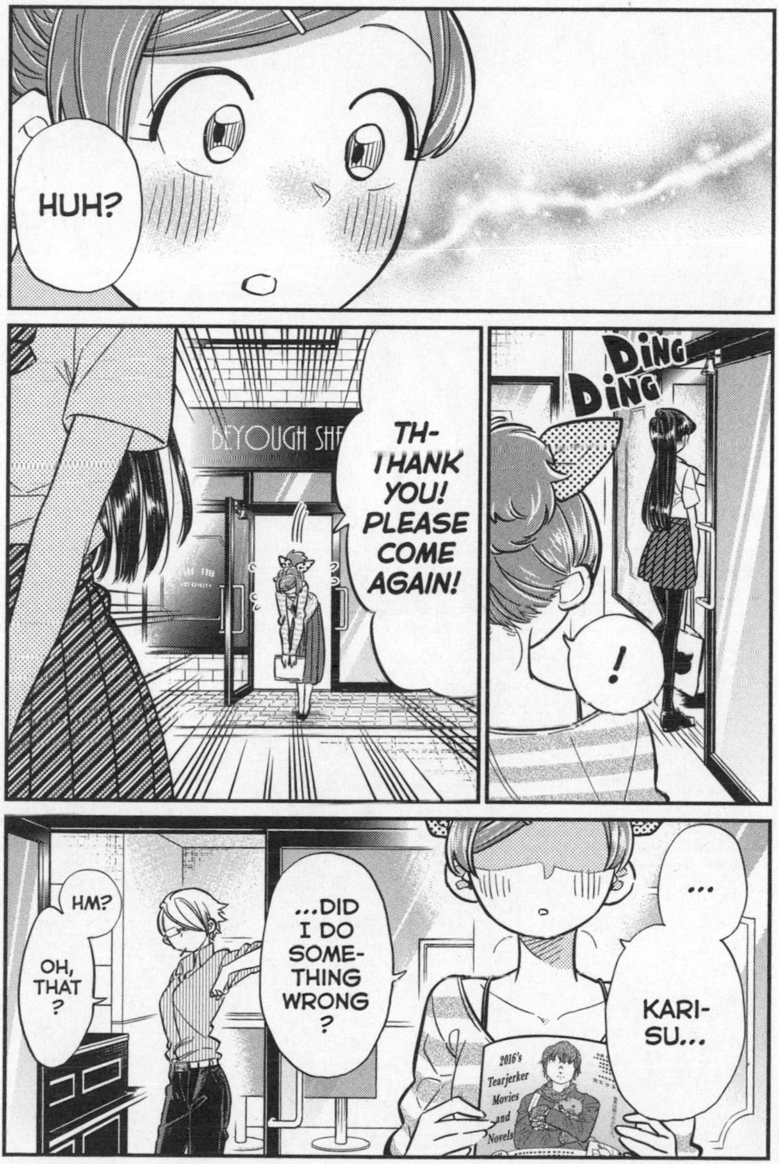
HUH?
DING DING
!
TH-THANK YOU! PLEASE COME AGAIN!
...
KARI-SU...
2016's Tearjerker Movies and Novels
...DID I DO SOMETHING WRONG?
HM?
OH, THAT?

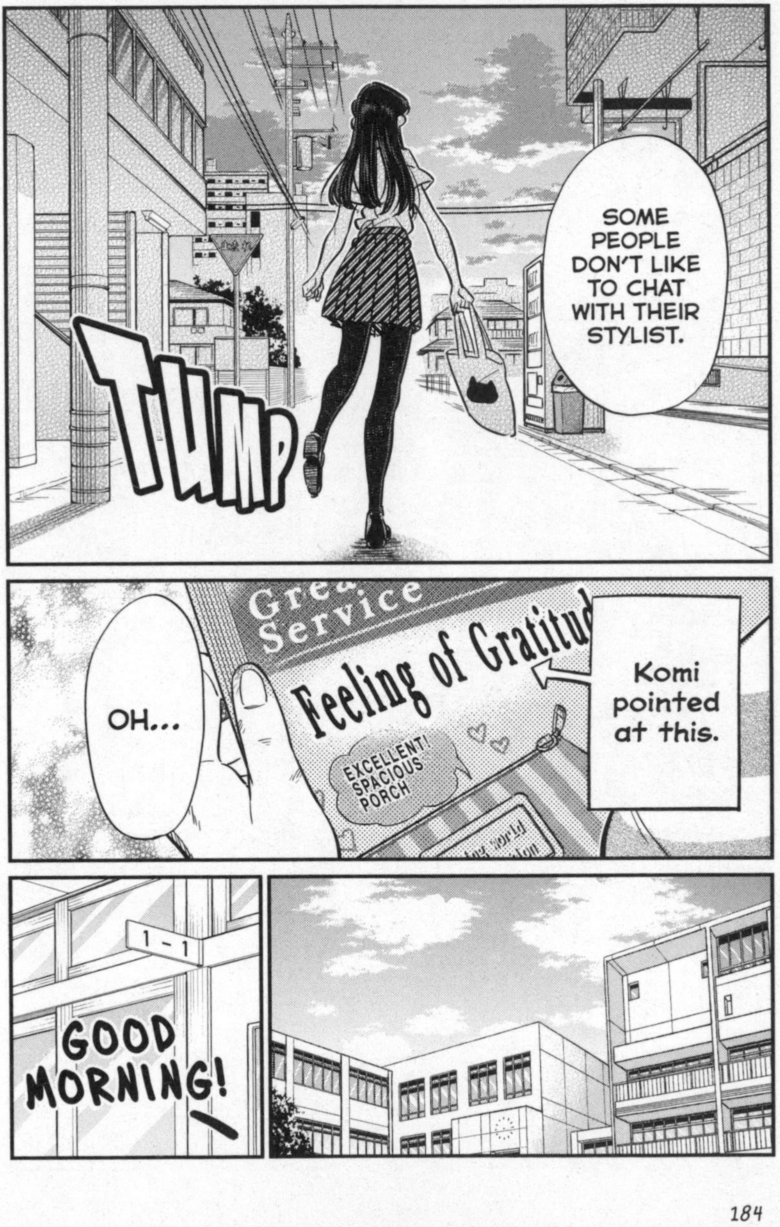
SOME PEOPLE DON'T LIKE TO CHAT WITH THEIR STYLIST.
THUMP
Komi pointed at this.
Service
Feeling of Gratitud
EXCELLENT! SPACIOUS PORCH
OH...
1-1
GOOD MORNING!

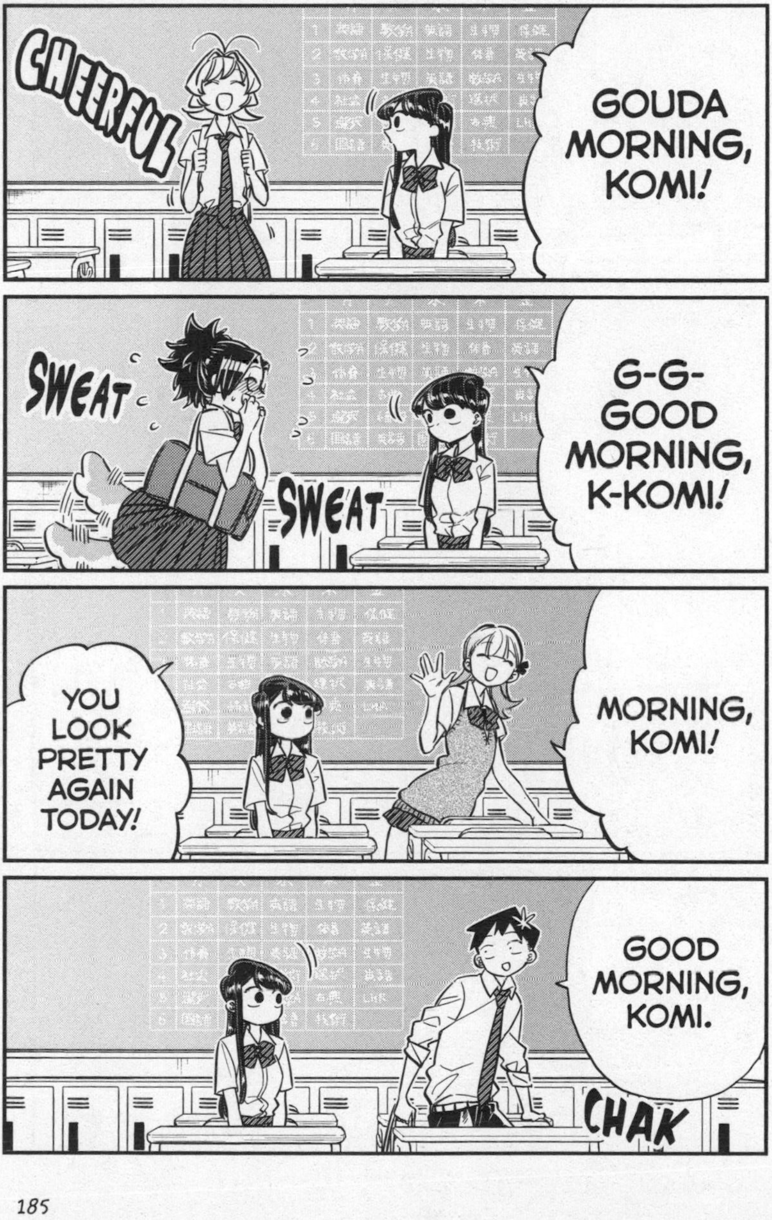
GOUDA MORNING, KOMI!
CHEERFUL
G-G-GOOD MORNING, K-KOMI!
SWEAT
SWEAT
MORNING, KOMI!
YOU LOOK PRETTY AGAIN TODAY!
GOOD MORNING, KOMI.
CHAK

...
HM?
DID YOU CUT YOUR HAIR?
...
BLUSH
Huh? You did?
It looks the same!
GLOOM
I totally failed...
Nooo! I can't believe I didn't notice!
?!

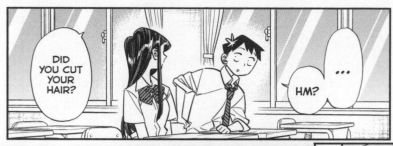

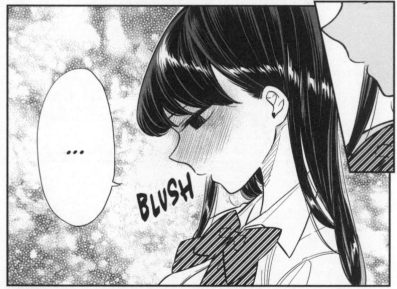

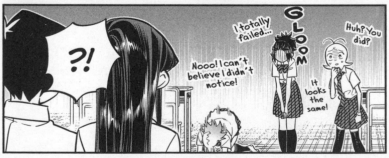

Communication 34 – The End

Komi Can't
Communicate

Komi Can't Communicate Bonus

Can Komi Make a Hundred Friends? -Greed, Love and Hate-

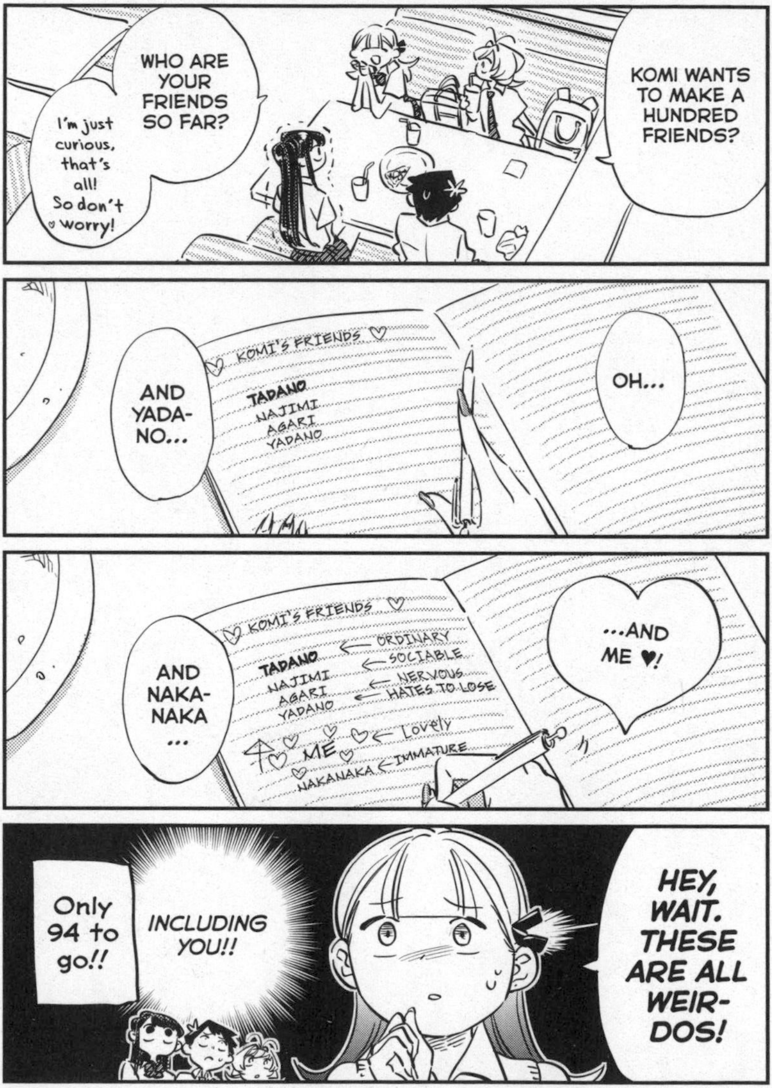
KOMI WANTS TO MAKE A HUNDRED FRIENDS?
WHO ARE YOUR FRIENDS SO FAR?
I'm just curious, that's all! So don't worry!
OH...
KOMI'S FRIENDS
TADANO
NAJIMI
AGARI
YADANO
AND YADA-NO...
...AND ME ♥!
KOMI'S FRIENDS
TADANO ← ORDINARY
NAJIMI ← SOCIABLE
AGARI ← NERVOUS
YADANO ← HATES TO LOSE
ME ← Lovely
NAKANAKA ← IMMATURE
AND NAKA-NAKA...
HEY, WAIT. THESE ARE ALL WEIR-DOS!
INCLUDING YOU!!
Only 94 to go!!

Komi Can't Communicate Bonus

Cut Scene: Tadano Tied Up

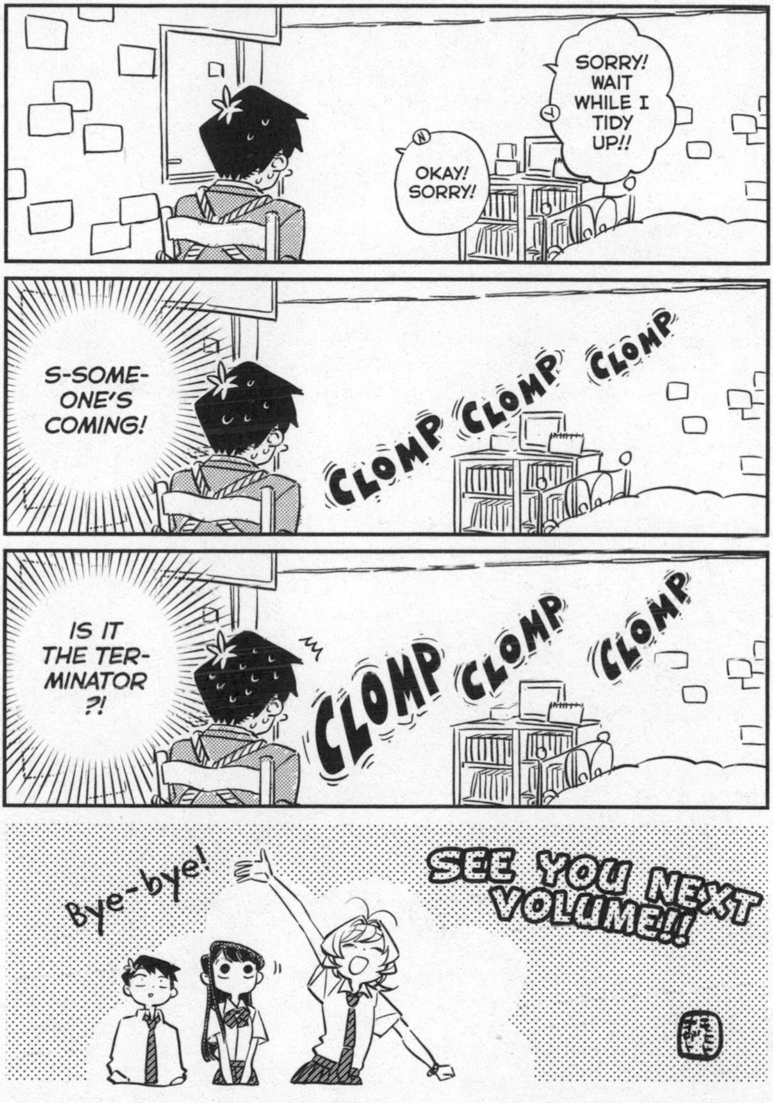
SORRY! WAIT WHILE I TIDY UP!!
OKAY! SORRY!
S-SOME-ONE'S COMING!
CLOMP CLOMP CLOMP
IS IT THE TER-MINATOR ?!
CLOMP CLOMP CLOMP
SEE YOU NEXT VOLUME!!
Bye-bye!

Komi Can't Communicate

VOL. 2
Shonen Sunday Edition

Story and Art by Tomohito Oda

English Translation & Adaptation/John Werry
Touch-Up Art & Lettering/Eve Grandt
Design/Julian [JR] Robinson
Editor/Pancha Diaz

COMI-SAN WA, COMYUSHO DESU. Vol.2
by Tomohito ODA
© 2016 Tomohito ODA
All rights reserved.
Original Japanese edition published by SHOGAKUKAN.
English translation rights in the United States of America, Canada, the United Kingdom, Ireland, Australia and New Zealand arranged with SHOGAKUKAN.

Printed in the U.S.A.

Published by VIZ Media, LLC
P.O. Box 77010
San Francisco, CA 94107

10 9 8 7 6
First printing, August 2019
Sixth printing, June 2021

viz.com

shonensunday.com

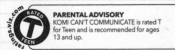

PARENTAL ADVISORY
KOMI CAN'T COMMUNICATE is rated T for Teen and is recommended for ages 13 and up.